Get the eBook FREE!

(PDF, ePub, Kindle, and liveBook all included)

We believe that once you buy a book from us, you should be able to read it in any format we have available. To get electronic versions of this book at no additional cost to you, purchase and then register this book at the Manning website.

Go to https://www.manning.com/freebook and follow the instructions to complete your pBook registration.

That's it!
Thanks from Manning!

grokking concurrency

grokking

concurrency

Kirill Bobrov

MANNING
SHELTER ISLAND

For online information and ordering of this and other Manning books, please visit
www.manning.com. The publisher offers discounts on this book when ordered in quantity.
For more information, please contact

    Special Sales Department
    Manning Publications Co.
    20 Baldwin Road, PO Box 761
    Shelter Island, NY 11964
    Email: orders@manning.com

Manning Publications Co.	Development editor: Ian Hough
20 Baldwin Road	Technical development editor: Arthur Zubarev
Shelter Island, NY 11964	Review editor: Adriana Sabo
	Production editor: Andy Marinkovich
	Copy editor: Tiffany Taylor
	Proofreader: Katie Tennant
	Technical proofreader: Mark Thomas
	Typesetter: Dennis Dalinnik
	Cover designer: Leslie Haimes
	Illustrator: Ekaterina Krivets

ISBN: 9781633439771
Printed in the United States of America

To my parents, Elena and Andrey, the dynamic duo who created this masterpiece (me); and to my wife, Katya, who helps me stay sane in a world full of bugs and glitches

contents

preface

Picture a world where technology evolves faster than a caffeinated cheetah runs, and the demand for efficient, concurrent programming reaches new heights. In this world, software engineers face a formidable challenge: building systems that can handle colossal amounts of data and provide high processing speeds while satisfying the insatiable demands of users. It's a place where concurrency is both a fascination and a puzzle to be solved. This is the world we live in now.

I was once caught in this fascinating web. Then I stumbled across the terms *concurrency* and *asynchrony*. What I discovered was a hidden treasure: a rich source of untapped power that, when harnessed, can transform ordinary programs into extraordinary displays of computational strength. However, this treasure was wrapped in complexity, and the various pieces of the puzzle—concurrency, parallelism, threads, processes, multitasking, and coroutines—were scattered throughout the technological landscape. I yearned for a guide, a mentor, someone to put it all together and reveal the full picture. Unable to find a resource that bridged the gap between theory and practice across different programming languages, I decided to take matters into my own hands. And thus, *Grokking Concurrency* was born—a companion that will accompany you, whispering secrets and illuminating the path through this intricate maze.

This is not your ordinary technical tome. No, it's a book that will captivate and involve you, interweaving tales and cultural references into its pages. This book has evolved from a theoretical guide to a journey packed with stories, cultural references (count them all!), and hilarious illustrations. It's a book that doesn't shy away from humor—and a deep love for dumplings and pizza—because why should learning concurrency be a dull and dreary experience?

Together, we will conquer the complexities of concurrency and decipher the mystery of asynchrony. From the basics of concurrency to the fascinating world of `async` and `await`, we'll use Python as our trusty companion and the language of choice. Don't worry if Python isn't your primary language—the concepts and techniques we'll cover go beyond specific implementations.

"But why Python?" you may wonder. Well, dear reader, it strikes the perfect balance between simplicity and expressiveness, allowing us to focus on the essence of concurrency without unnecessary distractions. Besides, I simply enjoy it, and I won't hide that fact.

Whether you're an experienced developer seeking to deepen your understanding of concurrent systems or a curious newcomer eager to grasp the intricacies of concurrency, this book has something for you. Together, we'll uncover the secrets of concurrency, empowering you to build scalable, efficient, and resilient software systems that can conquer any challenge.

Prepare to embark on a journey like no other, where the boundaries of time and space blur and programs dance to the beat of their own octopus-like rhythm. Yes, you heard it right—octopuses. Those delightful creatures of the deep, with their eight tentacles swirling in perfect harmony, symbolize the intricate and mesmerizing nature of concurrent systems we are about to explore together. Let the adventure begin!

acknowledgments

Before we delve into the depths of concurrency, I would like to take a moment to express my gratitude to the incredible people who have made this book possible. They say writing a book is like running a marathon, but I'd say it's more like a wild rollercoaster ride with a caffeine addiction. And boy, am I glad I had these folks by my side!

First and foremost, I want to express my utmost gratitude to my wife, Ekaterina Krivets, who sees me as creative even though she's the brilliant mind behind all the stunning illustrations in this book.

I'm also incredibly grateful for my family and relatives. Their love and support have been a huge motivator on my journey, and I'm lucky to have them in my corner.

Big ups to my squad who've been there for me every step of the way. Shout-out to Kristina Ialysheva, Mikhail Poltoratskii, Tatiana Borodina, Andrei Gavrilov, and Aleksandr Belnitskii for always having my back and believing in me. Special thanks to Vera Krivets for helping me finesse my English.

A special mention goes to Bert Bates and Brian Hanafee, whose teachings and ideas have forever shaped how I approach teaching and presenting complex concepts. Thank you for your invaluable insights and contributions to my growth as an author.

My deepest appreciation goes to the incredible team at Manning Publications. Mike Stephens, you're the one who started this wild adventure, and I can't thank you enough for taking a chance on me. Ian Hough, you've been my guide, patiently working with me chapter by chapter, fixing my English mishaps. You deserve a medal for surviving the editing process! Arthur Zubarev, thanks for slogging through the clunky first drafts and providing valuable feedback. Lou Covey, sorry for occasionally being rough, but your stories were always interesting and kept me going. Mark Thomas, your technical review and code assistance were game changers. Tiffany Taylor, your keen eye and expertise greatly enhanced the clarity and coherence of the text. Katie Tennant, your thorough review and keen editorial insights greatly polished the content, making it ready for publication.

To all the reviewers—Abhijith Nayak, Amrah Umudlu, Andres Sacco, Arnaud Bailly, Balbir Singh, Bijith Komalan, Clifford Thurber, David Yakobovitch, Dmitry Vorobiov, Eddu Melendez, Ernesto Arroyo, Ernesto Bossi, Eshan Tandon, Ezra Schroeder, Frans Oilinki, Ganesh Swaminathan, Glenn Goossens, Gregory Varghese, Imaculate Resto Mosha, James Zhijun Liu, Jiří Činčura, Jonathan Reeves, Lavanya M K, Luc Rogge, Manoj Reddy, Matt Gukowsky, Matt Welke, Mikael Dautrey, Nolan To, Oliver Korten, Patrick Goetz, Patrick Regan, Ragunath Jawahar, Sai Hegde, Sergio Arbeo Rodríguez, Shiroshica Kulatilake, Venkata Nagendra Babu Yanamadala, Vitaly Larchenkov, and William Jamir—thank you; your suggestions helped make this a better book.

I also want to give a big shout-out to the unsung heroes who worked tirelessly behind the scenes to make this book happen. You know who you are, and even though you don't have a flashy superhero cape, you're the secret sauce that makes it all come together. You're the real rock stars!

Finally, as Snoop Dogg would say, I want to thank myself, without whom this book would not have been possible!

about this book

This book aims to demystify concurrency, asynchrony, and parallel programming, providing fundamental insights and practical understanding. Unlike academic research papers or language-specific books, it focuses on explaining underlying ideas and principles rather than specific implementations. The book is written in a high-level, accessible manner, utilizing visual diagrams instead of complex mathematical explanations to foster a solid understanding. The knowledge you gain from this book will give you the context to comprehend concurrent frameworks and architect scalable solutions in your area of interest. The book fills a gap in available resources by providing a comprehensive and understandable guide for those seeking to grasp the concepts of concurrency and asynchrony, serving as a shortcut for developers who would otherwise need years of experience to acquire this knowledge independently.

Who should read this book?

Grokking Concurrency is perfect for everyone eager to learn the fundamentals of concurrency. To get the most benefit from this book, you should have a basic comfort level in working with computer systems, an understanding of programming language concepts and data structures, and experience with sequential programs. No prior knowledge of the OS is necessary, as all the essential information is provided in the book. While networking concepts are discussed, they aren't covered in great detail, so some basic understanding of networking fundamentals is assumed. You don't need deep knowledge on any of these topics, and if required, you can research them as you go.

How this book is organized: A roadmap

This book is divided into three parts. Part 1, "The octopus orchestra: Introduction to a symphony of concurrency," discusses the fundamental concepts and primitives of writing concurrent programs. Using a layered approach, Chapters 1 through 5 lay down the fundamental knowledge of concurrency from the hardware level to the application level.

Part 2, "The many tentacles of concurrency: Multitasking, decomposition, and synchronization," discusses the advantages of using abstractions and popular patterns to improve your code's performance, scalability, and resilience. In Chapters 6 through 9, you learn how to avoid some of the most frequent problems that arise when building concurrent systems.

Part 3, "Asynchronous octopuses: A pizza-making tale of concurrency," extends your concurrency knowledge beyond a single machine and scales it up to multiple machines connected via a network. In this context, events can occur asynchronously, meaning that one event may happen at a different time than another event. This concept of asynchrony will be a focus of Chapters 10 through 12, presenting another dimension of the topic. Asynchrony is used to present the impression of concurrent or parallel tasking, and in modern implementations, you can combine asynchronous and truly concurrent operations, giving the system a greater performance gain. Chapter 13 wraps up the book with a final set of concurrency problems that we solve step by step to make sure you've grokked concurrency.

About the code

You can get executable snippets of code from the liveBook (online) version of this book at https://livebook.manning.com/book/grokking-concurrency. The complete source code for the examples in the book is available for download from the Manning website at www.manning.com, and from GitHub at https://github.com/luminousmen/grokking_concurrency. The source code is intended to be a reference for how the programs could be implemented. These examples are optimized *for learning* and are *not for production* use. The code was written to serve as a tool for teaching. Using established libraries and frameworks is recommended for projects that will make their way into production, as they are usually optimized for performance, well tested, and well supported.

liveBook discussion forum

Purchase of *Grokking Concurrency* includes free access to liveBook, Manning's online reading platform. Using liveBook's exclusive discussion features, you can attach comments to the book globally or to specific sections or paragraphs. It's a snap to make notes for yourself, ask and answer technical questions, and receive help from the author and other users. To access the forum, go to https://livebook.manning.com/book/grokking-concurrency/discussion. You can also learn more about Manning's forums and the rules of conduct at https://livebook.manning.com/discussion.

Manning's commitment to our readers is to provide a venue where a meaningful dialogue between individual readers and between readers and the author can take place. It is not a commitment to any specific amount of participation on the part of the author, whose contribution to the forum remains voluntary (and unpaid). We suggest you try asking him some challenging questions lest his interest stray! The forum and the archives of previous discussions will be accessible from the publisher's website for as long as the book is in print.

about the author

KIRILL BOBROV is a seasoned and slightly grumpy software engineer who knows the ins and outs of developing and designing high-load applications. With a passion for data engineering, he now dedicates his efforts to implementing cutting-edge data engineering practices for companies worldwide. And guess what? This grumpy individual is also the cool cat behind the popular illustrated tech blog, https://luminousmen.com.

Part 1
The octopus orchestra: Introduction to a symphony of concurrency

Sitting in a coffee shop and enjoying your coffee, you find your attention caught by a nearby group of programmers in a passionate discussion of concurrency. They're throwing around terms like *parallel computing*, *threads*, and *interprocess communication* with ease, leaving you feeling a bit lost. But don't worry; you're not alone.

If you've ever been to an orchestra concert, you know the beauty of multiple musicians playing different instruments and melodies all at once. It's a beautiful chaos that somehow comes together to create an incredible performance. This chaos is much like concurrency: the idea of having multiple processes or threads running simultaneously to achieve a common goal.

In Chapters 1 through 5, you learn the fundamentals of concurrency, how computers work, and the different types of concurrency primitives. We explore sequential and parallel computing, delve into the hardware and software components that enable concurrency, and examine the various types of interprocess communication that allow multiple processes to work together seamlessly.

So, grab a latte and join the conversation—I promise it'll be worth it.

In this chapter

- You learn why concurrency is an important topic worth studying

- You learn how to measure the performance of the systems

- You learn that there are different layers of concurrency

Look out the window, and take a moment to observe the world around you. Do you see things moving in a linear, sequential fashion? Or do you see a complex web of interacting, independently behaving pieces all moving at the same time?

Although people tend to think sequentially—like going through to-do lists and doing things one step at a time— the reality is that the world is much more complex than that. It is not sequential but rather concurrent. Interrelated events happen simultaneously. From the chaotic rush of a busy supermarket to the coordinated moves of a football team to the ever-changing flow of traffic on the road, concurrency is all around us. Just as in the natural

world, your computer needs to be concurrent to be suited for modeling, simulating, and understanding complex real-world phenomena.

Concurrency in computing allows a system to deal with more than one task at a time. This could be a program, a computer, or a network of computers. Without concurrent computing, our applications would not be able to keep up with the complexity of the world around us.

As we delve deeper into the topic of concurrency, several questions may arise. First, if you're still not convinced—why should you care about concurrency?

Why is concurrency important?

Concurrency is essential in software engineering. The demand for high-performance applications and concurrent systems makes concurrent programming a crucial skill for software engineers.

Concurrent programming is not a new concept, but it has gained significant attention in recent years. With the increasing number of cores and processors in modern computer systems, concurrent programming has become a necessary skill for writing software. Companies are looking for developers who are proficient in concurrency, as it is often the only way to solve problems where computing resources are limited and fast performance is required.

The most important advantage of concurrency—and, historically, the first reason to start exploring this area—is the ability to increase system performance. Let's look at how that happened.

Increasing system performance

When we need to improve performance, why can't we just buy faster computers? Well, that was what people did a few decades ago, but we found out that, eventually, buying faster computers is no longer feasible.

Moore's law

In 1965, Gordon Moore, one of the founders of Intel, discovered a pattern. New processor models appeared about two years after their predecessors, and the number of transistors they contained roughly doubled each time. Moore concluded that the number of transistors, and consequently the processor's clock speed, would double every 24 months. This observation became known as Moore's law. For software engineers, that meant they had to wait only two years for an application to double in speed.

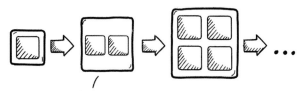

2x TRANSISTORS EVERY 1-2 YRS: 2,000 TRANSISTORS BY 2022

The problem was that around 2002, the rules changed. As the famous C++ expert Herb Sutter put it, "the free lunch was over."[1] We discovered a fundamental relationship between the physical size of the processor and the processing speed (processor's frequency). The time required to execute an operation depends on the circuit length and the speed of light. Simply put, we can add only so many transistors (the fundamental building block of computer circuitry) before we run out of space. Rising temperatures also play a major role. Further performance improvements could not depend on merely increasing the processor's frequency. Thus began what's become known as the *multicore crisis*.

The progress of individual processors in terms of clock speed stopped due to physical limitations, but the need to increase the performance of systems did not. Manufacturers' focus shifted to horizontal expansion in the form of multiprocessors, forcing software engineers, architects, and language developers to adapt to architectures with multiple processing resources.

The most important conclusion from this history tour is that by far the most relevant advantage of concurrency, and historically the first reason to start exploring this area, is to increase system performance in a way that makes efficient use of additional processing resources. This leads us to two important questions: how do we measure performance, and how can we improve it?

---

[1]   Herb Sutter, "The free lunch is over," blog post, http://www.gotw.ca/publications/concurrency-ddj.htm.

Latency vs. throughput

In computing, performance can be quantified a number of ways, depending on how we look at the computer system. One way to increase the amount of work done is to reduce the time it takes to perform individual tasks.

Let's say you use a motorcycle to travel between home and work, and it takes an hour for a one-way trip. You care about how fast you can get to work, so you measure system performance by this metric. If you drive faster, you get to work sooner. From a computing system perspective, this scenario is called *latency*. Latency is a measure of how long a single task takes from start to finish.

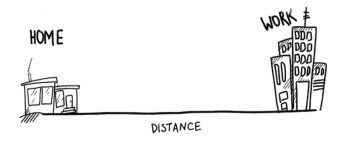

Now imagine you work for a transportation department, and your job is to increase the performance of the bus system. You aren't just concerned about getting one person to the office faster; you want to increase the number of people who can get from home to work per unit of time. This scenario is called *throughput*: the number of tasks a system can handle over a period of time.

It is very important to understand the difference between latency and throughput. Even if a motorcycle goes twice as fast as a bus, the bus has 25× greater throughput (the motorcycle transports 1 person a given distance in an hour, while the bus transports 50 people the same distance in 2 hours: averaged for time, that gives us 25 people per hour!). In other words, higher system throughput does not necessarily mean lower latency. When optimizing performance, an improvement in one factor (such as throughput) may lead to the worsening of another factor (such as latency).

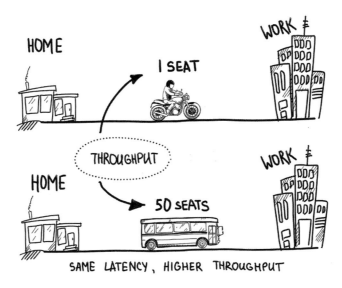

SAME LATENCY, HIGHER THROUGHPUT

Concurrency can help decrease latency. For example, a long-running task can be broken down into smaller tasks executed in parallel, thus reducing the overall execution time. Concurrency can also help increase throughput by allowing multiple tasks to be processed simultaneously.

In addition, concurrency can hide latency. When we are waiting for a call, waiting for the subway to take us to work, and so forth, we can just wait, or we can use our processing resources to do something else. For example, we can read our emails while catching a ride on the subway. This way, we're essentially doing multiple tasks at once and hiding the delay by making productive use of the waiting time. Hiding latency is key to responsive systems and is applicable to problems that involve waiting.

Therefore, using concurrency can improve system performance in three main ways:

- It can reduce latency (that is, make a unit of work faster).
- It can hide latency (that is, allow the system to accomplish something else during an operation with high latency).
- It can increase throughput (that is, make the system able to do more work).

Now that we've seen how concurrency is applied to system performance, let's look at another application of concurrency. Early in this chapter, we considered how concurrency is necessary if we want to model the complex world around us. Now we can get more specific about how concurrency can solve large or complex problems computationally.

Solving complex and large problems

Many problems that software engineers need to solve when developing systems that deal with the real world are so complex that it is impractical to solve them using a sequential system. Complexity can come from the size of the problem or how hard it is to understand a given piece of the systems we develop.

Scalability

A problem's size involves *scalability* or the characteristic of a system that can increase performance by adding more resources. Ways to increase the scalability of systems can be divided into two types: vertical and horizontal.

Vertical scaling (scaling up) increases system performance by increasing the amount of memory to upgrade existing processing resources or replacing a processor with a more powerful one. In this case, scalability is limited since it is very difficult to increase the speed of individual processors, making it easy to hit the performance ceiling. Upgrading to more powerful processing resources is also expensive (i.e., buying a supercomputer), as we have to pay higher prices for smaller and smaller gains for top-tier cloud instances or hardware.

Decreasing the processing time associated with a particular work unit will get us so far, but ultimately, we need to scale out our systems. *Horizontal scaling (scaling out)* involves increasing program or system performance by distributing the load between existing and new processing resources. As long as it is possible to increase the number of processing resources, we can increase system performance. In this case, scalability problems won't arise as quickly as in the case of vertical scaling.

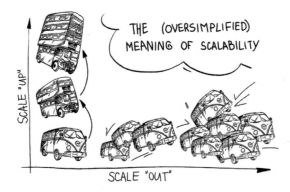

The industry decided to migrate toward a horizontally scalable approach. This trend is driven by demand for real-time systems, high volumes of data, reliability through redundancy, and improved utilization through resource sharing due to migration to cloud/SaaS environments.

Horizontal scaling requires system concurrency, and one computer may not be enough. Multiple interconnected machines, called *computing clusters*, solve data processing tasks in a reasonable time.

Decoupling

Another aspect of large problems is complexity. Unfortunately, the complexity of systems does not decrease over time without some effort on the part of the engineers. Businesses want to make their products more powerful and functional. This inevitably increases the complexity of the code base, infrastructure, and maintenance efforts. Engineers have to find and implement different architectural approaches to simplify the systems and divide them into simpler independent communicating units.

Separation of duties is almost always welcome in software engineering. A basic engineering principle called *divide and conquer* creates loosely coupled systems. Grouping related code (*tightly coupled* components) and separating unrelated code (*loosely coupled* components) makes applications easier to understand and test and reduces the number of bugs—at least, in theory.

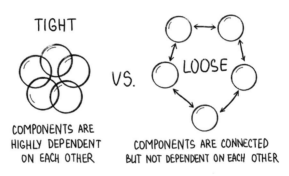

Another way of looking at concurrency is that it is a decoupling strategy. Dividing functionality between modules or units of concurrency helps individual pieces focus on specific functionality, makes them maintainable, and reduces overall system complexity. Software engineers decouple *what* gets done from *when* it gets done. That dramatically improves the performance, scalability, reliability, and internal structure of an application.

Concurrency is important and widely used in modern computing systems, operating systems (OSs), and large distributed clusters. It helps model the real world, maximizes the efficiency of systems from users' and developers' perspectives, and allows developers to solve large, complex problems.

As we explore the world of concurrency, the journey will change the way you think about computer systems and their capabilities. This book will reveal the lay of the land as you learn about the different layers of concurrency.

Layers of concurrency

Like most complex design problems, concurrency is built using multiple layers. In a layered architecture, it is important to understand that contradictory or seemingly mutually exclusive concepts can coexist at different levels *concurrently*. For example, it's possible to have concurrent execution on a sequential machine.

I like to think of concurrency's layered architecture as a symphony orchestra that plays, say, Tchaikovsky:

- At the top, we have the conceptual or design layer (the *application layer*). We can think of this as the composer's composition within the orchestra; within a computer system, like musical notation, algorithms tell the components of the system what should be done.

- Next, we have multitasking at runtime (the *runtime system layer*). This is like the musicians all playing different portions of the composition, using different instruments cooperatively. The music flow moves from one group to another, following the conductor's instructions. Within a computer system, various processes do their part to achieve an overall purpose.

- Finally, we have low-level execution (the hardware layer). Here, we zoom in on a specific instrument: the violin. Each note produced by a violinist results from one to four strings oscillating at a specific frequency determined by the length, diameter, tension, and density of the wire. Within a computer system, a single process performs tasks as dictated by instructions specific to that process.

Each layer describes the same process at different levels, but the details are different and sometimes contradictory.

The same happens in concurrency:

- At the *hardware layer*, we directly encounter machine instructions executed by the processing resources using signals to access hardware peripherals. Modern architectures continue to increase in complexity. Because of this, optimizing application performance on these architectures now requires a deep understanding of the application's interactions with the hardware components.

- Moving to the *runtime system layer*, many of the shortcomings associated with programming abstractions are hidden behind mysterious system calls, device drivers, and scheduling algorithms that significantly affect concurrent systems and therefore require a thorough understanding. This layer is frequently represented by the operating system, as described in some detail in Chapter 3.

- Finally, at the *application layer*, abstractions that are closer in spirit to how the physical world operates become available. Software engineers write source code that can implement complex algorithms and represent business logic. This code can also modify the execution flow using programming language features and generally represent very abstract concepts that only a software engineer can think of.

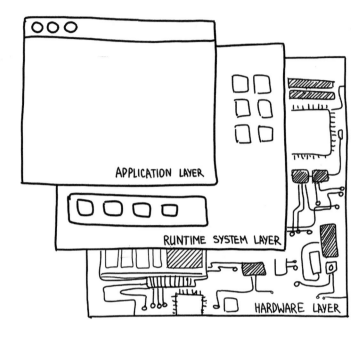

We use these layers extensively as a travel guide while moving up the ladder of knowledge about concurrency.

What you'll learn from this book

Concurrency has earned a reputation as a hard field. Some of its complexity lies in the lack of written wisdom from experienced practitioners. Oral tradition instead of formal writing has left this area shrouded in mystery. I wrote this book in an effort to make this area less mysterious.

This book won't teach you everything you will ever need to know about concurrency. It will get you started and help you understand what you need to learn more about. We will explore the problems involved in concurrent programming and gain insight into the best practices needed to create concurrent and scalable applications.

Beginner and intermediate programmers will get a basic understanding of how to write concurrent systems. To get the most out of the book, you should have some programming experience, but you don't need to be an expert. Concrete examples explain the key concepts in general terms, and then we demonstrate them in action using the Python programming language.

This book is organized into three parts covering different levels of concurrency. The first part discusses fundamental concepts and primitives of writing concurrent programs, covering knowledge from the hardware layer to the application layer.

The second part focuses on designing concurrent applications and popular concurrent patterns. It also covers how to avoid common concurrency problems that arise when building concurrent systems.

The third part of the book expands our knowledge of concurrency beyond a single machine and delves into scaling applications to multiple machines connected via a network. We explore asynchronous communication between tasks, which is crucial in this context. Additionally, we provide a step-by-step guide for how to write a concurrent application.

By the end of the book, you will be up to speed on concurrency and modern asynchronous and concurrent programming approaches. We move from low-level hardware operations to a higher level of application design and translate theory into practical implementation.

All the code in the book is written in the Python 3.9 programming language and tested on macOS and Linux OSs. The narrative is not tied to any specific programming language but references the Linux kernel subsystem. All the source code for the examples can be found in the GitHub repository (https://github.com/luminousmen/grokking_concurrency) and on the book's website (www.manning.com/books/grokking-concurrency).

Recap

- A concurrent system is a system that can deal with many things at once.
- In the real world, many things happen concurrently at any given time. If we want to model the real world, we need concurrent programming.
- Concurrency drastically enhances the throughput and performance of a system by reducing or hiding latency and utilizing the existing resources more efficiently.
- The concepts of *scalability* and *decoupling* are used throughout the book:
  - Scalability can be vertical or horizontal. Vertical scaling increases program and system performance by upgrading existing processing. Horizontal scaling increases performance by distributing the load between existing and new processing resources. The industry migrated toward a horizontally scalable approach to scaling architecture, for which concurrency is a prerequisite.
  - Complex problems can be decoupled into simple components that are linked together. In a way, concurrency is a decoupling strategy that can help us solve large and complex problems.
- A journey to an unfamiliar place usually requires a map if we want to find our way without getting lost. In this book, we navigate using layers of concurrency: the *application layer, runtime system layer*, and *hardware layer*.

In this chapter

- You learn the terminology to talk about a running program

- You learn different approaches at the lowest layer of concurrency: physical task execution

- You draft your first parallel program

- You learn the limitations of the parallel computing approach

For thousands of years (well, not quite, but for a long time), developers have been writing programs using the simplest model of computation: the sequential model. The serial execution approach is at the core of sequential programming, and this is our starting point in our introduction to concurrency. In this chapter, I introduce different execution approaches that lie at the low-level execution layer.

Review: What is a program?

The first problem with concurrency, and computer science in general, is that we're extremely bad at naming things. We sometimes use the same word to describe several distinct concepts, different words to describe the same thing, or even different words to describe different things where the meaning depends on context. And sometimes, we just make up words.

> **NOTE**   Did you know that CAPTCHA is a contrived acronym for "Completely Automated Public Turing test to tell Computers and Humans Apart"?

So, before we start looking at execution, it will be helpful to understand what is being executed and to establish the general terminology we use in this book. Generally speaking, a *program* is a sequence of instructions that a computer system performs or *executes*.

A program must be written before it can be executed. This is done by writing *source code* using one of many programming languages. The source code can be thought of as a recipe in a cookbook—a set of steps that helps the cook make a meal from raw ingredients. There are many components to cooking: the recipe itself, the cook, and the raw ingredients.

Executing a program is similar to executing a recipe. We have the source code of the program (the recipe), the chef (the processor, aka *CPU*), and the raw ingredients (the input data of the program).

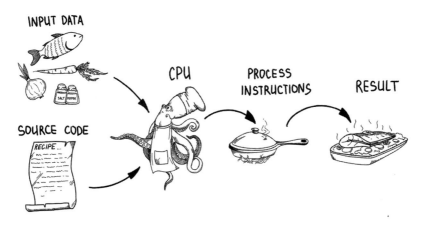

The processor cannot solve a single meaningful task on its own. It can't sort things or search for objects with specific characteristics; a processor can only do a limited number of simple tasks. All its "intellectual" power is determined by the programs it executes. No matter how much processing power you have, you can't accomplish anything unless that power is given direction. Turning a task into a set of steps that can be executed on a processor is what a *developer* does, not unlike the writer of a cookbook.

Developers normally describe the task they want to accomplish using a programming language. However, the CPU cannot understand source code written in a normal programming language. First, the source code has to be translated into machine code, which is the language the CPU speaks. This translation is done by special programs called *compilers*. A compiler creates a file, often called an *executable,* with machine-level instructions that the CPU can understand and execute.

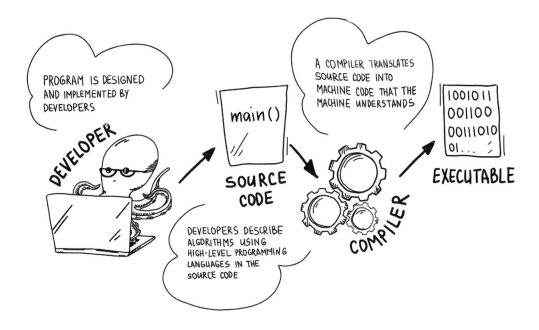

The CPU can take a few different approaches when it executes the machine code. The most fundamental approach for handling multiple instructions is *serial execution,* which is at the heart of *sequential* computing. We look at this next.

Serial execution

As stated earlier, a program is a list of instructions, and generally, the order of that list matters. Back to our recipe example: suppose you started cooking your favorite recipe and followed all the steps the recipe told you, but in the wrong order. For example, maybe you cooked the egg before you mixed it into the flour. You probably would not be happy with the outcome. For many tasks, the order of the steps matters a lot.

The same is true with programming. When we solve a programming problem, we first divide the problem into a series of small tasks and execute these small tasks one after another, or *serially*. Task-based programming allows us to talk about computations in a machine-independent manner and provides a framework for constructing programs modularly.

A task can be thought of as a piece of work. If we are talking about CPU execution, we can call that task an *instruction*. A task can also be a sequence of operations forming an *abstraction* of a real-world model, such as writing data to a file, rotating an image, or printing a message on a screen. A task can contain a single operation or many (which we talk more about in the following chapters), but it is a logically independent chunk of work. We use the term *task* as a general abstraction for the unit of execution.

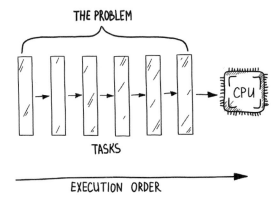

The *serial* execution of tasks is a sort of chain, where the first task is followed by the second one, the second is followed by the third, and so on, without overlapping time periods. Imagine that today is laundry day, and you have a pile of laundry to wash. Unfortunately, as in many homes, you have only one washing machine, and you regretfully remember how you once washed your favorite white T-shirt with a colored shirt. Tragic!

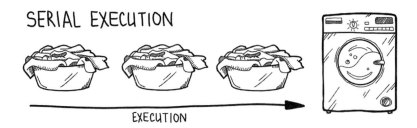

Chastened by that mistake, you start by washing white laundry in the washing machine, followed by washing dark laundry, then sheets, and finally, towels. The minimum time in which anybody can do laundry is determined by the speed of the washing machine and the amount of laundry. Even if we have a ton of laundry to wash, we still have to do it *serially*, one pile after another. Each execution blocks the entire processing resource; the washing machine can't wash half of the white clothes and then begin washing dark clothes. That's not the behavior you expect from it.

Sequential computations

On the other hand, to describe dynamic, time-related phenomena, we use the term *sequential*. This is a conceptual property of a program or a system. It's more about how the program or system has been designed and written in the source code, not actual execution.

Imagine that you need to implement a Tic-Tac-Toe game. The rules of the game are simple enough: there are two players, and one of the players chooses O and the other X to mark their respective cells. Players take turns putting their X or O on the board, one after another. If a player gets three marks on the board in a row, a column, or one of the two diagonals, that player wins. If the board is full and no player wins, the game ends in a draw.

Can you write such a game?

Let's discuss the game logic. Players take turns by typing the row number and column number in which they want to make a move. After a player makes a move, the program checks if this player has won or if there is a tie and then switches to the other player's turn. The game proceeds this way until a player wins or there is a draw. If a player wins, the program displays a message saying which player won, and then the user presses any button to exit the program.

The next illustration shows what a diagram of the game Tic-Tac-Toe might look like.

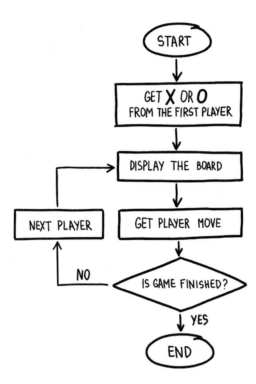

The program has serial steps to solve the problem. Each step relies on the result from the previous step. Hence, each step is *blocking* the execution of the subsequent steps. We can only implement such a program using a sequential programming approach.

As you can see, the computational model of the program here is determined by the rules of the game—the algorithm. There is a clear dependency between the tasks that cannot be broken down in any way. We can't check a move that wasn't made yet by the player, and we can't give the first player two moves in a row since that would be cheating.

> **NOTE**   In fact, there are not many tasks where the next step depends on the completion of the previous steps. Hence it is comparatively easy to exploit concurrency in most programming problems that developers face every day. We talk about that in the subsequent chapters.

What tasks can you think of where serial execution is required? Hint: That means no step can execute until the previous step has completed.

The opposite of sequential programming is *concurrent programming*. Concurrency is based on the idea that there are *independent* computations that can be executed in an arbitrary order with the same outcome.

Pros and cons of sequential computing

Sequential computation has several important advantages but also comes with pitfalls.

Simplicity (pro)

Any program can be written in this paradigm. It's a clear and predictable concept, so it's the most common. When we think of tasks, it is natural to consider a sequence. Cook first, then eat, and then wash the dishes is a reasonable sequence of tasks. Eating first, then washing the dishes, and then cooking makes less sense.

Sequential computing is a straightforward approach with a clear set of step-by-step instructions about what to do and when to do it. The execution guarantees that there is no need to check whether a dependent step has completed or not—the next operation will not start executing until the previous one finishes its execution.

Scalability (con)

Scalability is the ability of a system to handle an increasing amount of work, or the potential to increase the system's ability to handle work, to accommodate growth. A system is considered scalable if performance improves after adding more processing resources. In the case of sequential computing, the only way to scale the system is to increase the performance of system resources used—CPU, memory, and so on. That is vertical scaling, which is limited by the performance of CPUs available on the market.

Overhead (con)

In sequential computing, no communication or synchronization is required between different steps of the program execution. But there is an indirect overhead of underutilizing available processing resources: even if we are happy with the sequential approach inside the program, we may not use all available resources of the system, leading to decreased efficiency and unnecessary costs. Even if the system has a single one-core processor, it can still be underutilized. We go deeper into why in Chapter 6.

Parallel execution

If you're familiar with gardening, you may be aware that growing a tomato plant typically takes around four months. With this in mind, consider the following question: is it true or false that you can only grow three tomatoes in a year?

Clearly, the answer is false, because you can grow more than one tomato at a time.

As we've seen, in serial execution, only one instruction is performed at a time. Sequential programming is what most people learn first, and most programs are written that way: execution starts at the beginning of the main function and proceeds serially, one task/function, call/operation at a time.

When we remove the assumption that we can do only one thing at a time, we open up the possibility of working *in parallel*—just like growing more than one tomato plant. However, programs that can do things *in parallel* can be more difficult to write. Let's look at a simple analogy.

How to speed up the process of doing the laundry

Congratulations! You just won the lottery: free tickets to Hawaii. Sweet! But there's a catch—you have only a couple of hours before your plane leaves, and you need to do four loads of laundry. Your washing machine, no matter how efficient, cannot wash more than one load at a time, and you do not want to mix the laundry.

With programming, as with laundry, the time it takes for a sequential program to run is limited by the speed of the processor and how fast it can execute that series of instructions. But what if you use more than one washing machine? Because each load is independent of any other laundry load, you can cope with the task much faster if you have multiple machines, right?

So you decide to visit the nearest laundromat. It has a bunch of washing machines, and you can easily wash all four of your loads in four separate machines, all at the same time. In this case, we can say that all the washing machines are working in *parallel*—more than one load is being washed at a time. Thus, you have increased the throughput by four times.

Remember the horizontal scaling we talked about in Chapter 1? Here we have applied this approach.

Parallel execution means task execution is physically simultaneous. Parallel execution is the opposite of serial execution. *Parallelism* can be measured by the number of tasks that can be executed in parallel. In this case, you have four washing machines, so the parallelism equals four.

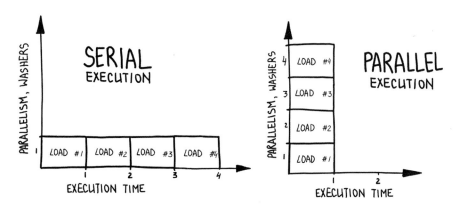

Now that we know what parallel execution is, we need to understand the requirements for it to be possible.

Parallel computing requirements

Before we go deeper into parallel execution, let's first consider the requirements to achieve it: task independence and hardware support.

Task independence

In sequential computing, all operations are accelerated by increasing the CPU clock speed. This is the simplest solution to the latency reduction problem. It does not require any special program design. All we need is a more powerful processor. Parallel computing is mainly used to decrease latency by dividing a problem into tasks that can be executed concurrently and independently of each other.

> **NOTE** Large programs often consist of many smaller ones. For example, a web server processes requests from web browsers and responds with HTML web pages. Each request is handled like a small program, and it would be ideal if such programs could run simultaneously.

The use of parallel computing is problem specific. To apply parallel computing to a problem, it must be possible for the problem to be decomposed into a set of independent tasks so that each processing resource can execute part of the algorithm simultaneously with the others. Independence here means processing resources can process tasks in whatever order they like and wherever they like, as long as the result is the same. Noncompliance with this requirement makes the problem non-parallelizable.

The key to understanding whether a program can be executed in parallel is to analyze which tasks can be decomposed and which tasks can be executed independently. We talk more about how to do decomposition in Chapter 7.

> **NOTE** In this case, the logic goes only in one direction—a program that can run in parallel can always be made sequential, but a sequential program cannot always be made parallel.

Task independence is not always possible because not every program or algorithm can be divided into independent tasks from start to finish. Some tasks can be independent, and some cannot if they depend on previously executed tasks. That requires developers to *synchronize* different dependent pieces of a program to get the correct results. Synchronization means *blocking* the execution of the task waiting for dependencies. In the Tic-Tac-Toe example, program execution is blocked by the individual players' moves. Coordinating interdependent parallel computations via synchronization can severely limit the parallelism of the program, presenting a significant challenge in writing parallel programs compared to simple sequential programs (as discussed in more detail in Chapter 8).

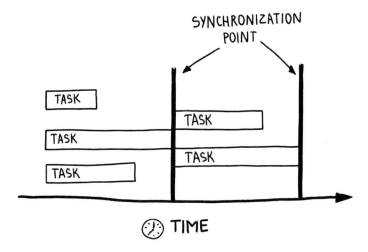

That extra work can be worth the effort. When done right, parallel execution increases the overall throughput of a program, enabling us to break down large tasks to accomplish them faster or accomplish more tasks in a given time frame.

Tasks that require little or no synchronization are sometimes called *embarrassingly parallel*. They can easily be broken down into independent tasks executed in parallel. Such tasks are often found in scientific computing. For example, distributing the work of finding prime numbers can be done by allocating subsets to each processing resource.

> **NOTE**   There is no shame in having an embarrassingly parallel task! On the contrary, embarrassingly parallel applications are cool because they are easy to program. In recent years, the term *embarrassingly parallel* has taken on a slightly different meaning. Algorithms that are embarrassingly parallel tend to have little communication between processes, which is the key to good performance, so *embarrassingly parallel* usually refers to an algorithm with low communication needs. We touch on this a little more in Chapter 5.

Thus, the extent of parallelism depends more on the problem than on the people trying to solve it.

Hardware support

Parallel computing requires hardware support. Parallel programs need hardware with multiple processing resources. Without at least two processing resources, we cannot achieve true parallelism. We talk about hardware and how it can support multiple simultaneous operations in the next chapter. Having all the requirements for parallel computing, we are now ready to explore what it actually is.

Parallel computing

Parallel computing uses decomposition to split large or complex problems into small tasks and then utilizes parallel execution of the runtime system to solve them effectively. In the next example, let's demonstrate how parallelism can save the world.

Imagine that you are working at the FBI IT department, and for the next mission, you must implement a program to crack a password (number combination of a particular length) and access a system that can destroy the whole world.

The usual approach for finding a correct password consists of repeatedly guessing the password (known as the *brute-force approach*), calculating its scrambled form (*cryptographic hash*), and comparing the resulting cryptographic hash with the one stored on the system. Let's assume that you already have a cryptographic hash of the password.

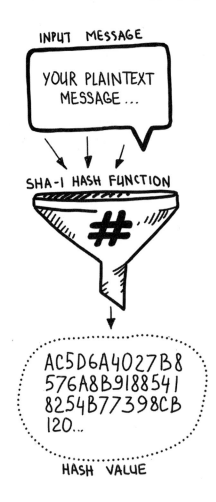

How do you implement such a program?

Brute force is understood as a general method of finding a solution to a problem that requires listing all possible combinations, iterating over this list, and checking whether each particular solution solves the problem. In this case, you need to go through a list of all possible number combinations and check whether each cryptographic hash corresponds to the hash found on the system.

After a couple of sleepless nights, you figure out how to check the cryptographic hash, go through all the possible number combinations, and finish implementing the program using your favorite programming language. The algorithm generates a number combination and checks the cryptographic hash. If it matches, the found password is printed out, and the program finishes; if not, it goes to the next combination and does the cycle again.

Essentially, you process all possible password combinations one by one using sequential computing. Here, you let your CPU process one task at a time and then get the next task and do it serially until all the tasks have been completed. The steps for how to use serial execution to solve a problem are shown in the previous figure and this code:

```python
# Chapter 2/password_cracking_sequential.py
import time
import math
import hashlib
import typing as T


def get_combinations(*, length: int, min_number: int = 0) -> T.List[str]:
    combinations = []
    max_number = int(math.pow(10, length) - 1)
    for i in range(min_number, max_number + 1):
        str_num = str(i)
        zeros = "0" * (length - len(str_num))
        combinations.append("".join((zeros, str_num)))
    return combinations
```

In a given range, generates a list of all possible passwords with a specified number of digits

```python
def get_crypto_hash(password: str) -> str:
    return hashlib.sha256(password.encode()).hexdigest()


def check_password(expected_crypto_hash: str,
                   possible_password: str) -> bool:
    actual_crypto_hash = get_crypto_hash(possible_password)
    return expected_crypto_hash == actual_crypto_hash
```

Compares the cryptographic hash of a possible password with the one stored in the system

```python
def crack_password(crypto_hash: str, length: int) -> None:
    print("Processing number combinations sequentially")
    start_time = time.perf_counter()
    combinations = get_combinations(length=length)
    for combination in combinations:
        if check_password(crypto_hash, combination):
            print(f"PASSWORD CRACKED: {combination}")
            break
```

Sequentially generates and tests all possible passwords of a specified length and stops as soon as it finds a password that produces the expected cryptographic hash

```python
    process_time = time.perf_counter() - start_time
    print(f"PROCESS TIME: {process_time}")


if __name__ == "__main__":
    crypto_hash = \
        "e24df920078c3dd4e7e8d2442f00e5c9ab2a231bb3918d65cc50906e49ecaef4"
    length = 8
    crack_password(crypto_hash, length)
```

The output will look similar to this:

```
Processing number combinations sequentially
PASSWORD CRACKED: 87654321
PROCESS TIME: 64.60886170799999
```

With absolute confidence in your heroism from solving the problem, you give the program to the next hero who will go on a mission. Agent 008 nods and finishes drinking a vodka martini.

We all know spies don't trust anyone, right? In less than an hour, Agent 008 bursts into your office and tells you that the program is taking too long—according to their calculations, it will take an hour to process all the possible password combinations on the super device! "I only have a couple of minutes before the building will burst into flames," says Agent 008 fearfully, sipping another vodka martini. They leave the room with a parting command: "Speed it up!" Ouch.

How do you speed up a program like this?

The obvious way would be to increase the performance of the CPU: by increasing the clock speed of the super device, you can process more passwords in the same amount of time. Unfortunately, we have already discovered that this approach has limits—there is a physical limit on how fast the CPU can be. And, after all, it's the FBI. You already have the fastest processor. There is no way you can increase its performance. This is the most significant disadvantage of sequential computing. It is not easily scalable, even if we have more than one processing resource on the computer system.

Another way to make the program's execution faster is to break it down into independent parts and distribute those tasks among multiple processing resources so they can be processed simultaneously. The more processing resources and smaller tasks we have, the faster the processing goes. This is the core idea behind parallel computing and something we look at in more detail in Chapters 8 and 12.

Do you think you can use parallel execution here? The super device uses a top-tier CPU with a lot of cores. So, the first condition is fulfilled—you have proper hardware that can execute tasks in parallel.

Is it possible to decompose the problem into independent tasks? Checking individual password combinations can be thought of as tasks, and they are not dependent on each other—you don't need to check all previous passwords before checking the current one. It does not matter which password is processed first, as they can be executed entirely independently of each other as long as you find the right one. Great!

So, you have met all the requirements for parallel computing. You have hardware support and task independence. Let's design a final solution!

The first step for every such problem is to decompose the problem into separate tasks. As we've already discovered, individual password checks can be considered independent tasks, and we can execute them in parallel. There are no dependencies, which leads to no synchronization points; hence, it is an embarrassingly parallel problem.

In the following illustration, you can see a diagram of the solution split into several steps. The first step is creating ranges of passwords (chunks) to check for each individual processing resource. Then we distribute those chunks between available processing resources. As a result, we have a set of password ranges that are assigned to each processing resource. The next step will be to run the actual execution.

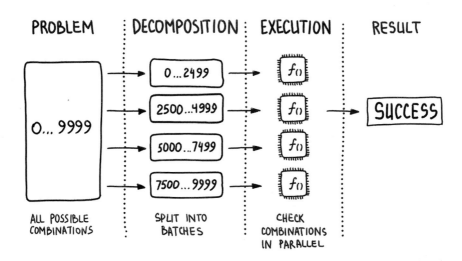

Here's the code:

Splits a large range of integers into smaller chunks, each containing roughly the same number of passwords that can be processed in parallel by multiple cores or processors

```python
ChunkRange = T.Tuple[int, int]

def get_chunks(num_ranges: int,
              length: int) -> T.Iterator[ChunkRange]:
    max_number = int(math.pow(10, length) - 1)
    chunk_starts = [int(max_number / num_ranges * i)
                   for i in range(num_ranges)]
    chunk_ends = [start_point - 1
                 for start_point in
                   chunk_starts[1:]] + [max_number]
    return zip(chunk_starts, chunk_ends)


def crack_password_parallel(crypto_hash: str, length: int) -> None:
    num_cores = cpu_count()
    chunks = get_chunks(num_cores, length)
```

Gets the number of available processors

```
# DO IN PARALLEL
# for chunk_start, chunk_end in chunks:
#     crack_chunk(crypto_hash, length, chunk_start, chunk_end)}
```

Pseudocode for processing each chunk in a separate process concurrently

We add a new function, `crack_password_parallel`, that should execute the `crack_password` function in parallel on multiple cores. It may look different in different programming languages, but the idea is the same: it should create a set of parallel units and distribute the password ranges between them for parallel execution. This requires the use of *pseudocode* (a human-readable representation of the logic of a program, written in a stylized language that mimics actual code), which we discuss further in Chapters 4 and 5.

> **NOTE** Even if we use pseudocode, our example is very realistic in terms of usage. For example, the MATLAB language has a `parfor` construct that makes it trivial to use parallel `for` loops. The Python language has a `joblib` package that makes parallelism incredibly simple using the `Parallel` class. The R language has a `Parallel` library with the same functionality. The standard Scala library has parallel collections to facilitate parallel programming, sparing users the low-level parallelization details.

Because of parallel computing, Agent 008 once again saves the world with seconds to spare. Unfortunately, most of us don't have the resources of the FBI; parallel execution has its limits and costs, which we need to consider before we apply it to our problems. We think about this in the next section.

Amdahl's law

One mother can deliver a baby in nine months. Does this mean nine people working together can deliver a baby in one month?

It seems that we can infinitely increase the number of processors and thus make the system run as fast as possible. But unfortunately, this is not the case. A famous observation of Gene Amdahl, known as *Amdahl's law*, demonstrates this clearly.

So far, we have analyzed the execution of a parallel algorithm. Although a parallel algorithm may have some sequential parts, it is common to think of execution in terms of some fully parallel parts and some fully sequential parts. Sequential parts may simply be steps that have not been parallelized, or they may be sequential, as we've seen before.

Imagine that you have a huge pile of index cards with definitions written on them. You want to find cards with information about concurrency and put them in a separate stack, but the cards are mixed up. Fortunately, you have two friends with you, so you can divide the cards, give each person a pile, and tell them what to look for. Then each of you can search your own pile of cards. Once someone finds a concurrency card, they can announce it and put it into a separate stack.

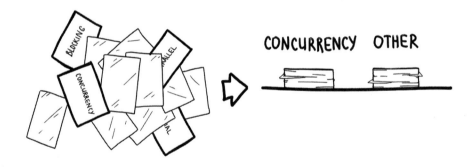

This algorithm might look like the following:

1. Divide the pile into stacks, and hand one stack to each person (serial).

2. Everyone looks for a "concurrency" card (parallel).

3. Put the concurrency cards in a separate pile (serial).

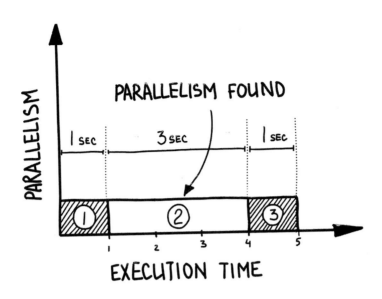

Steps 1 and 3 of this algorithm take 1 second, and step 2 takes 3 seconds. Thus, it takes 5 seconds to execute the algorithm from beginning to end if you do it yourself. Steps 1 and 3 are algorithmically sequential, and there is no way to separate them into independent tasks and use parallel execution. But you can easily use parallel execution in step 2 by dividing the cards into any number of stacks, as long as you have friends to execute this step independently. You reduce the execution time of that part to 1 second with the help of two friends. The whole program now takes only 3 seconds, which is a 40% speedup. The speedup here is calculated as a ratio of the time it takes to execute in a parallel manner with a certain number of processing resources, over the time it takes to execute the program in the optimal sequential manner with a single processing resource.

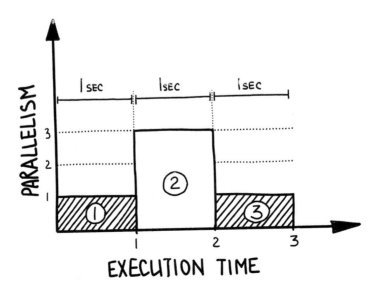

What happens if we keep increasing the number of friends? For example, suppose you add three more friends, making six people total. Now step 2 of the program takes only half a second to execute. The whole algorithm takes only 2.5 seconds to complete, which is a 50% speedup.

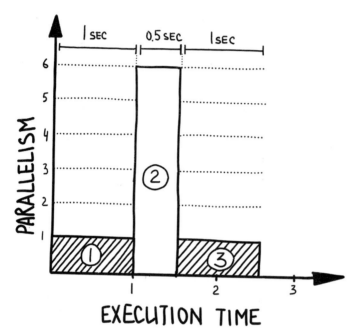

Following the same logic, you can invite all the people in the city and make the parallel part of the algorithm execute instantaneously (in theory, you have a communication cost overhead, discussed in Chapter 6). You still end up with latency of at least 2 seconds—the serial part of the algorithm.

A parallel program runs as fast as its slowest sequential part. An example of this phenomenon can be seen every time you go to the mall. Hundreds of people can shop at the same time, rarely disturbing each other. But when it comes time to pay, lines form because there are fewer cashiers than shoppers ready to leave.

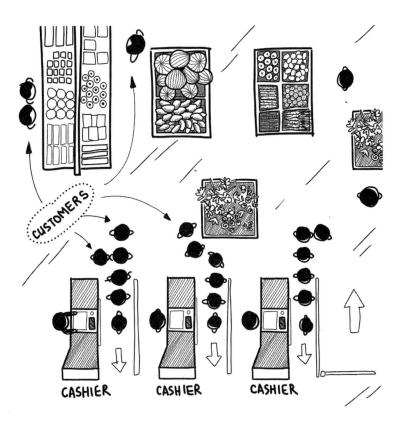

The same applies to programming. Since we cannot speed up sequential parts of a program, increasing the number of resources does not affect their execution. This is the key to understanding Amdahl's law. The potential speed of a program using parallel computing is limited to the sequential parts of the program. The law describes the maximum speedup we can expect when we add resources to the system, assuming parallel computing. For our example, Amdahl's law predicts that if two-thirds of a program are sequential, no matter how many processors we have, we never get more than 1.5× speedup.

More formally, the law is stated using this formula:

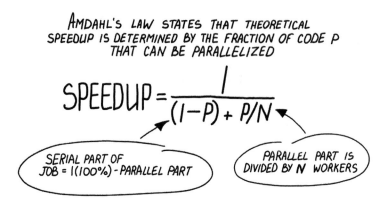

The formula may look harmless until we start putting in values. For example, if 33% of the program is sequential, adding 1 million processors can give no more than 3× speedup. We can't accelerate one-third of the program, so even if the rest of the program runs instantaneously, the performance gain is limited to 300%. Adding several processors can often provide significant acceleration, but as the number of processors grows, the advantage quickly diminishes. The following graphical representation shows the speedup versus the number of processors for different fractions of code that can be parallelized if we do not consider algorithms or coordination overhead.

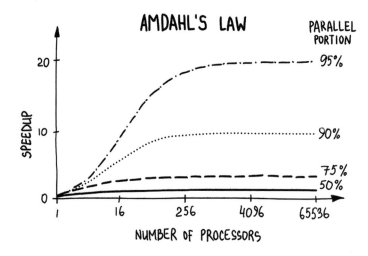

We can also do the math the other way around—for example, with 2,500 processors, what percentage of the program must be perfectly parallelizable to get 100× acceleration? Putting the values into Amdahl's law, we get $100 \leq 1/(S + (1 - S)/2500)$. By calculating S, we see that less than 1% of the program can be sequential.

To sum up, Amdahl's law illustrates why using multiple processors for parallel computing is only really useful for programs that are highly parallelizable. Just because you can write programs to be parallel doesn't mean you always should, because the costs and overhead associated with parallelization sometimes outweigh the benefits. Amdahl's law is a handy tool to estimate the benefits of parallelizing a program to determine whether it makes sense to do so.

Gustafson's law

With such disappointing results, it is tempting to abandon parallelism as a way to improve performance. You should not be completely discouraged. Parallelism does provide real acceleration of performance-critical parts of programs, but you can't speed up all parts of a program—unless it is an embarrassingly parallel problem. For other tasks, there is a hard limit to the possible gains.

But we can look at Amdahl's law from a different perspective. Our example program ran in 5 seconds—what if we double the amount of work done in the parallelizable part—not 3 but 6 tasks? So, we would get 6 tasks done simultaneously, and the program would still run in 5 seconds, resulting in a total of 8 tasks done—a 1.6× increase over two processors. And if we add a couple more processors, each doing the same amount of work, we can get 11 tasks done in the same 5 seconds: a 2.6× increase.

According to Amdahl's law, speedup shows how much less time it will take to execute a parallel program, assuming that the volume of the problem remains constant. However, the speedup can also be seen as an increase in the volume of the executed task in a constant time interval (throughput). Gustafson's law emerged from this assumption.

Gustafson's law gives a more optimistic perspective of parallelism limits. If we keep increasing the amount of work, the sequential parts will have less and less effect, and we can see speedup in proportion to the number of processors we have.

So if you ever hear Amdahl's law cited as a reason why parallelism won't work in your case, you can make the observation that Gustafson had an explanation for what to do. And that's the key to why supercomputers and distributed systems have been successful with parallelism—because we can keep increasing the volume of data.

Now that we are familiar with parallel computing, it's time to talk about how it relates to concurrency.

Concurrency vs. parallelism

Conversational meanings of the words *parallel* and *concurrent* are mostly synonymous, which is a source of significant confusion that extends even to the computer science literature. Distinguishing between parallel and concurrent programming is important because they pursue different goals at different conceptual levels.

Concurrency is about multiple tasks that start, run, and complete in overlapping time periods in no specific order. Parallelism is about multiple tasks running at the same time on hardware with multiple computing resources, like multicore processors. Concurrency and parallelism are *not* the same thing.

Imagine that one cook is chopping salad while occasionally stirring the soup on the stove. The cook has to stop chopping, check the stove, start chopping again, and repeat this process until everything is done.

As you can see, we have only one processing resource here—the cook—and their concurrency is mostly related to logistics. Without concurrency, the cook has to wait until the soup on the stove is ready before chopping the salad.

Parallelism is an *implementation property*. It is the simultaneous physical execution of tasks at runtime, and it requires hardware with multiple computing resources. It lies on the hardware layer.

Back in the kitchen, we now have two cooks: one who can do the stirring and one who can chop the salad. We've divided the work by having another processing resource—another cook. Parallelism is a subclass of concurrency: before we can do several tasks at once, we must first manage several tasks.

The essence of the relationship between concurrency and parallelism is that concurrent computations can be parallelized without changing the correctness of the result, but concurrency itself does not imply parallelism. Further, parallelism does not imply concurrency; it is often possible for an optimizer to take programs with no semantic concurrency and break them down into parallel components via such techniques as pipeline processing; wide vector operations; single instruction, multiple data (SIMD) operations; and divide and conquer (we talk about some of those later in the book).

As Unix and Go programming legend Rob Pike pointed out, "Concurrency is about dealing with lots of things at once. Parallelism is about doing lots of things at once."[1] The concurrency of a program depends on the programming language and how it is programmed, while parallelism depends on the actual execution environment. In a single-core CPU, we may get concurrency but not parallelism. But both go beyond the traditional sequential model in which things happen one at a time.

To get a better idea about the distinction between concurrency and parallelism, consider the following points:

- An application can be concurrent but not parallel. It processes more than one task over a given period (i.e., juggling more than one task even if no two tasks are executing at the same instant—this is described in more detail in Chapter 6).

- An application can be parallel but not concurrent, which means it processes multiple subtasks of a single task simultaneously.

---

[1] Rob Pike gave a talk at Heroku's Waza conference entitled "Concurrency is not parallelism," https://go.dev/blog/waza-talk.

- An application can be neither parallel nor concurrent, which means it processes one task at a time sequentially, and the task is never broken into subtasks.

- An application can be both parallel and concurrent, which means it processes multiple tasks or subtasks of a single task concurrently at the same time (executing them in parallel).

Imagine you have a program that inserts values into a hash table. In terms of spreading the insert operation between multiple cores, that's parallelism. But in terms of coordinating access to the hash table, that's concurrency. And if you still don't understand the latter, don't worry; the following chapters explain the concept in detail.

Concurrency covers various topics, including the interaction between processes, sharing and competition for resources (such as memory, files, and I/O access), synchronization between multiple processes, and allocation of processor time between processes. These problems arise not only in multiprocessor and distributed processing environments but also in single-processor systems. In the next chapter, we start by understanding the environment the program is running in—the computer hardware and runtime system.

Recap

- Every problem, when formulated into an application, is divided into a series of tasks that, in the simplest case, are executed serially.

- A *task* can be thought of as a logically independent piece of work.

- *Sequential computing* means each task in a program depends on the execution of all previous tasks in the order in which they are listed in the code.

- *Serial execution* refers to a set of ordered instructions executed one at a time on one processing unit. Serial execution is required when the input to each task requires the output of a previous task.

- *Parallel execution* refers to executing multiple computations at the same time. Parallel execution can be used when the tasks can be performed independently.

- *Parallel computing* uses multiple processing elements simultaneously to solve a problem. This often leads to significant program redesign—decomposition of the problem, creating or adapting an algorithm, adding synchronization points to the program, and so on.

- *Concurrency* describes working on multiple tasks at the same time. *Parallelism* depends on the actual runtime environment, and it requires multiple processing resources and task independence in a decomposed algorithm. The concurrency of a program depends on the programming language and how it is programmed, while parallelism depends on the actual execution environment.

- Amdahl's law is a handy tool to estimate the benefits of parallelizing a program to determine whether it makes sense to do so.

- Gustafson's law describes how to get more work out of systems despite the limitations of Amdahl's law.

How computers work | 3

....

In this chapter

- You learn the details of how code is executed
  on the CPU

- You learn about the functions and goals
  of the runtime system

- You learn how to choose hardware suitable
  for your problem

....

Twenty years ago, a working programmer could go for years without encountering a system that had more than two processing resources. Today, even a mobile phone has multiple processing resources. A modern programmer's mental model needs to encompass multiple processes running on different processing resources at the same time.

When describing concurrent algorithms, it is not necessary to know the specific programming language to implement a program. It is necessary, however, to understand the features of the computer system on which the algorithm will be executed. You can construct the most effective concurrent algorithm by selecting the types of operations that most fully utilize computer system hardware. Therefore, you need to understand the potential capabilities of different hardware architectures.

Since the goal of using parallel hardware is performance, the efficiency of our code is a major concern. This, in turn, means we need a good understanding of the underlying hardware we are programming. This chapter provides an overview of parallel hardware so you can make informed decisions when designing software.

Processor

The term *central processing unit (CPU)* originated in the misty days of the first computers when one massive cabinet contained the circuitry needed to interpret and execute machine instructions. The CPU also performed all operations for connected peripheral devices like printers, card readers, and early storage devices such as drum and disk drives.

The modern CPU has become a slightly different device, more focused on its primary task of executing machine instructions. The CPU can easily process these instructions thanks to the *control unit (CU)*, which interprets machine instructions, and the *arithmetic logic unit (ALU)*, which performs arithmetic and bitwise operations. Thanks to the CU and ALU together, the CPU processes more complex programs than a simple calculator can.

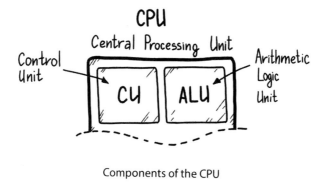

Components of the CPU

But another component of the CPU also plays an important role in speeding up execution.

Cache

The *cache* is temporary memory on the CPU. This chip-based feature of a computer lets us access information more quickly than from the computer's main memory.

Imagine a joinery workshop with one joiner. The joiner (CPU) has to fulfill incoming customer requests (instructions). To make the product the customer wants, the joiner creates nearby temporary storage for fresh wood and some resources without having to go to the warehouse where they keep all their supplies (hard disk drive [HDD]).

The temporary storage is the memory attached to the CPU—called *random access memory (RAM)*—that is used to store data and instructions. When a program starts to run, executable files and data are copied to the RAM and stored until the end of the program execution.

But the CPU never directly accesses RAM. The CPU's ability to perform calculations is much faster than the RAM's ability to transfer data to the CPU. Modern CPUs have one or more levels of *cache memory* to speed up access.

Going back to the workshop, in addition to having access to temporary storage in the workshop, the joiner always needs fast access to their tools, so those should always be at hand. The joiner stores them on a workbench for fast access. You can think of the cache memory as a workbench for the processor.

Cache memory is faster than RAM, and it is closer to the CPU because it is located on the CPU chip. Cache memory provides storage for data and instructions so the CPU doesn't have to wait for data to be retrieved from RAM. When the processor needs data—and program instructions are considered data—the cache controller determines whether the data is in the cache and provides it to the processor. If the requested data is not in the cache, it is retrieved from RAM and moved to the cache. The cache controller analyzes the requested data, predicts what additional data will be required from RAM, and loads it into the cache.

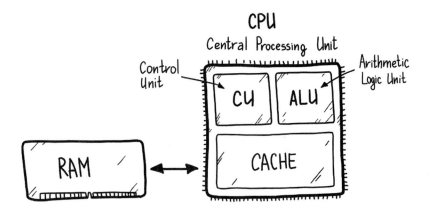

A processor has three levels of cache: levels 1, 2, and 3 (L1, L2, and L3). Levels 2 (L2) and 3 (L3) are designed to predict what data and instructions will be needed next, moving them from RAM to the L1 cache so they are closer to the processor and ready when needed. The bigger the level, the slower the communication channel is, and the more memory is available. The L1 cache is closest to the processor. Because of the additional cache levels, the processor can stay busy and not waste cycles waiting for the required data.

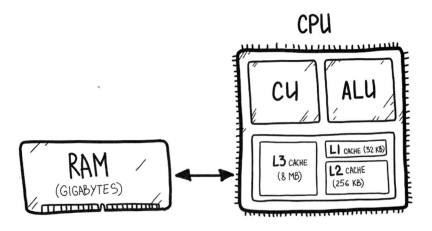

Almost all data access and communication add up to execution latency—the communication cost—and it's one of the biggest threats to system performance. Cache exists to mitigate or at least soften these communication costs. Let's take a look at how it would affect latency if things were scaled up into everyday units that humans can intuitively picture (this is called *scaled latency*).

System event	Actual latency	Scaled latency
One CPU cycle	0.4 ns	1 s
L1 cache access	0.9 ns	2 s
L2 cache access	2.8 ns	7 s
L3 cache access	28 ns	1 min
Main memory access (RAM)	~100 ns	4 min
High-speed SSD I/O	<10 µs	7 h
SSD I/O	50–150 µs	1.5–4 days
HDD I/O	1–10 ms	1–9 months
Network request, San Francisco to NYC	65 ms	5 years

Having said that, let's look at the actual execution cycle.

CPU execution cycle

Back to the workshop again. Our single joiner does all the work, from communicating with customers to the actual woodworking. This work includes getting customer ideas, translating those ideas into task items, executing tasks, and giving the results to the customers. The joiner spends all their time in this cycle, and that's what keeps the business running.

Similarly, the CPU carries out a continuous process of instruction execution through various stages. These sequences of stages are known as the *CPU cycle*. In their simplest form, processors operate in four different stages:

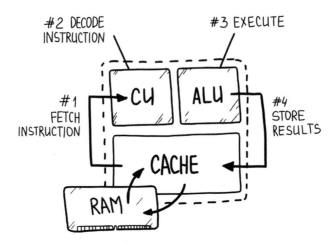

CPU execution cycle

1. *Fetch*. The CU fetches the instruction from memory or cache and copies it to the CPU. In this process, the CU uses various counters to understand what instruction to fetch and where to find it.

2. *Decode*. The previously fetched instruction is decoded and sent for processing. Different types of instructions do different things, so depending on the type of instruction and the operation code, we need to know which processing units the instructions will be sent to.

3. *Execute*. The compute instruction is then moved to ALU and starts the execution.

4. *Store the result*. Once the instruction is complete, the result is written into RAM, and the next instruction starts its execution. Then the processor goes back to step 1 until there are no more instructions left to fetch.

The processor spends all its time in this cycle, endlessly retrieving the next instruction, decoding it, executing it, and storing the result.

Runtime system

Working with the CPU is not a simple process. Developers have to handle everything ourselves, including the various operational tasks: controlling hardware resources, managing access to those hardware resources, managing the exact functionality that should be executed, providing isolation between programs in case of a crash, accessing shared resources, and so on.

Modern systems need to be multipurpose and hence are complex. Eventually, they become overgrown with many software systems related to specific management tasks, such as file management systems, graphics management systems, and task management systems. These are all examples of microprogram management systems that eventually evolved into an additional level of abstraction introduced between the application and the system: the *runtime system*, the common example of which is an *operating system*.

Going back to the workshop, our joiner starts getting strange orders from customers, like delivering wood, building a ship or bridge, or making products beyond the ability of the joiner's tools. The joiner realizes that these orders are coming to them from customers by mistake, since other businesses do the requested work. The joiner decides to hire someone to take care of these requests and give the workshop only the work the joiner can do. So, they arrange with the other business owners on the same street to hire a manager to handle incoming requests. This manager has the customer complete a predetermined form, determines the right business to fulfill the request, and passes the request to the joiner or other business.

The manager is the *operating system* (*OS*), a low-level system interface between the hardware component of the computer system and the developer. Those interfaces are called *system calls*. They interact with the computer hardware and provide services and utilities that user applications can use.

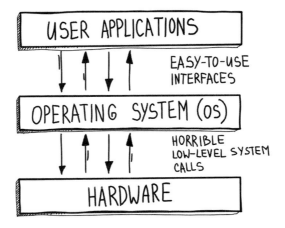

For example, when a program wants to write data to a disk, it delegates that task to the OS. The OS gives instructions to the disk using the disk controller that can send the right signals to the disk. The program that wants to use a disk doesn't worry about what kind of disk the system has or understand how it works. The OS handles the details and, if possible, tries to protect the hardware and other resources from improper use. This introduces overhead as the program uses OS functionality without directly communicating with the hardware. Sometimes this can be critical, and it is advantageous to do something at the user application level instead of introducing a system call. I describe specific examples in the following chapters.

To execute a program using the OS, the first step is loading the executable file and any static data (such as initialized variables) into memory. Then we start the program from the entry point: main(). When the OS switches to main(), control of the processor is transferred to the program, and thus our program begins its execution under the control and protection of the OS.

All modern computer systems follow these steps. The process may be more sophisticated than the one described, but overall, the design components are the same.

Design of computer systems

If you look at the organization of a computer system, you will see one or more processors, RAM that the processors can access, various peripheral devices (printers, card readers, hard drives, monitors, etc.), and device controllers or *drivers* that allow all of those devices to communicate with the processor or RAM. There is a channel to connect everything: the *system bus* allows communications between the CPU, RAM, and peripheral devices.

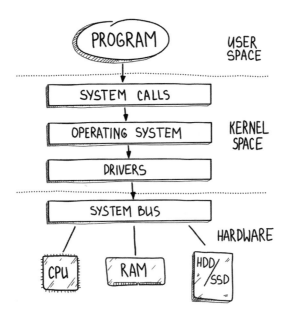

Let's now turn our attention to *user space* and *kernel space*, two distinct areas in a computer system. User space is where user-level applications run, and kernel space is where the OS's core functions and system calls run. The distinction is important because applications in user space cannot access or modify the underlying system, while the kernel has complete control over the system and its resources. The internal design of a computer system remains largely the same regardless of hardware platform specifics, such as the form factor, OS structure, or intended use.

With this understanding of the general components of the design, let's move on to look at the several levels of parallel hardware that this design can represent.

Multiple levels of concurrent hardware

CPUs are composed of many circuits (ALUs) that can perform basic arithmetic operations (like addition or multiplication). Because of this, the CPU can break up complex mathematical operations so that subparts of the operation run on separate arithmetic units simultaneously. This is called *instruction-level parallelism*. Sometimes this type of parallelism is taken to an even deeper level: *bit-level parallelism*. (Most developers rarely think about this level. The work of arranging instructions in the most convenient sequence for the processor is done by the compiler. Only a small group of engineers trying to squeeze all possible power from the processor or compiler are interested in this level.)

Another simple idea for creating parallel hardware is to install more than one chip in a computer system, replicating the processor, just like hiring a manager so all craftspeople can work together on incoming customer requests. This is a *multiprocessor*, which is what we can call any computer system with more than one processor.

A *multicore processor* is a special kind of multiprocessor with all processors on the same chip. Each core works independently, and the OS perceives each core as a separate processor. There are slight differences between these two approaches in terms of how quickly the processors can work together and how they access memory, but for this book, we treat them as the same.

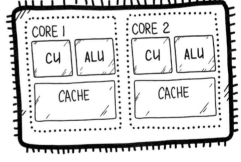

A multicore processor

Symmetric multiprocessing architecture

Computer memory usually operates at a much slower speed than processors do, resulting in the communication costs mentioned in Chapter 2. That's why most multiprocessor systems today use *symmetric multiprocessing* (*SMP*) architecture. SMP is a set of identical processors connected to shared memory with a single address space and operating under the same OS.

The processors in SMP architecture are linked by an interconnection network via the system bus. Although these networks are fast, if processors need to exchange data, the exchange is not instantaneous because it must go through one or more interconnections. These communication costs are not negligible, and this problem worsens the latency as the number of interacting resources and the distance between them increases. Thus, in the SMP architecture, all processors have their own private cache to reduce system bus traffic, resulting in lower latency.

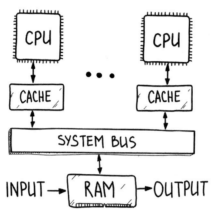

Symmetric multiprocessing (SMP) architecture consists of multiple interconnected processors that have shared memory.

The coolest feature of SMP is that the existence of multiple processors is transparent to the end user. The OS takes care of scheduling processes on individual processors and synchronization among those processors. However, in such systems, increasing the number of processors connected to a common system bus makes it a bottleneck. This problem is worsened by *cache coherence,* where multiple processor cores share the same memory hierarchy but have their own L1 data and instruction caches.

> **NOTE**   The development of the MESI protocol in the 1980s solved the problem of cache coherence in multiprocessor systems. By tracking the state of each cache line, MESI ensures that all processors have a consistent view of the data, allowing for efficient and conflict-free collaboration. Today, MESI is an essential part of modern computing.

The only way to move beyond SMP to large, massively parallel computers is to abandon the shared memory architecture and move to distributed memory systems called *computer clusters.* These clusters are distributed machines with their own CPUs, connected via a network. Computer clusters are very powerful parallel systems. One machine cannot share memory with another, as each operates independently. If one machine changes its local memory, that change is not automatically reflected in the memory of processors on other machines. Hence, clusters typically have distributed memory that leads to greater communication costs because we need to communicate via a network, which is much slower than transferring data between processes on the local machine.

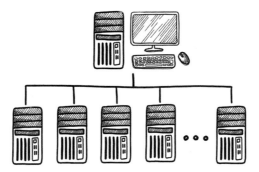

Clusters are appropriate for *loosely coupled* problems (which do not require frequent communication between processors but do require more power), while *tightly coupled* problems are more suitable for single-machine systems. The advantage of clusters is high scalability. The disadvantage is the high communication costs. We discuss distributed systems in detail in later chapters, but right now, we focus on the types of multiprocessor architectures.

Taxonomy of parallel computers

One of the most widely used systems for classifying multiprocessor architectures is Flynn's taxonomy. It distinguishes four classes of computer architectures based on two independent dimensions: *instructions* and *data flow*.

The first and second categories of computer architectures—*single instruction, single data (SISD)* and *multiple instruction, single data (MISD)*—involve processing one block of data with one or multiple instructions, respectively. However, as they lack parallelization, they are irrelevant for concurrent systems and are only mentioned here for reference.

The third category is *single instruction, multiple data (SIMD)*, which features shared control units across multiple cores. With this design, only one instruction can be executed simultaneously on all available processing resources, allowing the same operation to be performed on a large set of data elements simultaneously. However, the instruction set in SIMD machines is limited, making them suitable for solving specific problems that require high computing power but not much versatility. Graphics processing units (GPUs) are a well-known example of SIMD today.

The fourth category is *multiple instruction, multiple data (MIMD)*. Here, each processing resource has an independent control unit. So, it is not limited to certain types of instructions and executes different instructions independently on a separate block of data. Thus, it includes architectures with multiple cores, multiple CPUs, or even multiple machines so that different tasks can be executed simultaneously on several different devices.

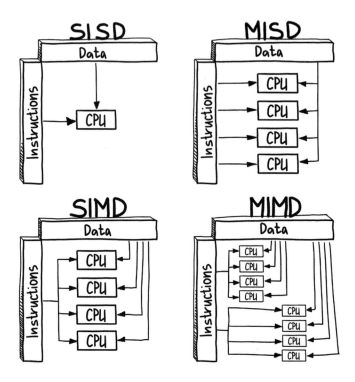

MIMD has a wider set of instructions, so the individual processing resources are more versatile than in SIMD. That's why MIMD is the most commonly used architecture in Flynn's taxonomy, and you'll find it in everything from multicore PCs to distributed clusters.

CPU vs. GPU

Even if you don't play video games, you can be grateful to the players because they have spawned a class of very powerful parallel processing devices: GPUs. The CPU and GPU are similar. They both have millions of transistors and can process a vast number of instructions per second. But how are these two important components different, and when should we use one or the other?

Standard CPUs are built using the MIMD architecture. A modern CPU is powerful because engineers have implemented a wide variety of instructions in them. And a computer system can complete a task because its CPU can complete that task.

The GPU is a specialized type of processor similar to SIMD architecture, optimized for a very limited set of instructions. The GPU operates at a lower clock speed than the CPU but has more cores—hundreds or even thousands that run simultaneously. That means it performs a huge number of simple instructions at incredible speed due to massive parallelism.

NOTE For example, the NVIDIA GTX 1080 graphics card has 2,560 cores with 1607 MHz clock speed. Thanks to these cores, the NVIDIA GTX 1080 can perform 2,560 instructions per clock cycle. If we want to make the picture 1% brighter, the GPU will cope with this without any difficulty. But the Intel Core i9-10940X CPU with 3.3 GHz can execute only 14 instructions per clock cycle.[1]

Although individual CPU cores are faster, based on clock speed, and have extensive instruction sets, the sheer number of GPU cores and the massive parallelism they provide more than compensate for the difference in CPU core clock speed and limited instruction set. CPUs are just better suited for complex linear tasks.

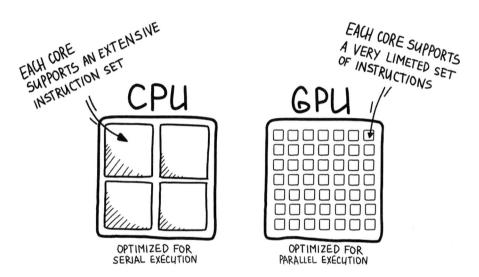

GPUs are best suited for repetitive and highly parallel computational tasks such as video and image processing, machine learning, financial simulations, and many other types of scientific computing. Operations such as matrix addition and multiplication are easily performed using a GPU because most of these operations in matrix cells are independent of each other and are similar and, therefore, can be parallelized.

Hardware architectures are highly variable and can affect the portability of programs between different systems. In addition, programs sometimes inherently accelerate differently depending on where they run. For example, many graphics programs run much better and faster on GPU resources, while ordinary programs with mixed logic make sense to run on the CPU.

In this book, we use the term *CPU* in a general sense that covers both types of processing resources. With all the components of physical execution in mind, in the next chapter, we add a couple of easy-to-use abstractions that represent instruction streams.

---

[1] Intel Core i9-10940X X-series processor specifications, http://mng.bz/JgGz.

Recap

- Execution depends on the actual hardware. Modern hardware has multiple processing resources—multiple *cores*, *multiprocessors*, or *computer clusters*—and they are optimized for executing programs.

- Flynn's taxonomy describes four types of architecture based on whether the system processes single or multiple instructions at a time (SI or MI) and whether each instruction acts on single or multiple blocks of data (SD or MD).

- A *GPU* is an example of *SIMD* architecture. It's optimized for highly parallel task execution.

- Modern multiprocessors and multicore processors are examples of *MIMD*. They are far more complex because they're multipurpose.

- The processor or CPU is the brain of the computer system, but it's difficult to work with directly. In programming, an additional level of abstraction is introduced between the application and the system: the *runtime system*.

- To exploit parallel execution, an application developer needs a processing unit that is suitable for the problem. A CPU has a higher clock frequency and a wider set of instructions that can be executed in parallel, while a GPU operates at a lower clock speed and executes only one instruction across all of the cores, but it does so at incredible speed due to massive parallelism.

Building blocks of concurrency | 4

In this chapter

- You learn more about the middle layer of concurrency: the runtime system, a popular example of which is the operating system

- You learn the internals of the two basic concurrency abstractions: threads and processes

- You learn how to implement concurrent applications using threads and processes

- You learn how to choose the concurrency abstraction suitable for your problem

Concurrent programming involves breaking down applications into independent units of concurrency. In previous chapters, we referred to these units as *tasks* for organizing the flow of the application. Now, with knowledge of the hardware being used, we need to map these abstractions onto the physical devices executing the code. Fortunately, another layer of abstraction can handle this task: the OS. Its role is to apply the available hardware as efficiently as possible, but it is not a magical solution. This chapter focuses on how developers can structure their programs to aid the OS in achieving optimal hardware utilization.

Concurrent programming steps

Concurrent programming is a set of abstractions that allow the developer to structure the program to generate small, independent tasks and pass them to the runtime system, queuing them for execution. The runtime system orchestrates tasks to optimally utilize system resources and passes them for execution on appropriate processing resources. The two main abstractions used to accomplish this in concurrent programming are *processes* and *threads*.

Processes

The informal definition of a *process* is relatively straightforward: it is a running program. The program itself is a lifeless thing. It sits on a disk, representing a set of instructions waiting to be executed. The OS takes these instructions and executes them on hardware, turning the program into something useful.

Imagine a car. A car is just a set of mechanical parts that together make up a car. Even though the car has great potential, it has no value if it stands still. But when someone turns the key and the engine starts running, the car can move. It evolves into the process of driving. It becomes not just a car but a trip from point A to point B, bringing value. The car facilitates the desired action.

Source code is like the car. It is just a passive sequence of instructions that operate with resource abstractions. When writing source code, developers do not have memory to store temporary data, files to read or write, or devices they want to send signals to. Developers write code using real-world models built upon abstractions provided by programming languages and runtime environments. Actual resources must be provided at the time of execution.

The abstraction provided by the OS for a running program is what we call a process. There is no concept of a process at the level of machine instructions.

The purpose of using processes in an OS is to isolate tasks and allocate hardware resources for their execution. All processes in an OS share hardware resources and are managed by the OS. To ensure that the OS knows the relationship between processes and resources, each process must have its own independent address space and file table. Therefore, processes are the unit for resource allocation in the OS.

OSs provide the illusion of full ownership of the computer system to each process, even though there are usually multiple processes running concurrently. To maintain this illusion, OSs take great care to control and protect processes and isolate them from each other. This includes controlling the allocation of CPU cores and memory for each process. The main advantage of processes is the complete independence and isolation of their execution from the rest of the system, preventing accidental interference with global objects and ensuring that crashes of one program do not affect others.

From this advantage, however, comes a disadvantage. Processes are independent of each other by design, which makes communication between them difficult. Formally, processes have almost nothing in common, and any nontrivial communication between processes requires using other mechanisms, which are usually several orders of magnitude slower than direct access to data. We talk about that in detail in Chapter 5; for now, let's look inside the process.

Process internals

As we have said, a process is just a running program. At any given time, we can assemble a process by making a list of the various parts of the computer system that it accesses or modifies at runtime:

- The data the process reads or writes to is stored in memory. Thus, the memory the process can see or access (the address space) is part of the running process.

- The executable file with all the machine instructions is part of the process.

- The process also needs an identifier: a unique name by which the process can be identified. It is called a *process ID* (*PID*).

- Finally, programs often access disks, network resources, or other third-party devices. Such information must include a list of files currently open by the process, open network connections, and any additional information about the resources it uses.

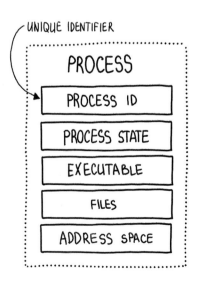

Thus, a process encapsulates many things: an executable file, the set of resources used (files, connections, etc.), and the address space with internal variables. All of this is called *execution context*. Because so many things exist inside processes, starting a new process is a pretty heavy thing to do. That's why they are often called *heavyweight* processes.

Process states

If you look at a process from a high level, everything appears trivial. At first, it seems the process doesn't exist. Then it is created and initialized, after which it exists somewhere in computer memory (the *Created* state). When the user code starts a process, it goes to the *Ready* state—it is ready to be executed on a processor core at any moment, but it doesn't do anything yet. It needs a processing resource to start the execution. Then the OS selects the next process to be executed on the CPU from the list of processes ready for execution. After the OS chooses a process, the chosen process goes into the *Running* state.

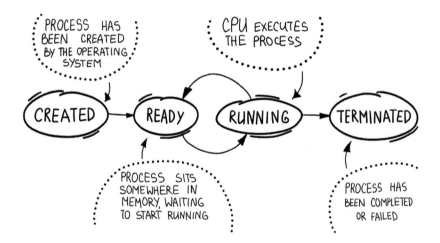

Processes are usually created by the OS. Apart from creating processes, the OS is also responsible for process termination. This is not a trivial task. The OS needs to understand that the process is finished—either the task is complete, the process failed and it's time to clean it up, or the parent process is dead. Creating or terminating a process is relatively expensive because, as we have seen, a process has many resources attached to it, and they must be created or freed up. Doing so takes system time and introduces additional latency.

Multiple processes

Processes can create their own processes—called *child processes*—through appropriate system calls, such as `fork()` or `spawn()`; this process is called *spawning*. Child processes are independent forks of the main process with a separate memory address space, which again means the process works independently and is isolated from others by the OS's control. It cannot directly access the data of other processes, and instructions belonging to each process are executed in the corresponding process independently and, ideally, in parallel.

Now we are moving into the territory of concurrency. Using spawning programs, execution can be decomposed into multiple processes that can be executed simultaneously on parallel hardware.

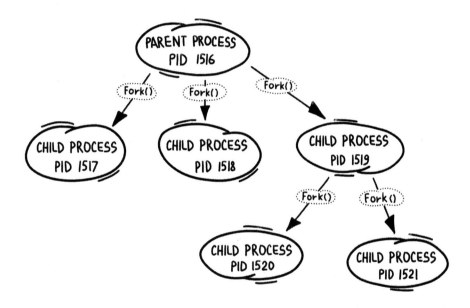

However, this is probably easier to understand in code than in theory. Here is an example of a program that makes three child processes using a forking mechanism:

```python
# Chapter 4/child_processes.py
import os
from multiprocessing import Process


def run_child() -> None:
    print("Child: I am the child process")
    print(f"Child: Child's PID: {os.getpid()}")
    print(f"Child: Parent's PID: {os.getppid()}")
```

```
def start_parent(num_children: int) -> None:
    print("Parent : I am the parent process")
    print(f"Parent : Parent's PID: {os.getpid()}")
    for i in range(num_children):
        print(f"Starting Process {i}")
        Process(target=run_child).start()

if __name__ == "__main__":
    num_children = 3
    start_parent(num_children)
```

Spawns a new process.
The start() method starts
the run_child function in
a separate process.

The code creates a parent process with three child processes that are copies of the parent process; the only difference is the process ID. The execution of the parent and child processes is independent.

> **NOTE**   It's important to note that when forking a process, the new process starts its execution from the point where the forking occurred, and its internal state is copied. It does not execute the script again from the beginning.

The program outputs messages from the parent and child processes with their respected PIDs, similar to the following:

```
Parent : I am the parent process
Parent : Parent's PID: 73553
Parent : Child's PID: 73554
Child: I am the child process
Child: Child's PID: 73554
Child: Parent's PID: 73553
Parent : I am the parent process
Parent : Parent's PID: 73553
Parent : Child's PID: 73555
Child: I am the child process
Child: Child's PID: 73555
Child: Parent's PID: 73553
Parent : I am the parent process
Parent : Parent's PID: 73553
Parent : Child's PID: 73556
Child: I am the child process
Child: Child's PID: 73556
Child: Parent's PID: 73553
```

Programming languages commonly have high-level abstractions or service methods for working with processes as they are easier to maintain and follow in the program source code.

NOTE This forking/spawning approach has been implemented in *prefork* mode in several popular server technologies. Preforking means a server creates forks at server startup, which then handle incoming requests. NGINX, Apache HTTP Server, and Gunicorn work in this mode, allowing them to handle hundreds of requests. But these solutions also support other methods.

Threads

Sharing memory between processes is possible on most OSs, but it requires additional effort (we discuss this in Chapter 5). Another abstraction allows us to share a bit more: *threads*.

In the end, a program is simply a set of machine instructions that must be executed one after the other in sequence. To make this happen, the OS uses the concept of a thread. Technically, a thread is defined as an independent stream of instructions whose execution can be scheduled by the OS.

Remember we said that a process is a running program plus resources? If we split the program into separate components, a process is a container of resources (address space, files, connections, etc.), and a thread is a dynamic part—a sequence of instructions executed inside this container. Therefore, in the OS context, a process can be seen as a unit of resources, while a thread can be viewed as a unit of execution.

But threads were born from the idea that the most efficient way to share data between interacting processes is to share a common address space. Thus, threads in a single process are like processes that can easily share resources with each other and their parent process, such as address space, files, connections, shared data, and so on.

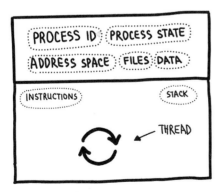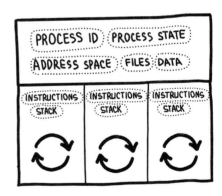

Threads also maintain their own state to allow for the safe, local, independent execution of their instructions. Each thread is unaware of the other threads unless it is interfering with them on purpose. The OS manages the threads and can distribute them among the available processor cores. Thus, creating a multithreaded program can be a convenient way to run multiple tasks concurrently.

To illustrate the difference between processes and threads, let's look at an example. Imagine that you are managing a construction company, and you hire three construction crews to work on three different projects.

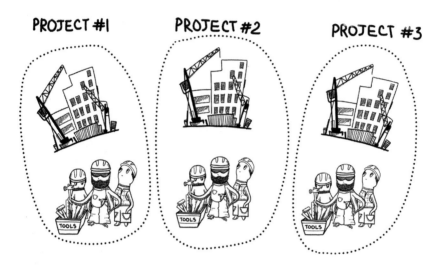

This is a process-like job. Each construction crew (process) is dedicated to one project (task) with its own tools, project plan, and resources. On the other hand, to save money, you could hire just one construction crew for all three different projects; they would use common tools and resources, but there would be a separate list of instructions for each project, similar to how threads work.

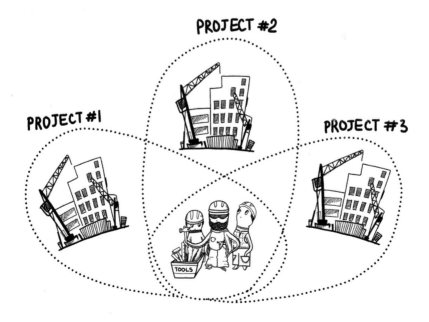

Historically, hardware vendors implemented their own versions of threads. These implementations differed significantly, making it difficult for developers to implement portable threaded applications. A standardized programming interface was needed.

For UNIX systems, this interface was defined by IEEE POSIX[1] and is available as an optional library for Windows-family OSs. Implementations that adhere to this standard are called *POSIX threads* or *Pthreads* (also the name of the C library implementation). Most hardware manufacturers use Pthreads, so we'll talk more about this standard.

In the standard, every program we run causes the OS to create a process, and every process has at least one thread; a process without a thread cannot exist. Each thread also maintains its independent execution context to ensure that its instructions are executed safely and independently.

Thread features

Properly implemented, threads have advantages and disadvantages compared to processes.

Advantage: Less memory overhead

Processes are completely independent, each with its own address space, set of threads, and copies of variables that are completely independent of the same variables in other processes. Threads have much less memory overhead than the standard `fork()` function as the parent thread is not copied—threads use the same process. Because of this, threads are also sometimes called *lightweight* processes.

Consequently, we can create more threads than processes on the same system. Creating and terminating threads is faster than processes because it takes less time for the OS to allocate and manage thread resources. Because of this, we can create threads whenever it makes sense in an application and not worry about wasting CPU time and memory.

Advantage: Less communication overhead

Each process works with its own memory. Processes can only exchange something through a process communication mechanism, which we discuss in Chapter 5.

Threads use the same address space and therefore can communicate with each other by writing and reading to the shared address space of their parent process without any problems or overhead: anything changed by one thread is immediately available to all. Hence, for widely used SMP systems, it is sometimes much more convenient to use threads than processes.

---

[1] IEEE POSIX 1003.1c (1995), https://standards.ieee.org/ieee/1003.1c/1393.

Disadvantage: Need for synchronization

The OS provides complete independence of processes from each other, so if one of them crashes, other processes are not harmed. This is not the case with threads: since all threads in a process use the same shared resources, if one crashes or is corrupted, the others will likely be affected. To prevent this from happening, developers need to synchronize access to shared resources and have more control over the behavior of threads (we discuss this in Chapter 8).

Thread implementation

A thread-based approach is a common way to achieve concurrency in many languages. This does not mean threads are explicitly used in programming languages. Instead, the runtime environment can map other programming language concurrency constructs to physical threads at runtime. Programming languages usually have higher-level abstractions for creating processes because they are easier to maintain and keep track of in the program's source code.

> **NOTE**   Avoid using low-level threads if you can get away with it. Look at libraries that abstract away the need to use low-level threads. A general implementation of POSIX is presented in C/C++ as a library of functions. Modern languages such as Python, Java, and C# (.NET) provide a set of abstractions on top of native threads that most closely match these languages' design characteristics. Similarly, the property of multiple threads can be idiomatically hidden in a language such as Go's goroutines, Scala parallel collections, Haskell's GHC, Erlang processes, OpenMP, and others. These implementations are portable in any OS that provides the runtime implementation required by these languages.

Here is an example in Python where we are creating five child threads:

```python
# Chapter 4/multithreading.py
import os
import time
import threading
from threading import Thread


def cpu_waster(i: int) -> None:
    name = threading.current_thread().getName()
    print(f"{name} doing {i} work")
    time.sleep(3)
```

```
def display_threads() -> None:
    print("-" * 10)
    print(f"Current process PID: {os.getpid()}")
    print(f"Thread Count: {threading.active_count()}")
    print("Active threads:")
    for thread in threading.enumerate():
        print(thread)

def main(num_threads: int) -> None:
    display_threads()

    print(f"Starting {num_threads} CPU wasters...")
    for i in range(num_threads):
        thread = Thread(target=cpu_waster, args=(i,))
        thread.start()

    display_threads()
```

Displays information about the current process, such as its PID, thread count, and active threads

Creates and starts a new thread

```
if __name__ == "__main__":
    num_threads = 5
    main(num_threads)
```

Here is the output:

```
----------
Current process PID: 35930
Thread Count: 1
Active threads:
<_MainThread(MainThread, started 8607733248)>
Starting 5 CPU wasters...
Thread-1 doing 0 work
Thread-2 doing 1 work
Thread-3 doing 2 work
Thread-4 doing 3 work
Thread-5 doing 4 work
----------
Current process PID: 35930
Thread Count: 6
Active threads:
<_MainThread(MainThread, started 8607733248)>
<Thread(Thread-1, started 12940410880)>
<Thread(Thread-2, started 12945666048)>
<Thread(Thread-3, started 12950921216)>
<Thread(Thread-4, started 12956176384)>
<Thread(Thread-5, started 12961431552)>
```

When we start our program, we create a process in which a main execution thread is created. Note that any thread, including the main thread, can create child threads at any time (that's why we have `Thread Count: 6` in the output). In our example, we create five new threads and run them concurrently.

Processes and threads are the building blocks of concurrency, and we talk a lot about them; but whether you work with threads or processes, you can think of them all as threads, because every process has at least one thread. Later in the book, we use the term *task* as a generic entity if the specific implementation is not important.

Before we move on, you've probably figured out by now that implementing concurrency is not easy work. Over the course of the last four chapters, we've outlined just how difficult it can be. After reading this far, you may wonder if it's right for you. But let's take a moment for some encouragement.

Think of kittens in a basket of yarn. They are inquisitive, experimental, and love a good time. Kittens don't look at the knitting basket with dismay—they see it as a playground to explore, disassemble, and make their own.

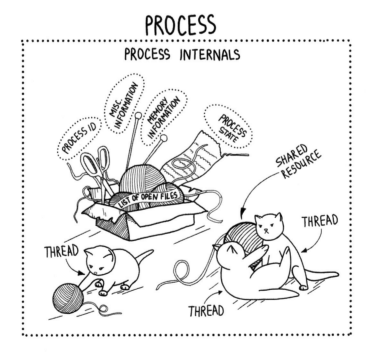

A good programmer is much the same way. You've got processes, shared resources, threads, open files, and data to work with, all to create a program that can solve real-world problems, automate tasks, or entertain millions of users.

So be encouraged, and press on. Grab that thread and unravel it. What you do from here on could change the world.

Recap

- The OS's job is to map execution onto the actual hardware.

- A *process* is an instance of a program running within a computer system. Each process has one or more threads of execution, and no thread can exist outside a process.

- A *thread* is a unit of computation, an independent set of programming instructions designed to achieve a particular result, which the OS independently executes and manages.

- Multiple execution threads can exist within the same process and share resources, while processes are almost independent.

- Using threads makes it easy to create concurrent applications because switching between threads is easier than switching between processes. Moreover, threads use a common address space, resulting in faster access to shared data. But there is also a risk of data corruption, which requires some caution to control access and synchronization to shared objects.

In this chapter

- You learn how to achieve effective task
  communication

- You learn how to choose a communication type for
  your applications

- You learn a popular programming pattern for creating
  concurrent applications: a thread pool

We can't always guarantee that concurrent tasks running on a computer are independent. Often, communication between tasks is necessary for efficient execution. For example, if one task depends on the result of another, the application has to know when to pause its work while it waits for the other task to finish.

Communication is therefore at the heart of any concurrent system. If we cannot ensure proper communication between tasks, the performance gains from concurrency are meaningless. In this chapter, you learn about the concepts provided by the OS to allow processes and threads to communicate and coordinate their work. We start by looking at the different types of communication you're likely to encounter in a concurrent system.

Types of communication

The OS provides mechanisms allowing processes and threads to communicate with each other. These mechanisms are called *interprocess communication* (IPC). Once you decide that your application will benefit from IPC, you must decide which of the available IPC methods to use on your system.

> **NOTE** IPC is called inter*process* communication, but that does not mean only processes need to communicate. Whether you work with threads or processes, you can think of them all as threads because every process has at least one thread, so de facto communication only occurs between threads. Ignore the confusing terminology—we use the term *task* as a general abstraction for the unit of execution.

The most popular types of IPC are via *shared memory* and *message passing*.

Shared-memory IPC

The simplest way to communicate between tasks is to use shared memory. Shared memory allows one or more tasks to communicate through common memory that appears in all their virtual address spaces as if they were reading and writing to local variables that were part of their address space. So, changes made by one process or thread are instantly reflected in the others without interacting with the OS.

Imagine that you live in the same house with several friends. There's a shared kitchen with a single refrigerator for everyone's use. You can get a beer for yourself and inform your friends that they can find a six-pack on the lowest shelf. The refrigerator serves as shared memory, used by all friends (tasks) to store beer (shared data).

Shared-memory IPC can be found if two processors (or processor cores) in the same computer refer to the same physical memory location or when threads within the same program share the same objects. In the code, it looks like this:

```
# Chapter 5/shared_ipc.py
import time
from threading import Thread, current_thread

SIZE = 5
shared_memory = [-1] * SIZE
```

Sets up shared memory of size SIZE

```
class Producer(Thread):
    def run(self) -> None:
        self.name = "Producer"
        global shared_memory
        for i in range(SIZE):
            print(f"{current_thread().name}: Writing {int(i)}")
            shared_memory[i - 1] = i
```

The producer thread writes data to shared memory.

```
class Consumer(Thread):
    def run(self) -> None:
        self.name = "Consumer"
        global shared_memory
        for i in range(SIZE):
            while True:
                line = shared_memory[i]
                if line == -1:
                    print(f"{current_thread().name}: Data not available\n"
                        f"Sleeping for 1 second before retrying")
                    time.sleep(1)
                    continue
                print(f"{current_thread().name}: Read: {int(line)}")
                break
```

The consumer thread continuously reads data from shared memory and waits if the data is not available yet.

```
def main() -> None:
    threads = [
        Consumer(),
        Producer(),
    ]

    for thread in threads:
        thread.start()

    for thread in threads:
        thread.join()
```

Starts all the child threads

Waits for all the child threads to finish

```
if __name__ == "__main__":
    main()
```

Here we create two threads: Producer and Consumer. Producer produces data and stores it in the shared memory; Consumer consumes the data stored in shared memory. Hence, they communicate with each other using a shared array. The output of the program is as follows:

```
Consumer: Data not available
Sleeping for 1 second before retrying
Producer: Writing 0
Producer: Writing 1
Producer: Writing 2
Producer: Writing 3
Producer: Writing 4
Consumer: Read: 1
Consumer: Read: 2
Consumer: Read: 3
Consumer: Read: 4
Consumer: Read: 0
```

This sharing of memory is both a blessing and a curse for the developer.

Advantages

The blessing of the approach is the fact that it provides the fastest and least resource-intensive communication possible. Although the OS helps allocate the shared memory, it does not participate in communication between tasks. Thus, in this case, the OS is completely removed from the communication and all the overhead of working with it, resulting in higher speed and less data copying.

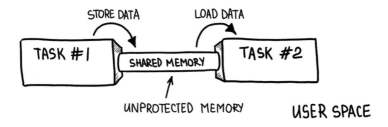

Disadvantages

The "curse" of this approach is that it is not necessarily the safest communication between tasks. The OS no longer provides the interfaces and protection of the shared memory. For instance, two friends may want to drink the last bottle of beer. That's a conflict (even war, sometimes). Similarly, tasks running the same program may want to read or update the same data structures. For that reason, using this approach is sometimes more error-prone, and developers have to redesign the code by protecting shared-memory objects (we talk more about that in Chapter 8).

Another disadvantage of this approach is that it does not scale beyond one machine. Shared memory can be used only for local tasks. This creates problems in large distributed systems where data that needs to be processed can't fit into one machine, but it's a perfect fit for symmetric multiprocessing (SMP) architecture systems.

In an SMP system, all processes or threads on the various CPUs share a unique logical address space mapped to physical memory. And that's why the shared-memory approach is popular for SMP systems, especially using threads: they have been built around the shared-memory idea in mind from the beginning. However, in such systems, increasing the number of processors connected to a common system bus makes it a bottleneck (see Chapter 3).

Message-passing IPC

Probably the most widely used type of IPC mechanism today (which is often supported by OSs) is *message passing*. In message-passing IPC, each task is identified by a unique name, and tasks interact by sending and receiving messages to and from named tasks. The OS establishes a communication channel and provides proper system calls for tasks to pass messages through this channel.

The advantage of this approach is that the OS manages the channel, providing easy-to-use interfaces to send and receive data without conflicts. On the other hand, there is a huge communication cost. To transfer any piece of information between tasks, it must be copied from the task's user space to the OS channel through system calls (as discussed in Chapter 3) and then copied back to the address space of the receiving task.

Message passing has another advantage: it can be easily scaled beyond one machine to distributed systems. But there's more to it, so let's move on for now.

> **NOTE** Many programming languages choose to use only message-passing IPC. The Go language philosophy is to share memory through communication. Here's the idea in a slogan from the Go language documentation: "Do not communicate by sharing memory; instead, share memory by communicating." Another example is Erlang, where processes don't share any data and communicate with each other exclusively by message passing.

There are a lot of technologies to implement the message-passing approach. We cover some of the most common ones in modern OSs—pipes, sockets, and message queues—in the following sections.

Pipes

This is probably the simplest form of IPC. A pipe is a simple, synchronized way of transferring information from one task to another. As the name implies, a pipe defines a one-way flow of data between tasks—data is written to one end and read from the other. A pipe allows for data flow in one direction; when bidirectional communication is needed, two pipes must be created.

You can imagine a pipe in IPC as being like a water pipe. If you put a rubber duck into a stream, it will travel downstream to the end of the waterway. The writer end is the upstream location where you put a rubber duck into the pipe, and the reader end is where the rubber duck ends up downstream.

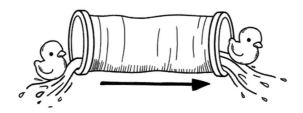

In the code, one section calls methods on the writer end to send data, while another section reads incoming data. A pipe is a temporary object that can be used by only two tasks and will be closed if either the sender or receiver half is dropped.

> **NOTE** Channels are a popular data type in Go and provide synchronization and communication between Go concurrency primitives, or goroutines. Channels can be thought of as pipes that are used by goroutines to communicate.

Pipes come in two kinds: *unnamed* and *named*. *Unnamed pipes* can only be used by related tasks (i.e., child–parent or sibling processes, or threads in the same process) because related tasks share file descriptors. Unnamed pipes disappear after the tasks finish using them.

Since a pipe is essentially a file descriptor (in UNIX systems), pipe operations are similar to file operations but have no connection to the filesystem. When writers want to write data to a pipe, they use a `write()` OS system call on the pipe. To retrieve data from a pipe, the `read()` system call is used. `read()` handles pipes like it handles files, but it is blocked until there is no data to be read. Pipes may be implemented differently in different systems.

By creating a pipe in the main thread and then passing file descriptors to the child threads, we can pass data from one thread to another through the pipe. This is exactly how a standard pipe works. Let's look at the code:

```
# Chapter 5/pipe.py
from threading import Thread, current_thread
from multiprocessing import Pipe
from multiprocessing.connection import Connection


class Writer(Thread):
    def __init__(self, conn: Connection):
        super().__init__()
        self.conn = conn
        self.name = "Writer"

    def run(self) -> None:
        print(f"{current_thread().name}: Sending rubber duck...")
        self.conn.send("Rubber duck")
```

Writes a message
into the pipe

```
class Reader(Thread):
    def __init__(self, conn: Connection):
        super().__init__()
        self.conn = conn
        self.name = "Reader"

    def run(self) -> None:
        print(f"{current_thread().name}: Reading...")
        msg = self.conn.recv()
        print(f"{current_thread().name}: Received: {msg}")
```

Reads the message
from the pipe

```
def main() -> None:
    reader_conn, writer_conn = Pipe()
    reader = Reader(reader_conn)
    writer = Writer(writer_conn)

    threads = [
        writer,
        reader
    ]
    for thread in threads:
        thread.start()

    for thread in threads:
        thread.join()


if __name__ == "__main__":
    main()
```

Establishes an unnamed pipe
for communication between
two threads with two pipe
connections for reading and
writing

We create an unnamed pipe with two threads. The writing thread writes a message to the reader through the pipe. Here is the output of the program:

```
Writer: Sending rubber duck...
Reader: Reading...
Reader: Received: Rubber duck
```

> **NOTE** `pipe()` and `fork()` make up the famous functionality behind the pipe operator (|) in `ls | more` in the popular UNIX shell and command language Bash.

Named pipes allow the transfer of data between tasks according to the FIFO (first in, first out) principle, which means the request is processed in the order it arrives. Because of that, named pipes are often referred to as *FIFOs*.

Unlike unnamed pipes, FIFOs are not temporary objects; they are entities in the filesystem and can be freely used by unrelated tasks that have appropriate permissions to access them. Using named pipes allows tasks to interact even if they don't know which tasks are on the other end of the pipe, even over a network. Otherwise, FIFOs are treated exactly like unnamed pipes and use the same system calls.

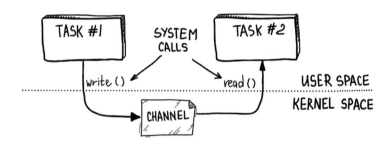

Because of this unidirectional nature of pipes, probably the best use of pipes is to transfer data from producer programs to consumer programs. For other uses, they are rather limited, and other IPC methods often work better.

Message queues

Another popular message-passing IPC implementation is the *message queue*. Like named pipes, message queues keep data organized using the FIFO principle, which is why they have *queue* in the name; but they also support multiple tasks to write or read messages.

Message queues provide a powerful means of decoupling tasks in a system, allowing producers and consumers to interact with the queue instead of directly with each other. That gives developers a lot of freedom to control execution. For example, workers can put messages back in the message queue if they have not been processed for some reason. Here's how message queues look in code:

```python
# Chapter 5/message_queue.py
import time
from queue import Queue
from threading import Thread, current_thread


class Worker(Thread):
    def __init__(self, queue: Queue, id: int):
        super().__init__(name=str(id))
        self.queue = queue

    def run(self) -> None:
        while not self.queue.empty():
            item = self.queue.get()
            print(f"Thread {current_thread().name}: "
                    f"processing item {item} from the queue")
            time.sleep(2)


def main(thread_num: int) -> None:
    q = Queue()
    for i in range(10):
        q.put(i)

    threads = []
    for i in range(thread_num):
        thread = Worker(q, i + 1)
        thread.start()
        threads.append(thread)

    for thread in threads:
        thread.join()


if __name__ == "__main__":
    thread_num = 4
    main(thread_num)
```

Gets the next item from the queue to be processed. This method blocks until an item is available in the queue.

Creates a queue with values put into it for processing in the threads.

Here we create a message queue and place 10 messages in it for our 4 children to process. Our threads process all the messages in the queue until it is empty. Note that the queue is not just a single thread interaction point but also holds the messages until they are processed—creating a loosely coupled system. The output of the program looks like this:

```
Thread 1 : processing item 0 from the queue
Thread 2 : processing item 1 from the queue
Thread 3 : processing item 2 from the queue
Thread 4 : processing item 3 from the queue
Thread 1 : processing item 4 from the queue
Thread 2 : processing item 5 from the queue
Thread 3 : processing item 6 from the queue
Thread 4 : processing item 7 from the queue
Thread 1 : processing item 8 from the queue
Thread 3 : processing item 9 from the queue
```

As we've seen, message queues are used to implement loosely coupled systems. They are used everywhere: in OSs to schedule processes and in routers as buffers to store packets before they are processed. Even cloud applications consisting of microservices use message queues to communicate. Also, message queues are widely used for asynchronous processing. We get to the practical use of queues at the end of this chapter, but for now, let's move on to a discussion of UDSs.

UDSs

Sockets can be used to communicate in a wide variety of domains, and in this chapter, we talk about UNIX domain sockets (UDSs) used between threads on the same system. We talk about network and network sockets, other common domain sockets, in Chapter 10.

We can create two-way, FIFO communications via sockets implementing message-passing IPC. In this IPC, one thread can write information to the socket, and a second thread can read information from the socket. A socket is an object that represents the end point of that connection. Threads from both ends have their own socket, which is connected to another socket. So, to send information from one thread to another, we write it to the output stream of one socket and read it from the input stream of the other socket.

Speaking of sending messages between two entities, let's take a moment to imagine sending a Christmas card to your mom. You need to write some sweet holiday wishes on the card and put your mom's name and address on it. Then you need to drop it in your local mailbox. You've done your part. Now the postal service will do the rest: it will send the card to your mom's local post office, and the mail carrier will deliver your card to your mom's door and see the happy look on her face.

In the case of a Christmas card, you first put the sender's and recipient's addresses on the card. With sockets, you have to establish a connection first, and then the message exchange starts.

The `Sender` thread puts the information it wants to send in the message and sends it explicitly over a dedicated channel to the `Receiver` thread, and the `Receiver` thread then reads it. We need at least two primitives: `send(message, destination)` and `receive()`. The threads in this exchange can be executed either on the same machine or on different machines connected by a network.

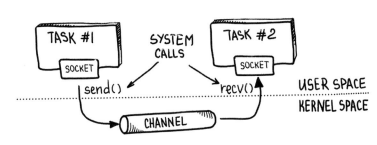

Here's the code:

In UNIX, everything is a file. This socket file will be used to facilitate communication between threads.

```python
# Chapter 5/sockets.py
import socket
import os.path
import time
from threading import Thread, current_thread

SOCK_FILE = "./mailbox"
BUFFER_SIZE = 1024


class Sender(Thread):
    def run(self) -> None:
        self.name = "Sender"
        client = socket.socket(socket.AF_UNIX, socket.SOCK_STREAM)
        client.connect(SOCK_FILE)

        messages = ["Hello", " ", "world!"]
        for msg in messages:
            print(f"{current_thread().name}: Send: '{msg}'")
            client.sendall(str.encode(msg))

        client.close()
```

Creates a new socket for the sender thread. AF_UNIX (UNIX domain socket) and SOCK_STREAM are constants that represent the socket family and socket type, respectively.

Buffer size for receiving data from the socket connection

Connects the sender thread's socket to the "channel"—a UNIX socket file

Sends a series of messages over the sender thread's socket

Creates a new socket for the receiver thread with
the same configuration as the sender socket

```python
class Receiver(Thread):
    def run(self) -> None:
        self.name = "Receiver"
        server = socket.socket(socket.AF_UNIX, socket.SOCK_STREAM)
        server.bind(SOCK_FILE)
        server.listen()
```

Binds and starts the receiver thread's
socket listening for incoming connections.

```python
        print(f"{current_thread().name}: Listening to incoming messages...")
        conn, addr = server.accept()
```

Accepts a connection on
the receiver thread's
socket and returns a new
connection and the
address of the sender

```python
        while True:
            data = conn.recv(BUFFER_SIZE)
            if not data:
                break
            message = data.decode()
            print(f"{current_thread().name}: Received: '{message}'")

        server.close()


def main() -> None:
    if os.path.exists(SOCK_FILE):
        os.remove(SOCK_FILE)

    receiver = Receiver()
    receiver.start()
    time.sleep(1)
    sender = Sender()
    sender.start()

    for thread in [receiver, sender]:
        thread.join()

    os.remove(SOCK_FILE)


if __name__ == "__main__":
    main()
```

Receives data from
the connected sender
socket until the
connection is closed

We create two threads, Sender and Receiver. Each has its own socket. The only difference between them is that Receiver is in listening mode, waiting for incoming senders to send their messages. Here is the output:

```
Receiver: Listening of incoming messages...
Sender: Send: 'Hello'
Sender: Send: ' '
Receiver: Received: 'Hello'
Receiver: Received: ' '
Sender: Send: 'world!'
Receiver: Received: 'world!'
```

This is probably the simplest and best-known way to implement IPC, but it is also costly because it requires serialization, which in turn requires the developer to think about what data needs to be transmitted. On the bright side, sockets are generally more flexible and can be extended to network sockets if needed with almost no changes, letting you easily scale your program to multiple machines. We talk more about that in part 3 of the book.

> **NOTE** This is not a complete list of types of IPC, only the most popular and those we need later in the book. For example, *signals* are among the oldest methods of IPC; and there are unique things, such as *mailslots*,[1] that are only available in Windows.

Having discussed IPC, we have covered the concurrency fundamentals. We are ready to start with our first concurrency pattern: the *thread pool*.

Thread pool pattern

Developing software using threads can be a daunting task. Not only are threads low-level concurrency constructs that require manual management, but the synchronization mechanisms typically employed with threads can complicate software design without necessarily improving performance. Moreover, since the optimal number of threads for an application can vary dynamically based on the current system load and hardware configuration, creating a robust thread management solution is exceedingly challenging.

Despite the challenges, most concurrent applications actively use multiple threads. However, this does not mean threads are explicit programming language entities. Instead, the runtime environment can map other programming language concurrency

---

[1] Microsoft documentation, "Mailslots," https://learn.microsoft.com/en-us/windows/win32/ipc/mailslots.

constructs to actual threads at runtime. One of the commonly implemented and widely used patterns in various frameworks and programming languages is the *thread pool*.

As the name implies, a thread pool is made by creating a small collection of long-running worker threads at program startup and then putting them into a pool (a container). When a task needs to be executed, the pool takes one of the pre-created threads and executes it; the developer does not need to create them. Sending tasks to the thread pool is similar to adding them to the to-do list for worker threads.

Reusing threads with a thread pool eliminates the overhead associated with creating new threads and protects against the unexpected failure of the task, such as raising an exception, without affecting the worker thread. Reusing threads becomes a real advantage when the time required to perform a task is less than the time required to create a new thread.

NOTE   The thread pool creates, manages, and schedules worker threads, which can become complex and costly tasks if not handled carefully. Thread pools come in different types, with different scheduling and execution techniques and either a fixed number of threads or the ability to dynamically change the size of the pool depending on the workload.

Suppose we have a large set of tasks to process using multiple threads, such as cracking passwords, as described in Chapter 2. By dividing the possible passwords into smaller chunks and assigning them to separate threads, we can achieve concurrency in our processing. In this scenario, we need a main thread that generates tasks for the worker threads running in the background.

To facilitate communication between the main thread and the worker threads running in the background, we need a storage mechanism that can act as a link between them. This storage should prioritize processing tasks in the order they are received. Moreover, any free worker thread should be able to pick up and process the next available task from this storage.

How do we build such communication between threads?

Message queues are a means of communication between threads within a pool. A queue logically consists of a list of tasks. Threads in the pool retrieve tasks from the message queue and process them concurrently.

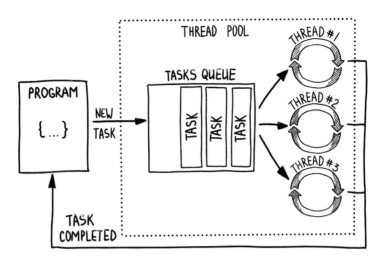

The implementation in different programming languages may differ. The following is an example of a thread pool implementation in Python:

```
# Chapter 5/thread_pool.py
import time
import queue
import typing as T
from threading import Thread, current_thread

Callback = T.Callable[..., None]
Task = T.Tuple[Callback, T.Any, T.Any]
TaskQueue = queue.Queue


class Worker(Thread):
    def __init__(self, tasks: queue.Queue[Task]):
        super().__init__()
        self.tasks = tasks

    def run(self) -> None:
        while True:
            func, args, kargs = self.tasks.get()
            try:
                func(*args, **kargs)
            except Exception as e:
                print(e)
            self.tasks.task_done()
```

Worker thread gets a task from the queue, runs the function associated with the task, and marks the task as done when it's finished. It does this indefinitely.

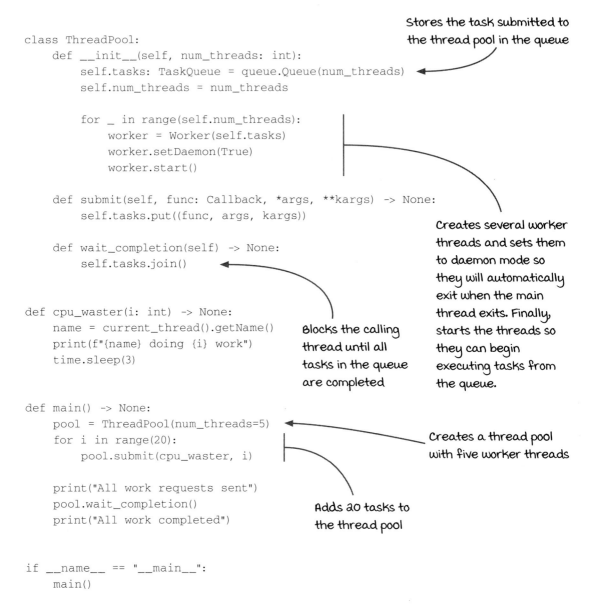

```
class ThreadPool:
    def __init__(self, num_threads: int):
        self.tasks: TaskQueue = queue.Queue(num_threads)
        self.num_threads = num_threads

        for _ in range(self.num_threads):
            worker = Worker(self.tasks)
            worker.setDaemon(True)
            worker.start()

    def submit(self, func: Callback, *args, **kargs) -> None:
        self.tasks.put((func, args, kargs))

    def wait_completion(self) -> None:
        self.tasks.join()


def cpu_waster(i: int) -> None:
    name = current_thread().getName()
    print(f"{name} doing {i} work")
    time.sleep(3)


def main() -> None:
    pool = ThreadPool(num_threads=5)
    for i in range(20):
        pool.submit(cpu_waster, i)

    print("All work requests sent")
    pool.wait_completion()
    print("All work completed")


if __name__ == "__main__":
    main()
```

Stores the task submitted to the thread pool in the queue

Creates several worker threads and sets them to daemon mode so they will automatically exit when the main thread exits. Finally, starts the threads so they can begin executing tasks from the queue.

Blocks the calling thread until all tasks in the queue are completed

Creates a thread pool with five worker threads

Adds 20 tasks to the thread pool

When we create this thread pool, it automatically creates several threads and a message queue where incoming tasks are stored. Next, in the main thread, we add a lot of tasks for the pool to process and wait for them to finish.

When a new task arrives, an available thread wakes up, executes the task, and returns to the Ready state. This avoids the relatively costly creation and termination of a thread for each task in progress and takes thread management out of the developer's control, passing it to a library or OS better suited to optimizing program execution.

NOTE   Check the file Chapter 5/library_thread_pool.py (available with the book's downloadable files) for the Python library implementation of the thread pool pattern.

Thread pooling is a good default choice for most concurrent applications, but in some scenarios it makes sense to create and manage your threads instead of using a thread pool:

- You want to control various thread priorities.
- You have tasks that cause the thread to block for a long time. Most thread pool implementations have a maximum number of threads, so many blocked threads might prevent tasks from starting in the thread pool.
- You need a static identifier associated with the thread.
- You want to dedicate a whole thread to one specific task.

As promised, let's dive into implementing communication concepts and summarize our knowledge of concurrent application execution along the way.

Cracking passwords, revisited

We have acquired some new knowledge, so let's proceed with the unfinished implementation of the password-cracking program from Chapter 2 using pools and processes (there is a Python limitation on using threads,[2] but it should not matter for other languages):

```
# Chapter 5/password_cracking_parallel.py
def crack_chunk(crypto_hash: str, length: int, chunk_start: int,
                chunk_end: int) -> T.Union[str, None]:
    print(f"Processing {chunk_start} to {chunk_end}")
    (reformat)
    combinations = get_combinations(
        length=length,
        min_number=chunk_ start,
        max_number=chunk_end
    for combination in combinations:
        if check_password(crypto_hash, combination):
            return combination
    return
```

Found a password

Did not find the password in this chunk

---

[2]   Python documentation, "Thread State and the Global Interpreter Lock," http://mng.bz/wvDB.

```
def crack_password_parallel(crypto_hash: str, length: int) -> None:
    num_cores = os.cpu_count()
    print("Processing number combinations concurrently")
    start_time = time.perf_counter()
```

Gets the number of available CPU cores on the system

Processes each chunk in a separate process concurrently

```
    with Pool() as pool:
        arguments = ((crypto_hash, length, chunk_start, chunk_end) for
                     chunk_start, chunk_end in
                     get_chunks(num_cores, length))
        results = pool.starmap(crack_chunk, arguments)
        print("Waiting for chunks to finish")
        pool.close()
        pool.join()

    result = [res for res in results if res]
    print(f"PASSWORD CRACKED: {result[0]}")
    process_time = time.perf_counter() - start_time
    print(f"PROCESS TIME: {process_time}")


if __name__ == "__main__":
    crypto_hash = \
        "e24df920078c3dd4e7e8d2442f00e5c9ab2a231bb3918d65cc50906e49ecaef4"
    length = 8
    crack_password_parallel(crypto_hash, length)
```

Closes the pool to indicate that no more tasks will be submitted to it

Waits for all submitted tasks to complete before continuing with the rest of the program

Here the main thread creates a number of worker threads equal to the number of available CPU cores using the thread pool pattern. Each worker thread does the same thing as in the original version from Chapter 2, and we process all of the password chunks concurrently. The output will look similar to this:

```
Processing number combinations concurrently
Chunk submitted checking 0 to 12499998
Chunk submitted checking 12499999 to 24999998
Chunk submitted checking 24999999 to 37499998
Chunk submitted checking 37499999 to 49999998
Chunk submitted checking 49999999 to 62499998
Chunk submitted checking 62499999 to 74999998
Chunk submitted checking 74999999 to 87499998
Chunk submitted checking 87499999 to 99999999
Waiting for chunks to finish
PASSWORD CRACKED: 87654321
PROCESS TIME: 17.183910416
```

We get more than a 3× speedup from our original sequential implementation. Great job!

We can implement many things with parallel hardware, but sometimes we have to use only one core, so parallel hardware is a luxury. That is not a reason to give up concurrency, because this is where concurrency beats parallelism. More in the next chapter.

Recap

- The mechanism by which threads and processes synchronize themselves and exchange data is called *interprocess communication* (*IPC*).

- Each IPC mechanism has advantages and disadvantages. Each is the optimal solution for a particular problem:

  - A shared-memory mechanism is used when threads or processes need to efficiently exchange large amounts of data but have a problem with synchronizing access to the data.

  - Pipes provide an efficient way to implement synchronous communication between producer–consumer processes. Named pipes provide a simple interface for transferring data between two processes, whether on the same computer or on a network.

  - A message queue between processes or threads is a way of asynchronously exchanging data. Message queues are used to implement weakly coupled systems.

  - Sockets are a two-way communication channel that can use networking capabilities. Here, data communication takes place through the socket interface instead of the file interface. In most cases, sockets provide the best combination of performance, scalability, and ease of use.

- A *thread pool* is a collection of worker threads that efficiently execute incoming tasks on behalf of the program's main thread. Worker threads in a thread pool are designed to be reused once the task is completed and protect against the unexpected failure of the task, such as raising an exception, without affecting the worker thread itself.

Part 2
The many tentacles of concurrency: Multitasking, decomposition, and synchronization

Have you ever seen a plate spinner in a circus juggle multiple plates that are spinning on sticks? They effortlessly keep all the plates spinning in perfect harmony. That's the power of multitasking! Similarly, in concurrent programming, we need to be able to juggle multiple tasks, ensuring that each task gets the required attention and resources.

In Chapters 6 through 9, we show you how to apply this same concept to creating a Pac-Man-like game and many other real-world scenarios. We explore the intricacies of designing concurrent programs, including multitasking, task decomposition, and the effect of granularity on performance.

But with great power comes great responsibility (I read that somewhere), and concurrency can lead to race conditions, deadlocks, and starvation. But fear not—we provide you with the tools to solve these problems, including synchronization techniques like mutual exclusion, semaphores, and atomic operations. Just like the musicians in an orchestra, the key to successful concurrency is coordination and synchronization. And we even tackle classic problems like the dining philosophers and learn a few well-known patterns. By the end of this part of the book, you'll be equipped with the knowledge to design and optimize concurrent programs that can handle any challenge thrown your way.

Are you ready to spin some plates? Or maybe juggle a few tasks at once?

Multitasking | 6

In this chapter

- You learn how to identify and analyze possible
  bottlenecks in your application

- You learn how to run multiple tasks concurrently
  in the absence of parallel hardware

- You learn about the preemptive multitasking
  technique: pros, cons, and using it to solve
  I/O-bound problems

Do you ever stop to marvel at the sheer multitasking ability of your computer? It's truly incredible how it can handle multiple applications running at the same time, all while you continue to work on a text editor without a hitch. It's a feat that we often take for granted, but it's a testament to the impressive capabilities of modern computing.

Have you ever wondered how your computer accomplishes all this? How does it manage to juggle so many tasks at once? Even more interestingly, what types of tasks are being handled, and how are they classified?

In this chapter, we take a deeper dive into the concept of concurrency and explore the fascinating world of multitasking. By introducing multitasking into the runtime layer, we gain a better understanding of how our machines can handle a variety of tasks simultaneously. But before we delve into the intricacies of multitasking, we first take a closer look at the different types of tasks our computers can handle.

CPU-bound and I/O-bound applications

Applications consist of numerical, arithmetic, and logical operations, which require intensive CPU work. They can also read from a keyboard, hard drive, or network card and produce output in the form of writing files, printing to "high-speed" printers, or sending signals to the display. These operations communicate with devices by sending and receiving signals. Most of the time, that does not require CPU as there is nothing to compute; we're just waiting for the response from the device. Such operations are also known as *input-output operations (I/O)*. Consequently, it does not always make sense to give some tasks the use of the CPU. First, we need to understand the type of load.

An application is considered *bound* by something when a required resource for its work is a bottleneck for achieving increased performance. There are two main types of operations: *CPU-bound* and *I/O-bound*.

CPU-bound

So far, we've mostly been talking about CPU-bound applications. An application is bound by the CPU if it would run faster if the CPU was faster—that is, it spends most of its time using the CPU to do some kind of computation.

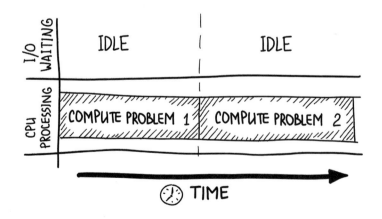

Here are some examples of CPU-bound operations:

*   Mathematical operations like addition, subtraction, division, and matrix multiplication

- Encryption and decryption algorithms that involve a lot of computationally intensive operations, like prime factorization and computing cryptographic functions

- Image processing and video processing

- Executing algorithms like binary search and sorting

I/O-bound

An application is bound by I/O if it would run faster if the I/O subsystem were faster. The kind of I/O subsystem can vary, but you can associate it with reading from disk, getting user input, or waiting for a network response. An application that goes through a huge file looking for a search term can become I/O bound because reading a lot of data from the disk creates a bottleneck.

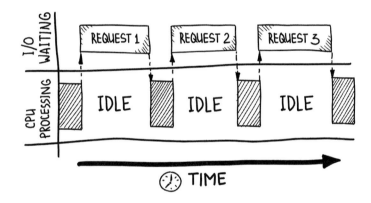

Idle sections in the illustration represent periods of time when a particular task is pending and thus cannot advance. A common reason is waiting for I/O to be performed. But to perform various I/O operations, the CPU often does nothing but wait for data to be transferred to or from an external device, and CPU time is expensive. Examples of I/O-bound operations are as follows:

- Most graphical user interface (GUI) applications, even if they never read from or write to the disk, because they spend most of their time waiting on user interaction via the keyboard or mouse

- Processes that spend most of their time doing disk I/O or network I/O, like databases and web servers

Identifying bottlenecks

When determining our application's bottleneck, we must think about which resource we need to improve so our application performs better. This directly relates to the connection between operations and the corresponding resources they rely on. Often, CPU and I/O operations are identified as the most important to address.

> **NOTE** Of course, this isn't just about I/O-only work and CPU-only work; we can also think about memory and cache work. But for the majority of developers and the purposes of this book, it is enough to consider the difference between CPU and I/O.

Imagine two programs. The first program performs the multiplication of two gigantic matrixes and returns the answer. The second program writes a huge amount of information from the network to a file on a disk. It is clear that these programs will not be equally accelerated by faster CPU clock speed or an increased number of cores. What does it matter how many cores there are if most of the time they are waiting for the next batch of data to be transferred to disk? One core or a thousand, we will not get a performance increase with an I/O-bound load. But if we have a CPU-bound load, there is a chance to get a boost when we parallelize our program so it can utilize multiple cores.

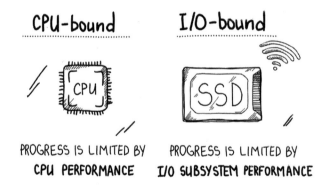

The need for multitasking

Applications naturally become more and more I/O-bound. This is because CPU speed has historically increased, allowing more instructions to be executed in a given time, while data-transfer speed has not increased much. Therefore, the limiting factor in programs is often I/O-bound operations that block the CPU. But they can be identified and executed in the background, and most modern runtime systems do this.

Imagine that your friend Alan finds an ancient arcade machine in his parents' attic. It has an old single-core processor, a big pixel screen, and a joystick. He approaches you, his only developer friend, and asks you to implement a Pac-Man-like game for the machine.

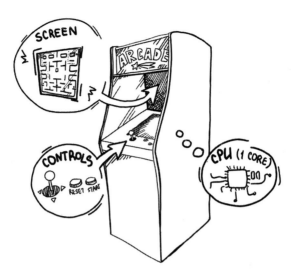

The game is interactive and needs the player's input to move the character in the game. At the same time, the world inside the game is dynamic. Ghosts need to move at the same time the gamer controls the character. And the gamer should see how the world is changing as well as how their character is moving.

Your first steps are to create game functionality divided among three functions:

- `get_user_input()`—Gets input from the controllers and saves it in the game's internal state. It is an I/O-bound operation.

- `compute_game_world()`—Computes the game world according to the game rules, the player's input, and the game's internal state. It is a CPU-bound operation.

- `render_next_screen()`—Gets the game's internal state and renders the game world on the screen. It is an I/O-bound operation.

Given those three functions, you can see that you have a problem—many things should be happening simultaneously for the gamer, but you only have an old one-core CPU. How can you solve this problem?

Let's start by trying to create a parallel program using one of the OS abstractions. We utilize threads for this problem, so we have one process and three threads. Using threads is beneficial, as we need to share data between tasks, and easier, as they can share the same process address space. So, our program looks like the following:

```python
# Chapter 6/arcade_machine.py
import typing as T
from threading import Thread, Event

from pacman import get_user_input, compute_game_world, render_next_screen

processor_free = Event()
processor_free.set()


class Task(Thread):
    def __init__(self, func: T.Callable[..., None]):
        super().__init__()
        self.func = func

    def run(self) -> None:
        while True:
            processor_free.wait()
            processor_free.clear()
            self.func()


def arcade_machine() -> None:
    get_user_input_task = Task(get_user_input)
    compute_game_world_task = Task(compute_game_world)
    render_next_screen_task = Task(render_next_screen)

    get_user_input_task.start()
    compute_game_world_task.start()
    render_next_screen_task.start()


if __name__ == "__main__":
    arcade_machine()
```

Simulates one processor/thread environment

Runs the function inside its own endless loop. The loop will run continuously until the program is stopped or the thread is terminated.

Defines and runs tasks in separate threads concurrently

Here, we initialize three threads, each corresponding to one of the three functions. Each function inside a thread runs in its own endless loop (assuming we don't stop a thread after a single execution) so that our threads are always kept working as a gamer continues playing.

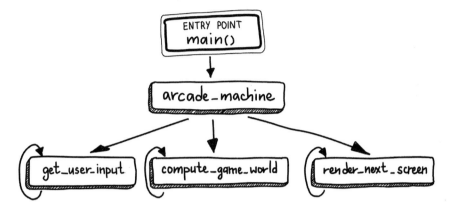

Unfortunately, if we start this program, it gets stuck on the first thread, asking for user input in the infinite loop, and does nothing else as our CPU has room for only one thread. So, we cannot utilize parallelism here, as it requires us to have the proper hardware. Don't worry. We can still utilize concurrency with multitasking!

Before we apply multitasking to our arcade problem, we need to understand its fundamentals. Let's put our problem to one side as we learn more about multitasking in the next section.

Multitasking from a bird's-eye view

In today's world, multitasking is everywhere. We multitask as we listen to music while walking, take a call while cooking, or eat while reading a book.

Multitasking is the concept of performing multiple tasks over a period of time by executing them concurrently. Multitasking can be compared to a plate spinner in a circus who juggles multiple plates that are spinning on sticks. The performer rushes from plate to plate, trying to keep them spinning so they won't fall off the sticks.

In a true multitasking system, operations run in parallel—but parallel execution requires appropriate hardware support. However, the appearance of multitasking can be achieved even on older processors by using several tricks.

Preemptive multitasking

The main task of the OS is resource management, and one of the most important resources for it to manage is the CPU. The OS must be able to allow every program to be executed on the CPU. This means it should be able to run a task for a while but then park it and allow another task to run. The problem is that most applications are not written to be attentive to other running applications. So, the OS needs a way to preemptively suspend the execution of an application.

The idea behind *preemptive multitasking* is to define a period of time a single task is allowed to run. This period is also known as a *time slice* because the OS tries to guarantee a slice of CPU time for each running task. And that's why this scheduling technique is called a *time-sharing* policy.[1] The CPU will execute the task in the Ready state during this time slice if it does not perform any blocking operations.

When the time slice expires, the scheduler *interrupts* the task (*preempts* it) and allows another task to run in its place while the first task waits its turn again. An interrupt is a signal to the CPU to stop the task and resume it later. There are three types of interrupts: hardware interrupts with a special interrupt controller (e.g., pressing a keyboard button or completing a write to a file); software interrupts (e.g., system calls) caused by the application itself; and errors and timer interrupts.

Imagine that a processor allocates a small amount of time to each running task and then quickly switches between them, allowing each task to execute in an interleaved fashion. By switching quickly and passing control to the tasks in the queue, the OS creates the illusion of multitasking, although only one task is executing at any given time. The following diagram shows the progress of the three tasks as a function of time. Time moves from left to right, and the lines indicate which task is in progress at any given moment. The illustration shows the perceived simultaneous execution model.

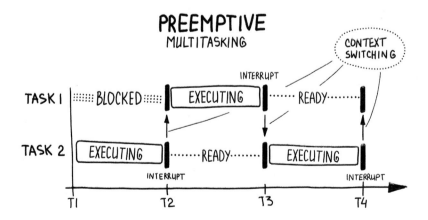

---

[1] If you're interested in learning more, here is a good video on the topic: "1963 Timesharing: A Solution to Computer Bottlenecks," https://youtu.be/Q07PhW5sCEk.

Most OSs developed in the last decade provide preemptive multitasking (we contrast it with cooperative multitasking in Chapter 12). If you work on Linux, macOS, or Windows, you work on an OS with preemptive multitasking. To better understand how multitasking can be implemented, let's go back to our arcade machine example.

Arcade machine with preemptive multitasking

We have two I/O-bound operations that are waiting for an event to occur and hence are blocking the CPU. For example, the `get_user_input_task` thread is waiting for the gamer to press a button on the controller.

We have an old one-core CPU on the arcade machine, but it's still very fast compared to human reflexes. It takes what would seem like an unimaginable amount of time to the CPU for a person to move their finger over the button and press it. The fastest possible conscious human reactions take around 0.15 seconds; if we have a 2 GHz processor, it can execute 300 million cycles in the same amount of time—roughly the number of instructions. While we wait for human input (the gamer pressing the button), we waste CPU computation resources as the CPU core does nothing. We can utilize this unoccupied CPU time by passing control to computational tasks during idle time.

Essentially, we need to implement part of the OS. This can be done via preemptive multitasking—giving each thread a CPU time to run and then passing the processor to the next thread. We can use a simple time-sharing policy and divide all available CPU time into equal time slices.

This is where the timer comes to the rescue. Timers tick at regular intervals and can be set to interrupt after a certain number of ticks. This interrupt pauses the current thread, allowing us to let another thread use the processor. So, the diagram of our program looks like this.

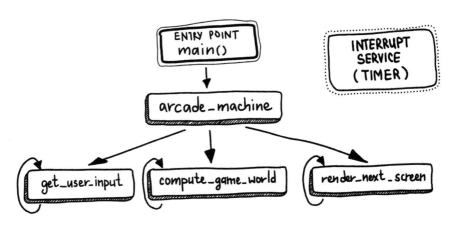

Implementing the time-sharing policy, runtime system divides the processor time between the threads into time slices to give the impression that they are running concurrently.

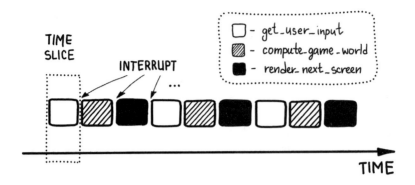

In the code, it looks like the following:

```
# Chapter 6/arcade_machine_multitasking.py
import typing as T
from threading import Thread, Timer, Event

from pacman import get_user_input, compute_game_world, render_next_
screen

processor_free = Event()
processor_free.set()
TIME_SLICE = 0.5
```

Defines the
processor time slice

```
class Task(Thread):
    def __init__(self, func: T.Callable[..., None]):
        super().__init__()
        self.func = func

    def run(self) -> None:
        while True:
            processor_free.wait()
            processor_free.clear()
            self.func()


class InterruptService(Timer):
    def __init__(self):
        super().__init__(TIME_SLICE, lambda: None)

    def run(self):
        while not self.finished.wait(self.interval):
            print("Tick!")
            processor_free.set()
```

Sets a timer to
indicate that the
processor is free
(the timer interrupts
the processor)

```
def arcade_machine() -> None:
    get_user_input_task = Task(get_user_input)
    compute_game_world_task = Task(compute_game_world)
    render_next_screen_task = Task(render_next_screen)

    InterruptService().start()
    get_user_input_task.start()
    compute_game_world_task.start()
    render_next_screen_task.start()


if __name__ == "__main__":
    arcade_machine()
```

We implement multitasking by putting threads into one infinite control loop where we can, in an interleaved manner, provide each thread with a CPU time slice. If the interleaving happens fast enough (say, 10 milliseconds), gamers get the impression of simultaneous execution. It seems to the player that all of the game's attention is devoted to them, when in fact the processor and the computer system as a whole may be working on a completely different task at the moment. The gamer gets the impression of parallel execution because of the extremely fast switching between threads.

So, physically, we still have serial execution of tasks because we have limited processing resources. But, conceptually, all three of our threads are in progress, making them run concurrently.

Concurrent computations have overlapping lifetimes. As we've seen, with the proper hardware, we can achieve true parallelism with physically simultaneous task execution, while multitasking helps us abstract away overlapping execution to the runtime system. Thus, true parallelism is essentially an implementation detail of the execution, while multitasking is part of the computational model.

There is one pitfall here that we have missed, so let's step back a bit.

Context switching

The *execution context* of a task contains the code that's currently running (the instruction pointer) and everything that aids in its execution on a CPU core (CPU flags, key registers, variables, open files, connections, etc.); it must be loaded back into the proces-  sor before the code resumes execution. Consequently, *context switching* is a physical act of swapping from one task's context to another without losing the data so that it can be recovered to the same moment when it was switched. The task selected from the Ready queue moves into a Running state.

Imagine that you're having an engaging conversation with a friend, but then your phone starts ringing, and you get distracted. You say, "Wait a minute" to your friend, and pick up the phone. Now you enter a new conversation—a new context. When it's clear to you who's calling and what they want, you can focus on their request. After the phone call ends, you return to the initial conversation. Sometimes you forget the context where you left off, but once your friend reminds you of what you were talking about, you can continue. It happens quickly but not instantly.

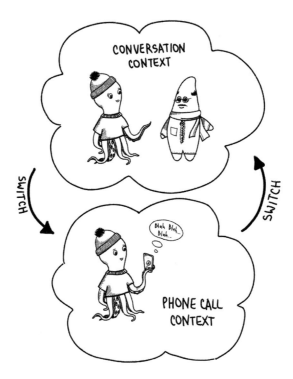

Like you, the processor needs to find the context where the task was and reconstruct it. From the point of view of the task, everything around it is in the same state as before. It doesn't matter whether the task started just now or 25 minutes ago. Context switching is a procedure performed by the OS, and it's one of the key mechanisms that provide the OS with a multitasking feature.

Context switches are considered costly because they require system resources. Switching from one task to another requires certain actions. First, the context of a running task must be saved somewhere, and then the new task starts. If the new task was previously in progress, it also has a stored context, which must be preloaded before it can continue execution. When the new task completes, the scheduler saves its final context and restores the context of the preempted task. The preempted task resumes execution as if nothing happened (except the time shift).

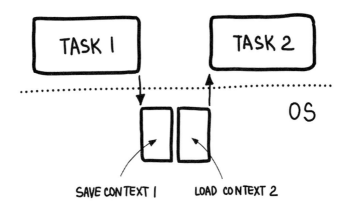

The overhead associated with saving and restoring state when switching contexts negatively affects program performance as the application loses the ability to execute instructions when switching contexts. It all depends on the type of operations your program is performing.

> **NOTE** The amount of latency incurred during context switching depends on various factors, but let's take a reasonable ~800 to ~1300 nanoseconds per context switch (the numbers I get using LMbench (https://lmbench. sourceforge.net) on my laptop). Given that the hardware should be able to reasonably execute, on average, 12 instructions per nanosecond per core, context switching could cost roughly ~9,000 to ~15,000 executed instructions.

Be careful when using multiple tasks in an application, because system performance can degrade if too many tasks are running. The system will waste a lot of usable time in the context-switching loop.

Now that we understand what multitasking is, let's integrate it into the runtime environment and combine all the other concurrency concepts.

Multitasking environments

In the early days of computers, people didn't think of doing more than one task at the same time on a single machine because the OS and the applications were not designed for multitasking. We had to exit one application and open a new one every time.

Today, the ability to perform multiple tasks concurrently has become one of the most important requirements for runtime systems. This requirement is addressed by multitasking. Although real parallel processing is not achieved, and some overhead is associated with switching between tasks, interleaved execution provides significant advantages in processing efficiency and program structuring.

For the user, the advantage of a multitasking system is the ability to have multiple applications running at the same time. For example, a user can edit a document in one application while watching a movie in another.

For the developer, the advantage of multitasking is the ability to create applications using more than one process and to create processes using more than one execution thread. For example, a process may have a user interface thread that handles user interaction (keyboard and mouse input) and worker threads that perform computational tasks while the user interface thread waits for user input.

Delegating the scheduling and coordination of tasks to a runtime system simplifies the development process while allowing flexibility to adapt transparently to different hardware or software architectures. Using different runtime environments (computer OS, Internet of Things [IoT] runtime environment, manufacturing OS, etc.) allows developers to optimize for different purposes. For example, minimizing power consumption may require a different scheduler than maximizing throughput.

> **NOTE**   In the 1960s and 1970s, the development of multitasking OSs such as IBM's OS/360 and UNIX allowed multiple programs to run on a single computer but required more memory than was physically available. To solve this problem, virtual memory was developed, a technique that temporarily transfers data from RAM to disk storage, allowing computers to use more memory than they have. This development enabled computers to run more programs simultaneously, and virtual memory remains an essential component of modern OSs.

Multitasking OSs

Multitasking in multiprocessor environments can be supplemented by distributing different tasks to the available CPU cores. The CPU does not know anything about processes or threads. The CPU's job is just to execute machine instructions. Thus, from the CPU's point of view, there is only one execution thread: serial execution of all incoming machine instructions from the OS. To make that happen, the OS uses thread and process abstractions. And the task of the OS when there are multiple running threads for a single processor core is to somehow juggle the threads, simulating parallel execution for the user but making them run concurrently.

Multitasking is a runtime system–level feature; there is no concept of multitasking at the hardware level. However, implementing multitasking is not without challenges and often requires the runtime system to have strong task isolation and an efficient task scheduler.

Task isolation

By the definition of multitasking, there are multiple tasks in the OS. You may have already guessed that we will now refer to processes and thread abstractions provided by the OS, but if you are creating a runtime system, things can be different.

There are two ways to create multiple tasks:

- As a single process with multiple threads

- As multiple processes, each having one or more threads

As previously discussed, each option has its pros and cons, but they all provide, to a greater or lesser extent, isolation of the execution of tasks. The OS, in turn, takes care of how these abstractions are mapped to the physical threads of the computer system and how they are executed on the hardware.

The OS abstracts from how the hardware works, and even if the system has only one core, the OS gives the developer the illusion that it doesn't. So even if the system cannot use parallelism, developers can still use concurrent programming and take advantage of the OS's multitasking. A program divided in this way can be written as if the processor is at its full disposal.

It is generally more efficient to implement multitasking by creating a single multi-threaded process rather than multiple processes, for the following reasons:

- The system can perform context switching faster for threads than for processes because a process has more overhead than a thread (a process context is larger than a thread context).

- All process threads share address space and can access global process variables, simplifying communication between threads.

Task scheduling

The scheduler is the core of multitasking OSs. From all the tasks in the Ready state, the scheduler chooses which one should be executed next.

The idea behind scheduling execution is simple. Something should always be running, to make better use of processor time. If there are more tasks than processors in the system, which is common, some tasks do not run at all times but wait in the Ready state. The choice of which task should be executed at the next moment is the fundamental decision of the scheduler from the information about the tasks that are ready to run.

Since the scheduler allocates a limited resource (CPU time), the logic it follows is based on balancing conflicting goals and priorities. Typical goals are to maximize throughput (number of tasks a system can handle over a period of time) or fairness (prioritizing or aligning computation) or minimize response time (time to complete the action) or delay (making it react faster).

The scheduler can forcefully take control away from a task (e.g., by a timer or when a task with a higher priority emerges) or wait until the task gives control explicitly (by calling a system procedure) or implicitly (when it finishes) to the scheduler. This means the scheduler is unpredictable regarding what task will be selected for execution at any given time. Thus, the developer should never write a program based on previously seen behavior, because it is not guaranteed to happen every time. We must control the synchronization and coordination of tasks to achieve determinism in our application. We talk about this in the following chapters.

Most importantly, the scheduler opens the door to implementing new methods of improving system performance without changing the program. Of course, introducing an additional layer between the application and the OS increases execution overhead. For this approach to work, the performance benefits that the runtime environment can provide must exceed the runtime management overhead.

> **NOTE**   We focused on the OS in this chapter, but other runtime environments implement the same multitasking concepts. For example, multitasking is used with `await` in languages like JavaScript and Python that feature a single-threaded event loop in their runtime. V8, one of the most efficient JavaScript execution engines on the market, and the Go programming language, known for its scalability and small memory footprint, do their own multitasking, lying on top of the OS (at the user level). We touch on this topic in Chapter 12 when we talk about cooperative multitasking and asynchronous communication.

Recap

- There are two types of bottlenecks in programs based on the resources used the most—CPU-bound and I/O-bound:

  - CPU-bound operations mostly require processor resources to finish their computation. In this case, the limitation is the speed at which the system can compute something.

  - I/O-bound operations mostly do I/O and don't depend on computation resources, such as waiting for a disk operation to finish or an external service to answer a request. In this case, the limit is the speed of the hardware, such as how fast a disk can read data or how fast a network can transmit it.

- *Context switching* is a physical act of swapping from one task's context to another so that the task can later be recovered to the same moment when it was switched. Context switching is a procedure handled by the OS, and it's one of the key mechanisms that provides multitasking to the OS.

Context switching is not free, so be careful when using multiple tasks in an application. System performance can degrade if too many tasks are running—the system will waste a lot of usable time in the context-switching loop.

- The ability to perform multiple tasks simultaneously is critical for runtime systems. It is solved by *multitasking*. This mechanism controls the interleaving and alternating execution of tasks. By constantly switching tasks, the system can maintain the illusion of simultaneous execution of tasks, although in fact the tasks are not executed in parallel.

- *Multitasking* is the concept of performing multiple tasks over a period of time by executing them concurrently. Multitasking is a runtime system–level feature; there is no concept of multitasking at the hardware level.

  - In preemptive multitasking, the scheduler prioritizes tasks and forces the tasks to pass control to other tasks.

  - It is generally more efficient to implement multitasking by creating a single multithreaded process rather than multiple processes.

  - It is important for the runtime system scheduler to distinguish between I/O-bound and CPU-bound tasks to ensure optimal use of system resources.

Decomposition | 7

In this chapter

- You learn decomposition techniques to efficiently break down programming problems into separate, independent tasks

- You learn popular concurrency patterns for creating concurrent applications: the pipeline, map, fork/join, and map/reduce patterns

- You learn how to choose the granularity of your applications

- You learn how to use agglomeration to reduce communication overhead and increase system performance

Previously, we learned that concurrent programming implies decomposing a problem into independent units of concurrency or tasks. Deciding how to decompose a problem into concurrent tasks is one of the more difficult but important steps. Automatically decomposing programs using a concurrent programming approach is a difficult research topic. Thus, in most cases, decomposition falls on the shoulders of the developers.

In this chapter, we discuss methods and popular programming patterns for designing concurrent applications. We talk about the application layer of concurrency, where we focus on where we can find independence of tasks and how to structure and design a program rather than how it will be executed (although we also touch on this part).

Dependency analysis

Decomposing a problem into concurrent tasks is one of the first necessary steps in writing concurrent applications and is the key to concurrent programming. When you decide to decompose a programming problem into tasks, don't forget that tasks can have dependencies on other tasks. Therefore, the first step to decompose the problem is to find the dependencies of all its constituent tasks and identify those that are independent. One method to help model how the tasks in a program relate to each other is to build a *task dependency graph*.

Dependency graphs help describe relationships between tasks. Consider the steps for cooking a simple chicken soup. To make chicken soup, you need to boil the chicken to make broth, remove the bones, chop carrots, chop celery, chop onions, mix these ingredients into the soup, and cook until the chicken is tender. You can't start to simmer the soup until you've done all of the preceding tasks. Each step represents a task, and going backward from the result through each task dependency, we can build a dependency graph that looks like this.

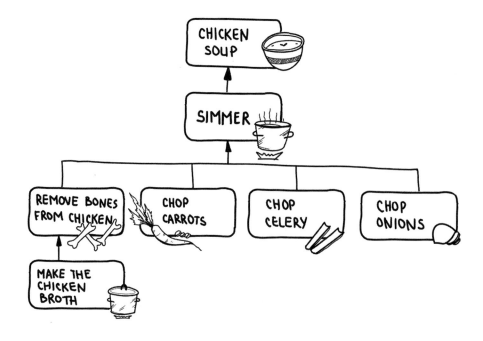

There are several ways to draw these types of computational graphs, but their general purpose is to provide an abstract representation of the program. They help visualize relationships and dependencies between tasks. Each node represents a task, and edges represent dependencies.

Dependency graphs can also be used to get an idea of how concurrent a program can be. The fact that there are no direct edges between the tasks of making broth and chopping vegetables indicates that concurrency is possible at this point. Thus, if this program could be implemented using threads, we would be able to create four separate threads: one for making broth and three others for chopping vegetables. All of them can be executed simultaneously. The same concept is used in runtime systems when scheduling individual tasks.

Building a dependency graph is the first step toward program or system design. It helps to identify portions of work that can be performed concurrently. For now, we are ignoring problems of practical implementation, such as the number of processors or cores that can be used; all our attention is focused on the possible concurrency of the original problem. Having said that about the dependency graph, let's look at it from different angles.

The two types of dependencies in code are control dependency and data dependency. The corresponding ways of dividing a problem into smaller tasks are *task decomposition* and *data decomposition*.

Task decomposition

Task decomposition answers the question, "How can a problem be decomposed into independent functionality that can be executed concurrently?" or, to put it in plain English, "How can we split a problem into a bunch of tasks that we can perform all at once?"

Let's imagine that there has been a major snowfall. You want to clear the area around the house by shoveling snow and scattering salt. Your friend comes over to help you finish the job faster, but you have only one shovel. So while one shovels, the other waits to take a turn. Remember, although this process makes sense, having only one resource (the shovel) does not speed up the work—it only slows it down. Overhead from context switching makes this process inefficient as it constantly interrupts the shoveling process.

Having the same goal of clearing the area around the house, you decide to give your friend another subtask. While you clear the snow with your only shovel, your friend scatters salt. By eliminating the wait for the shovel, you make the job more efficient. This is essentially what task decomposition (also known as *task parallelism*) gives you.

This is an example of breaking down the problem into tasks by functionality. But task decomposition is often far from obvious: it's complex and very subjective.

Task decomposition implies the decomposition of the application into functionally independent tasks based on application functionality. Such decomposition is possible when the problem to be solved naturally consists of different types of tasks, each of which can be solved independently.

For example, an email management application would have a lot of functional requirements: standard features should include a user interface, a way to reliably receive new emails, and the ability for the user to write, send, and search through emails.

The tasks of finding emails and the UI that lists those emails depend on the same data but are completely independent of each other, so they can be split into two tasks and executed independently. The same applies to sending and receiving emails. For example, we can use different processors, each working with the same data but doing their tasks concurrently.

As we have seen, the functionality of the different tasks in task decomposition is diverse, with a wide range of operations used. Therefore it can only be used on multiple instruction, multiple data (MIMD) and multiple instruction, single data (MISD) systems.

Task decomposition: Pipeline pattern

The most common pattern in task decomposition is so-called *pipeline processing*. The essence of pipeline processing is to decompose the algorithm into several separate consecutive steps. Pipeline steps can then be distributed among the different cores. Each core is like one worker on an assembly line; having completed its work, it passes the result to the next core while accepting a new portion of data. Hence, cores can execute multiple chunks of data simultaneously, starting new computations while others are still running.

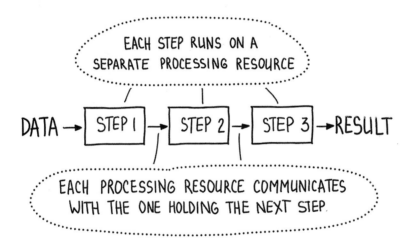

NOTE   Remember how we talked about the infinite CPU execution cycle? The execution of a single instruction includes passing through the steps of fetching instructions, decoding, executing, and storing the results. In modern processors, stages are designed so that instructions can be executed using pipeline processing at such a low level.

In Chapter 2, we did laundry in a hurry. Let's bring that example closer to reality. In addition to washing the laundry, which takes a decent amount of time, you need to dry the laundry and then fold it—you don't want to wear crumpled laundry to Hawaii, do you?

If you're not using pipeline processing, washing, drying, and folding four loads of laundry with one washer and dryer looks like this.

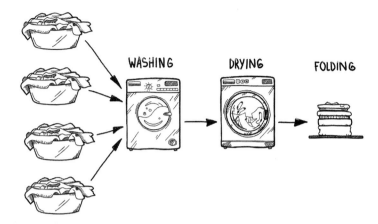

With this approach, your resources (washer, dryer) are not fully utilized—there are times when they are idle while some other action is performed.

Using pipeline processing ensures that you are constantly using the washer and dryer without wasting any time—you divide the three steps of the laundry process into three different workers: washer, dryer, and folder (the latter is probably you). Each worker has a lock on a common resource.

The first batch of laundry is ready to be washed and placed in the washer. When the laundry is washed and removed from the washer, it is transferred to the next stage of your pipeline, the dryer. While the first batch of laundry is drying in the dryer, the second batch can begin washing because the washing machine is idle.

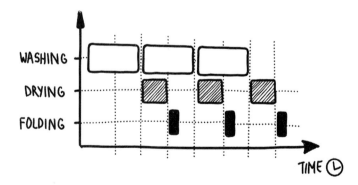

Concurrency occurs when a second load going through the pipeline ends up executing at the same time as the first load. The coincidence of previously separated operations definitely has a positive effect on processing speed.

NOTE   One of the most popular patterns in the big data world is ETL (extract, transform, load)—a popular paradigm for collecting and processing data from various sources that implements a pipeline pattern. Using ETL tools, we *extract* data from the source(s) and *transform* it into structured information, which we *load* into the target data warehouse or other target system.

To implement this type of functionality in our code, we need two things: a way to create independently running tasks and a way for tasks to communicate with each other. This is where threads and queues come to the rescue. Let's see what the example looks like in this code:

```python
# Chapter 7/pipeline.py
import time
from queue import Queue
from threading import Thread

Washload = str


class Washer(Thread):
    def __init__(self, in_queue: Queue[Washload], out_queue:
Queue[Washload]):
        super().__init__()
        self.in_queue = in_queue
        self.out_queue = out_queue

    def run(self) -> None:
        while True:
            washload = self.in_queue.get()
            print(f"Washer: washing {washload}...")
            time.sleep(4)
            self.out_queue.put(f'{washload}')
            self.in_queue.task_done()


class Dryer(Thread):
    def __init__(self, in_queue: Queue[Washload], out_queue:
Queue[Washload]):
        super().__init__()
        self.in_queue = in_queue
        self.out_queue = out_queue
```

- Gets the washload from the previous stage
- Simulates actual work
- Sends the washload to the next stage

```
    def run(self) -> None:
        while True:
            washload = self.in_queue.get()
            print(f"Dryer: drying {washload}...")
            time.sleep(2)
            self.out_queue.put(f'{washload}')
            self.in_queue.task_done()
```

Gets the washload from the previous stage

Simulates actual work

Sends the washload to the next stage

```
class Folder(Thread):
    def __init__(self, in_queue: Queue[Washload]):
        super().__init__()
        self.in_queue = in_queue

    def run(self) -> None:
        while True:
            washload = self.in_queue.get()
            print(f"Folder: folding {washload}...")
            time.sleep(1)
            print(f"Folder: {washload} done!")
            self.in_queue.task_done()
```

Gets the washload from the previous stage

Simulates actual work

Sends the washload to the next stage

```
class Pipeline:
    def assemble_laundry_for_washing(self) -> Queue[Washload]:
        washload_count = 8
        washloads_in: Queue[Washload] = Queue(washload_count)
        for washload_num in range(washload_count):
            washloads_in.put(f'Washload #{washload_num}')
        return washloads_in

    def run_concurrently(self) -> None:
        to_be_washed = self.assemble_laundry_for_washing()
        to_be_dried: Queue[Washload] = Queue()
        to_be_folded: Queue[Washload] = Queue()

        Washer(to_be_washed, to_be_dried).start()
        Dryer(to_be_dried, to_be_folded).start()
        Folder(to_be_folded).start()
```

Assembles a queue of laundry loads to be washed and starts the threads in the correct order, linked by the queues

```
        to_be_washed.join()
        to_be_dried.join()
        to_be_folded.join()                    Waits for all the washloads in
        print("All done!")                      the queue to be processed
```

```
if __name__ == "__main__":
    pipeline = Pipeline()
    pipeline.run_concurrently()
```

We implement three main classes: `Washer`, `Dryer`, and `Folder`. In this program, each of our functions runs on separate threads concurrently. The output looks like this:

```
Washer: washing Washload #0...
Washer: washing Washload #1...
Dryer: drying Washload #0...
Folder: folding Washload #0...
Folder: Washload #0 done!
Washer: washing Washload #2...
Dryer: drying Washload #1...
Folder: folding Washload #1...
Folder: Washload #1 done!
Washer: washing Washload #3...
Dryer: drying Washload #2...
Folder: folding Washload #2...
Folder: Washload #2 done!
Dryer: drying Washload #3...
Folder: folding Washload #3...
Folder: Washload #3 done!
All done!
```

Since more loads can be washed at the same time, a pipeline pattern provides more efficiency than washing one load at a time. Suppose it takes three steps to wash the clothes, and these steps take 20, 10, and 5 minutes, respectively. Then if all three steps were performed in sequence, you would complete one load of laundry every 35 minutes.

Using a pipeline pattern, you can complete the first load in 35 minutes and every subsequent load in 20 minutes because as soon as the first load finishes washing, the second load goes into the washing phase while the first load dries. Thus, the first load leaves the pipeline 35 minutes after the start of washing, the second load after 55 minutes, the third load after 75 minutes, and so on.

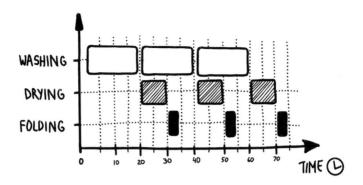

It would seem that pipeline processing could be successfully replaced by simple parallelism. But even in our example, to maintain parallelism, you would need to own four washers and four dryers. I would say this is impossible, if only because of the cost of all that equipment and available space.

The pipeline allows us to limit the number of threads, such as in the thread pool, needed for a particular pipeline step if there are a limited number of shared resources, rather than wasting threads that would otherwise be left idle. This is why pipelining is most useful when the number of shared resources is limited.

> **NOTE** For example, filesystems can usually handle a limited number of concurrent read/write requests before they become overloaded. This puts an upper bound on the number of threads that give a concurrency benefit to this step.

Pipeline processing is often combined with other decomposition approaches, such as data decomposition. Speaking of which . . .

Data decomposition

Another commonly used concurrent programming model, *data decomposition*, allows developers to exploit the concurrency that occurs when the same operation is applied to multiple elements of a collection, such as multiplying all the elements of an array by 2 or increasing the taxes of all citizens with salaries greater than a tax bracket. Each task performs the same set of instructions but with its own chunk of data.

Therefore, data decomposition answers the question, "How do you decompose task data into chunks that can be processed independently of each other?" Thus, data decomposition is based on the data, not the type of task.

Let's go back to our shovel problem. You have only one shovel, and the goal is to clear the snow from the area around the house. But if you have not one but two shovels, you can divide the area (data) into two zones (chunks of data) and clean them in parallel, using the independence of operations on the different data.

Data decomposition is achieved by dividing the data into *chunks*. Since each operation on each chunk of data can be treated as an independent task, the resulting concurrent program consists of a sequence of such operations. We already used data decomposition in Chapter 3 in the password-cracking example. The possible passwords (data) were divided into independent groups (parts of the task), which were evenly processed on different computing resources.

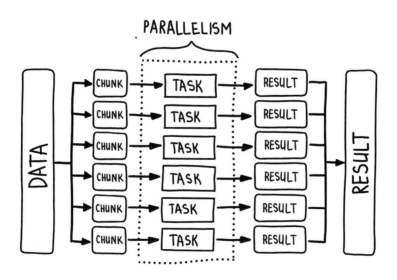

NOTE Although in this chapter we talk about concurrency at the application layer, data decomposition depends more on the actual parallelism at the hardware layer because without it, there is little point in using this method.

Data decomposition can be achieved in a distributed system by dividing the work between several computers or in one computer between different processor cores. Regardless of the amount of input data coming in, we can always horizontally scale resources to increase system performance as the specifically distributed system performs the same steps on all available computing resources simultaneously. If this sounds familiar, you are right. It is similar to the single instruction, multiple data (SIMD) architecture, and this type of architecture is best suited for this category of tasks.

Loop-level parallelism

The main candidate for using data decomposition is a program that has an operation that can be executed independently for each chunk of data. In general, loops in any form (for loop, while loop, and for-each loop) often fit this category perfectly, and that's why it's also referred to as *loop-level parallelism*. Loop-level parallelism is an approach often used to extract concurrent tasks from loops. It can even be used automatically by some compilers that can automatically translate sequential parts of a program into semantically equivalent concurrent code.

Imagine that you have the task of creating an application that searches a computer for files containing some search term. The user enters a directory path and a text string to search, and the program outputs the names of the files containing the search term.

How would you implement such functionality?

If we implement the program in a simple sequential form without using concurrency, it is a simple for loop:

```python
# Chapter 7/find_files/find_files_sequential.py
import os
import time
import typing as T


def search_file(file_location: str, search_string: str) -> bool:
    with open(file_location, "r", encoding="utf8") as file:
        return search_string in file.read()


def search_files_sequentially(file_locations: T.List[str],
                              search_string: str) -> None:
        result = search_file(file_name, search_string)
        if result:
            print(f"Found word in file: `{file_name}`")
```

```
if __name__ == "__main__":
    file_locations = list(
        glob.glob(f"{os.path.abspath(os.getcwd())}/books/*.txt"))
    search_string = input("What word are you trying to find?: ")

    start_time = time.perf_counter()
    search_files_sequentially(file_locations, search_string)
    process_time = time.perf_counter() - start_time
    print(f"PROCESS TIME: {process_time}")
```

Creates a list of file locations to search

Gets the search term from the user

To use this script, enter the directory to search for files when prompted and the word you're searching for. The script will search for the word in all files in the specified directory and print the name of any file that contains the word. Here is some sample output:

```
What word are you trying to find?: brillig
Found string in file: `Through the Looking-Glass.txt`
PROCESS TIME: 0.75120013574
```

Looking at this code, we see that in the for loop, we do the same actions on different data (files) at each iteration independently of each other—we don't need to finish processing file *N* to process file *N* + 1. So why can't we separate these chunks of data and start processing them in multiple threads instead? Of course, we can:

```
# Chapter 7/find_files/find_files_concurrent.py
import os
import time
import typing as T
from multiprocessing.pool import ThreadPool


def search_file(file_location: str, search_string: str) -> bool:
    with open(file_location, "r", encoding="utf8") as file:
        return search_string in file.read()


def search_files_concurrently(file_locations: T.List[str],
                              search_string: str) -> None:
    with ThreadPool() as pool:
        results = pool.starmap(search_file,
                               ((file_location, search_string) for
                                file_location in file_locations))
```

Searches for the same word in each thread concurrently

```
        for result, file_name in zip(results, file_locations):
            if result:
                print(f"Found string in file: `{file_name}`")


if __name__ == "__main__":
    file_locations = list(
        glob.glob(f"{os.path.abspath(os.getcwd())}/books/*.txt"))
    search_string = input("What word are you trying to find?: ")

    start_time = time.perf_counter()
    search_files_concurrently(file_locations, search_string)
    process_time = time.perf_counter() - start_time
    print(f"PROCESS TIME: {process_time}")
```

This code searches for a specified word in all files in a given directory and its subdirectories using multiple threads. Here's some sample output:

```
Search in which directory?: /Users/kirill/books/
What word are you trying to find?: brillig
Found string in file: `Through the Looking-Glass.txt`
PROCESS TIME: 0.04880058398703113
```

> **NOTE** In this example, we want to use all available CPU cores to process multiple files simultaneously. But keep in mind that getting files from the hard disk is an I/O operation, so the data will not be in memory when we start the execution; thus we may not get chunks of data processed simultaneously (even with parallel hardware). However, using loop-level parallelism, the program can start useful execution as soon as at least one of the data chunks is read. The execution system can even be single-threaded; it still helps multitasking, where the work completes as soon as it can be executed.

In the example code, threads do the same work but on different iterations and hence different pieces of data. *N* threads can each work on 1/*N* pieces of data concurrently.

Map pattern

We have just implemented a new programming pattern: the *map pattern*. The idea is based on the technique of functional programming languages. It is used in cases where a single operation is applied to all elements of a collection, but all individual tasks are processed autonomously and have no side effects (they don't change the program state but only convert input data into output data).

The map pattern is used to solve embarrassingly parallel tasks: tasks that can be decomposed into independent subtasks that do not require communication/synchronization. Those subtasks are executed on one or more processes, threads, or SIMD tracks or multiple computers.

MAP PATTERN

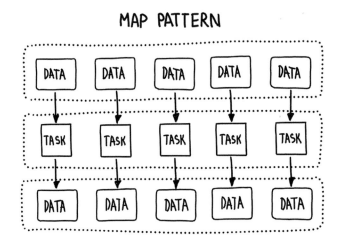

Loops take up a significant portion of execution time in many programs, especially in science and analytical systems, and they can take many forms. To understand whether your problem fits this pattern, you need to analyze at or close to the source code level. It is important to understand the dependencies between different loop iterations—whether data from the previous iteration is used in subsequent iterations.

> **NOTE** Many libraries and frameworks in the wild use loop-level parallelism. Open Multi-Processing (OpenMP) uses loop-level parallelism for multicore processor architectures. NVIDIA's CUDA library provides loop-level parallelism for GPU architectures. Map patterns are widely implemented in most modern programming languages, such as Scala, Java, Kotlin, Python, Haskell, and so on.

As you can see, data decomposition is widely used, but another pattern is even more common.

Fork/Join pattern

Unfortunately, an application is likely to have sequential parts (those that are not independent and must be executed in a particular order) and concurrent parts (which can be executed out of order or even in parallel). There is another common concurrency pattern for those types of applications.

Imagine that you're responsible for organizing a vote-counting process for the local mayoral elections (please note that this is a fictional scenario, so take it with a grain of salt). The work is simple—just go through the ballots and count the number of votes for one candidate or another.

As it's your first election, you don't put much thought into organizing the process and decide to do it all by yourself after the polls close on Election Day. You go through the pile of ballots sequentially, one after another. It takes the whole day to finish, but you make it. The sequential solution looks similar to the following:

```python
# Chapter 7/count_votes/count_votes_sequential.py
import typing as T
import random

Summary = T.Mapping[int, int]


def process_votes(pile: T.List[int]) -> Summary:
    summary = {}
    for vote in pile:
        if vote in summary:
            summary[vote] += 1
        else:
            summary[vote] = 1
    return summary


if __name__ == "__main__":
    num_candidates = 3
    num_voters = 100000
    pile = [random.randint(1, num_candidates) for _ in range(num_voters)]
    counts = process_votes(pile)
    print(f"Total number of votes: {counts}")
```

Generates a huge pile of votes for three candidates, where each vote is an integer representing the selected candidate

The function takes an array of votes as an argument, with each element representing a vote for a particular candidate, and returns an associative array of the number of votes for each candidate.

As a result of this campaign, you get a promotion to Election Day organizer of the vote-counting process—not for a local election, but for national presidential elections! And as an enormous number of votes from different states will come your way, you realize that it's not feasible to use the same sequential approach again.

How would you organize the process to make it possible to process a huge number of votes in a limited amount of time?

The obvious way to process the big pile of votes is to split it into several smaller piles and give each pile to a separate staff member to process in parallel. By distributing the work among multiple people or even groups of people, you can easily speed up the process. But that's not all. You need to produce a report with the total number of votes for each candidate, not piles of summaries—they should be merged. So, you decide to organize the process of splitting the votes at the beginning, distribute that work among your staff members, and combine their individual results yourself when they are done.

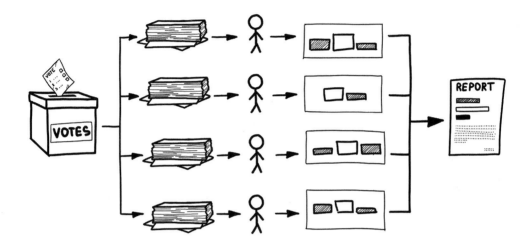

To exploit parallel execution, you hire more staff members whose job will be to count votes. Suppose you hire four staff members. Then you can do the following:

- Use the first staff member to sum the first quarter of the ballots.
- Use the second staff member to sum the second quarter of the ballots.
- Use the third staff member to sum the third quarter of the ballots.
- Use the fourth staff member to sum the fourth quarter of the ballots.
- Then you get all four results and combine them, returning the answer.

The first four tasks can be executed in parallel, but the last task is sequential as it depends on the results from previous steps.

Before looking at the following code, think of how you would solve the problem yourself:

```
# Chapter 7/count_votes/count_votes_concurrent.py
import typing as T
import random
from multiprocessing.pool import ThreadPool
```

```python
Summary = T.Mapping[int, int]


def process_votes(pile: T.List[int], worker_count: int = 4) -> Summary:
    vote_count = len(pile)
    vpw = vote_count // worker_count

    vote_piles = [
        pile[i * vpw:(i + 1) * vpw]
        for i in range(worker_count)
    ]

    with ThreadPool(worker_count) as pool:
        worker_summaries = pool.map(process_pile, vote_piles)

    total_summary = {}
    for worker_summary in worker_summaries:
        print(f"Votes from staff member: {worker_summary}")
        for candidate, count in worker_summary.items():
            if candidate in total_summary:
                total_summary[candidate] += count
            else:
                total_summary[candidate] = count

    return total_summary


def process_pile(pile: T.List[int]) -> Summary:
    summary = {}
    for vote in pile:
        if vote in summary:
            summary[vote] += 1
        else:
            summary[vote] = 1
    return summary


if __name__ == "__main__":
    num_candidates = 3
    num_voters = 100000
    pile = [random.randint(1, num_candidates) for _ in range(num_voters)]
    counts = process_votes(pile)
    print(f"Total number of votes: {counts}")
```

Fork step—divides the votes among workers and runs them concurrently

Join step—merges the staff worker summaries

This example utilizes a popular programming pattern for creating concurrent applications. It's called the *fork/join pattern.*

The idea is as follows. We split the data into multiple smaller chunks and process them as independent tasks. In the example, smaller piles of votes are divided between staff members. This step is called a *fork*. As in loop-level parallelism, it can be scaled horizontally by adding more processing resources.

Then we go through the process of combining the results of individual tasks until the solution to the original topmost problem is obtained. In the example, we need to aggregate the final election results for each candidate's votes from the results of each staff member summary. You can think of it as a synchronization point—in that step, we are just waiting for all the dependent tasks to be completed before calculating the final result. This step is called a *join*.

Combining the two steps, we get the fork/join pattern. As mentioned, this pattern is one of the most popular nowadays; many concurrent systems and libraries are written in this style.

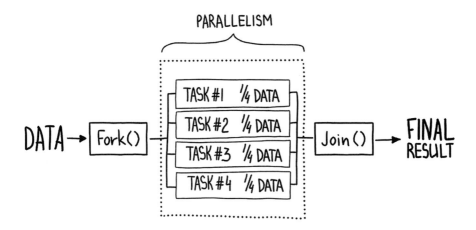

Map/Reduce pattern

Map/reduce is another concurrency pattern and is closely related to fork/join. The idea of the map step is the same as the map pattern: one function maps all inputs to get new results (e.g., "multiply by 2"). The reduce step performs an aggregation (e.g., "sum up individual votes" or "take the minimum value"). The map and reduce steps are typically performed in sequence, with the map step producing intermediate results that are then processed by the reduce step.

In map/reduce, as in fork/join, a set of input data is processed in parallel by multiple processing resources. The results are then combined until a single response is obtained. Although structurally identical, the type of work performed reflects a slightly different philosophy. The map and reduce steps are more independent than the standard fork/join as they can scale beyond a single computer, utilizing a fleet of machines to perform a single operation on a large volume of data. Another distinction from the fork/join pattern is that the map step can sometimes be done without reduction and vice versa.

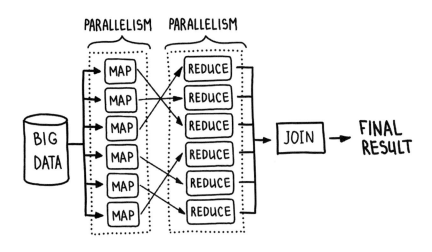

This is one of the key concepts behind Google's MapReduce framework and Yahoo's open source variant of Apache Hadoop. In these systems, the developer simply writes operations that describe how to map and reduce data. The system then does all the work, often using hundreds or thousands of computers to process gigabytes or terabytes of data. Developers just need to wrap the necessary logic into the computing primitives provided by the framework, leaving everything else to the runtime system.

> **NOTE** Another currently popular framework is inspired by MapReduce's model: Apache Spark. This framework uses functional programming and pipeline processing to implement a map/reduce pattern. Instead of writing data to disk for each job as MapReduce does, Spark can cache the results across jobs. Moreover, Spark is the underlying framework many different systems are built on, including Spark SQL and DataFrames, GraphX, and Streaming Spark. That makes it easy to mix and match the use of these systems in the same application. These features make Spark the best fit for iterative jobs and interactive analytics and help it provide better performance.

Data decomposition and task decomposition are not mutually exclusive and can be implemented simultaneously by combining them for the same application. In this way, applications get the maximum boost from the use of concurrency.

Granularity

In the previous voting example, we made two rather questionable assumptions:

- We assumed that we would have exactly four processing resources—the staff members—and that each processing resource would get about the same amount of work. However, limiting the number of processing resources used doesn't make sense. We want concurrent applications to efficiently use all the processing resources available to them. Constantly using exactly four threads is not the best approach. If a program runs on a system with three cores, it will take longer than if evenly distributed among three threads on one core. On the contrary, if we have a system with eight cores, four will be idle.

- We assumed that every processing resource was available exclusively for our application at runtime. However, our application is not the only one in the system, and some processing resources may be needed by other applications or the system itself.

Putting these assumptions aside, a problem arises: How can we use all available resources on the system to perform tasks as efficiently as possible? Ideally, the number of tasks in decomposed problems should be at least as large as the number of available processing resources, preferably larger, to provide greater flexibility for the runtime system.

The number and size of tasks into which a problem is decomposed determine the *granularity* of the decomposition. Granularity is usually measured by the number of instructions executed in a particular task. For example, in our previous problem, dividing the work into eight threads instead of four makes the program *finer-grained* and, in this case, more flexible. It can be executed on more computing resources, if available. If the system has only four cores available, not all threads will execute simultaneously because a core can physically execute only one thread at a time. But that's okay, as the runtime system will keep track of which threads are waiting their turn and ensure that all the cores are busy. For example, the scheduler may decide that the first four threads will start running in parallel, and when they are finished, the remaining four will be executed. If there are eight cores available in the system, the system can execute all tasks in parallel.

With a *coarse-grained* approach, the program is split into larger tasks. As a consequence, a large amount of computation falls on the processors. This can lead to load imbalance, with some tasks processing most of the data and others idle, which limits concurrency in the program. But the advantage of this type of granularity is the lower communication and coordination overhead.

GRANULARITY

When fine granularity is used, the program is broken into many small tasks. Using fine granularity leads to more parallelism and therefore increases the system's performance since these tasks are evenly distributed among several processors, so the amount of work associated with a concurrent task is small and executed very quickly.

But creating a large number of small tasks has a downside: by increasing the number of tasks that need to communicate, we significantly increase the cost of communication. To communicate, tasks have to stop computation to send and receive messages. In addition to communication costs, we may have to look at the cost of creating tasks. As we've said before, some overhead costs are associated with creating threads and processes. Increasing the number of tasks to, say, 1,000,000 will significantly increase the load on the OS scheduler and significantly reduce system performance. Thus, optimal performance is achieved between the two extremes, fine-grained and coarse-grained.

Many algorithms developed using task decomposition have a fixed number of tasks of the same size, as well as structured connectivity, both local and global. In such cases, efficient mapping is straightforward. We map tasks in a way that minimizes interprocessor communication. We can also combine tasks mapped to a single processor, if this has not already been done, to get coarse-grained tasks, one per processor. This process of grouping tasks is called *agglomeration* (more about it in Chapter 13).

In talking about data decomposition, our effort should be to define as many smaller tasks as possible. This is useful because it forces us to consider a wide range of possibilities for parallel execution. If necessary, tasks are merged into larger tasks—an agglomeration process occurs to improve performance or reduce communication.

In more complex algorithms based on task decomposition, with variable workloads per task and/or unstructured communication schemes, effective agglomeration and matching strategies may not be obvious to the developer. Consequently, we can use load-balancing algorithms that seek to identify efficient agglomeration and mapping strategies, usually using heuristics.

Recap

- There is no magic formula for how to decompose a programming problem. One tool that can help is to visualize the dependencies of the tasks in the algorithm by building a *task dependency graph* and finding independent tasks in it.

- If an application has clear functional components, it may be advantageous to decompose that application into functionally independent tasks using *task decomposition* and then use MIMD/MISD systems for execution. Task decomposition answers the question, "How can a problem be decomposed into tasks that can execute concurrently?"

- *Pipeline processing* is a popular task decomposition pattern that can help increase the system's throughput when the number of shared resources is limited. It can be used together with other decomposition approaches.

- If an application has steps that can be performed independently on different data chunks, it may be advantageous to utilize *data decomposition* and use SIMD systems for execution. Data decomposition answers the question, "How can a problem's data be decomposed into units that can be operated on relatively independently?"

- *The map pattern, fork/join pattern,* and *map/reduce pattern* are popular data decomposition patterns used extensively in many popular libraries and frameworks.

- Task number and size determine the *granularity* of the system. Ideally, the number of tasks into which a problem is decomposed should be at least the number of available processing resources, preferably more, to provide flexibility for the runtime system.

Solving concurrency problems: Race conditions and synchronization

8

....

In this chapter

- You learn how to identify and solve one of the most common concurrency problems: race conditions

- You learn how to share resources between tasks safely and reliably using synchronization primitives

....

In sequential programs, code execution follows a happy path of predictability and determinism; looking at it and understanding what it does is as easy as understanding how each function works, given the current state of the program. But in a concurrent program, the state of the program changes during execution. External circumstances, such as the OS scheduler, cache coherency, or platform compilers, can affect the order of execution and resources the program accesses. In addition, concurrent tasks conflict with each other when they compete for the same resources, such as CPU, shared variables, or files, which often cannot be controlled by the OS. This can all affect the result of the program.

The importance of concurrency control was made clear in May 2012 during Facebook's highly anticipated initial public offering (IPO). A glitch in NASDAQ's system caused a 30-minute delay in Facebook's opening. This race condition led to chaotic order changes and cancellations, resulting in significant losses for traders. The IPO's underwhelming performance overshadowed NASDAQ's role in facilitating one of the largest IPOs in US history, high-lighting the crucial need for effective concurrency control (http://mng.bz/Bmr2).

Hence, we cannot simply rely on the runtime system to manage and coordinate our program's tasks and shared resources since the detailed requirements and program flow may not be obvious. In this chapter, we learn how to write code that provides synchronized access to shared resources, look at common concurrency problems, and discuss possible solutions and popular concurrency patterns.

Shared resources

Let's go back to our recipe example from earlier in the book. Often a recipe has several steps that can be done at the same time if there are several cooks in the kitchen. But if there is only one oven, you cannot cook a turkey and another dish at different tempera-tures simultaneously. In this case, the oven is a shared resource.

In short, multiple cooks provide an opportunity to increase efficiency, but they also make the cooking process more difficult because of required *communication* and *coordination*. It is the same with programming: the OS runs tasks concurrently, and these tasks also depend on limited resources. These tasks operate independently, often unaware of each other's existence and actions. Consequently, conflicts may arise when they attempt to utilize shared resources during runtime. To prevent such conflicts, it is essential for each task to leave the state of any resource it employs unaffected. For instance, consider a scenario where two tasks concurrently attempt to use a printer. Without proper control over printer access, an error could arise, leading the application (or even the whole system) into an unknown and potentially invalid state.

A function or operation is *thread safe* if it behaves correctly when accessed from multiple tasks, regardless of how those tasks are scheduled or interleaved by the execution environment. When it comes to thread safety, good application design is the best protection a developer can have. Avoiding resource sharing and minimizing communication between tasks make it less likely that these tasks will mess with each other. However, it is not always possible to create an application that does not use shared resources.

> **NOTE** It's easy to provide thread safety by using immutable objects and pure functions. Since they cannot change state, they cannot be corrupted by thread interference or observed in an inconsistent state. Immutability can be provided by the programming language or application so we don't mutate data while multiple threads are using it. These methods are not covered in this book.

To understand what thread safety is, let's first understand what an unsafe thread is, starting, as always, with an example.

Race conditions

Imagine that you are writing banking software where there is an object for each bank account. Different tasks (such as tellers or ATMs) can deposit or withdraw funds from the same account. Suppose the bank has ATMs that use a shared-memory approach so all ATMs can read and write the same account objects.

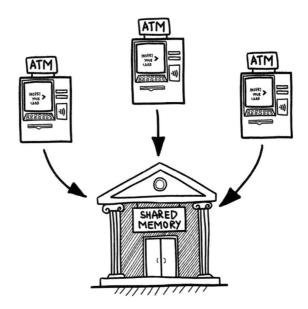

As an example, suppose the bank account class has methods for depositing and withdrawing money:

```
# Chapter 8/race_condition/unsynced_bank_account.py
from bank_account import BankAccount

class UnsyncedBankAccount(BankAccount):
    def deposit(self, amount: float) -> None:
        if amount > 0:
            self.balance += amount
        else:
            raise ValueError("You can't deposit a negative amount of money")

    def withdraw(self, amount: float) -> None:
        if 0 < amount <= self.balance:
            self.balance -= amount
        else:
            raise ValueError("Account does not have sufficient funds")
```

Here we have a class that implements a bank account with an internal variable `balance`, representing the amount of money in the account, and two methods, `deposit()` and `withdraw()`, which increase or decrease `balance`, respectively.

Imagine that you have a bunch of ATMs that execute the same transactions concurrently, as we usually assume in the real world. Here's how it looks in the code:

```
# Chapter 8/race_condition/race_condition.py
import sys
import time
from threading import Thread
import typing as T

from bank_account import BankAccount
from unsynced_bank_account import UnsyncedBankAccount

THREAD_DELAY = 1e-16

class ATM(Thread):
    def __init__(self, bank_account: BankAccount):
        super().__init__()
        self.bank_account = bank_account
```

```
    def transaction(self) -> None:
        self.bank_account.deposit(10)
        time.sleep(0.001)
        self.bank_account.withdraw(10)

    def run(self) -> None:
        self.transaction()

def test_atms(account: BankAccount, atm_number: int = 1000) -> None:
    atms: T.List[ATM] = []
    for _ in range(atm_number):
        atm = ATM(account)
        atms.append(atm)
        atm.start()

    for atm in atms:
        atm.join()

if __name__ == "__main__":
    atm_number = 1000
    sys.setswitchinterval(THREAD_DELAY)

    account = UnsyncedBankAccount()
    test_atms(account, atm_number=atm_number)

    print("Balance of unsynced account after concurrent transactions:")
    print(f"Actual: {account.balance}\nExpected: 0")
```

One transaction consists of consecutive deposits and withdrawals from a bank account.

Creates a number of ATM threads that execute transactions on a bank account concurrently

Waits for the ATM threads to finish executing

Greatly increases the chance of an operation being interrupted by a context switch, thus testing synchronization effectively

We've implemented an ATM as a thread that simply calls the deposit() method followed by a call to the withdraw() method with the same amount of money (say, $10). We run 1,000 ATMs concurrently. So the account balance should remain the same, as we add and remove the same amount of money—we expect the balance to be zero at the end of the program, right?

But if we run this code, we often find that the balance at the end of the program is different:

```
Balance of unsynced account after concurrent transactions:
Actual: 380
Expected: 0
```

How is that possible?

Let's zoom in on how the method breaks down into low-level instructions.

deposit()	withdraw()		Balance
Get balance		←	0
Add 10			0
Write back the result		→	10
	Get balance	←	10
	Remove 10		−10
	Write back the result	→	0

Suppose that two ATMs, let's call them A and B, deposit concurrently to a single bank account. In many scenarios, running the two method calls concurrently will not cause problems.

ATM A deposit()	ATM B deposit()		Balance
Get balance		←	0
Add 10			0
Write back the result		→	10
	Get balance	←	10
	Add 10		10
	Write back the result	→	20

This looks great—we end up with the correct balance of $20, so both A and B executed their transactions correctly.

But when ATMs A and B execute concurrently, these low-level instructions can interleave with each other, something like the following.

ATM A `deposit()`	ATM B `deposit()`		Balance
Get balance		←	0
	Get balance	←	0
Add 10			
	Add 10		
Write back the result		→	10
	Write back the result	→	10

In this case, ATMs A and B simultaneously read the balance, calculate different final balances, and then save the new balance, which does not take into account the contribution of the other ATM—so one of the deposits is lost. The balance is now $10: a $10 deposit has been lost!

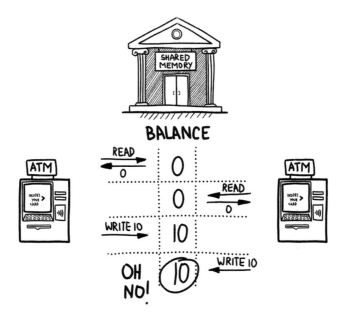

The two threads run simultaneously on different processor cores, or the OS scheduler stops one thread and starts the other at any time, switching between them any number of times. If more than one call to the `deposit()` method is executed concurrently, the balance may end up in an incorrect state. If one thread deposits and another thread withdraws, the exception thrown by the withdrawing thread may depend on the order of operations.

This is an example of a *race condition*. When we have a race condition, tasks access shared resources or common variables that can be used concurrently by other tasks, and as a result, the correctness of the program depends on the relative timing of concurrent operations. When this happens, we say, "One task is in a race with the other tasks."

There are many reasons for a race condition. Compilers usually perform various optimizations to achieve faster code execution without changing the semantics of the code. If we force compilers to never do interleaving and other code optimizations, it's difficult for the compilers to be efficient. Similarly, in hardware, no single shared-memory area contains a single copy of all the data in a program. Instead, there are various caches and buffers, allowing the processor to access one memory area faster than another, as we saw in Chapter 3. As a result, the hardware has to keep track of different copies of the data and move them around. In doing so, memory operations can become "visible" to other threads in a different order than they occur in the program. As with compilers, requiring the hardware to run all read and write operations in the order they occur is considered too burdensome from a performance standpoint. All the optimizations and reordering are completely hidden from developers, and we never have to worry about them if we avoid race conditions.

Errors caused by race conditions are hard to reproduce and isolate. They are a kind of *heisenbug*: a program error that disappears or changes its behavior when we try to investigate it. Because a race condition is a semantic bug, it can only be detected at runtime and is difficult to understand just by looking at the code without running the program. So, unfortunately, there is no universal way to detect race conditions. Sometimes placing `sleep` operators in different places in the code can help us detect potential race conditions by changing the timing and therefore the order of threads.

> **NOTE**   Make sure the libraries you are using are thread safe; if they are not, you will have to synchronize library calls. Also, be aware that global variables within a library may cause issues if the code is not designed to handle multiple concurrent calls. In such cases, you may need to abandon using the library.

As a result, we need mechanisms to provide synchronized access that prevents multiple tasks from alternating their operations in a way that leads to incorrect results and provides thread security.

Synchronization

Synchronization is one solution to these problems. Synchronization is a mechanism that controls access to shared resources between multiple tasks. This is especially important when multiple tasks require access to resources that cannot be accessed simultaneously. The right synchronization mechanism ensures exclusivity and orderly access to a resource across tasks. In Chapters 2 and 6, we talked about coordination by synchronizing execution points and waiting for dependencies. Developers can also use synchronization to protect a *critical section* of code.

A critical section is a piece of code that can be executed simultaneously by multiple tasks and has access to shared resources. For example, in the critical section, the developer may manipulate particular data structures or use a resource that supports no more than one client at a time, like a printer.

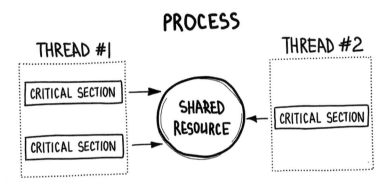

We cannot simply rely on the OS to understand and enforce this restriction, since the detailed requirements may not be obvious to the OS scheduler. For example, in the case of a printer, we want any individual process to have control over the printer as long as it prints the entire file. Otherwise, lines from competing processes will alternate. There must be some kind of mutual exclusion mechanism within the critical section that allows only one task to perform a printing operation at a time.

However, processors have instructions that can be used to implement synchronization. These instructions enable the temporary disabling of interrupts within specific sections of code, ensuring that they cannot be interrupted. This feature is valuable when safeguarding critical code sections that require uninterrupted execution. While these synchronization instructions find frequent application among compiler and OS developers, they are also abstracted as library functions in various programming languages. As a result, programmers can utilize these language-specific functions to shield critical code segments, even without directly manipulating the underlying processor-level instructions.

A popular primitive for synchronization called a *lock* controls access to critical sections. There are different types of locks with different behavior and semantics.

Mutual exclusion

The idea behind locks is that a task hangs a "Do not disturb" sign on the resource it is working with before the operation begins and does not remove it until the operation is complete (holding the lock). All other tasks check for a "Do not disturb" sign before trying to hang the sign and perform the operation themselves. If there is such a sign, the task is blocked and waits until the sign is removed to ensure that only it performs the operation, thus avoiding conflicting operations.

We have just introduced another state a process or thread can be in: the *Blocked* state. The following illustration shows the thread lifecycle (the same applies to processes) from being created, to readiness, to running, to possible blocking and, finally, to completion or termination.

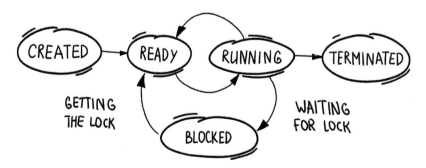

To be able to work with the shared resource, a task must first get a lock on it. If another thread already holds the lock, the first thread must wait until the lock is released before it can acquire it, entering a Blocked state until then. This technique is called *mutual exclusion*, or *mutex* for short, because it ensures that only one task has exclusive access to the shared resource at any given time. There is a concurrency abstraction of the same name in many programming languages and OSs.

Only two states are possible for a mutex: locked and unlocked. The primitive is created in the unlocked state and contains two methods: acquire() and release(). The acquire() method locks the mutex and blocks execution until the release() method unlocks it. The release() method is used to unlock the mutex and can only be called in the locked state. When the release method is called, the mutex is set to the unlocked state, and control is immediately returned to the calling thread.

Let's use a mutex to solve our money problem. For the mutex to protect the internal balance variable, blocks of code that work with that variable—critical sections of our program—must be wrapped with calls to the acquire() and release() methods:

```python
# Chapter 8/race_condition/synced_bank_account.py
from threading import Lock
from unsynced_bank_account import UnsyncedBankAccount

class SyncedBankAccount(UnsyncedBankAccount):
    def __init__(self, balance: float = 0):
        super().__init__(balance)
        self.mutex = Lock()

    def deposit(self, amount: float) -> None:
        self.mutex.acquire()
        super().deposit(amount)
        self.mutex.release()

    def withdraw(self, amount: float) -> None:
        self.mutex.acquire()
        super().withdraw(amount)
        self.mutex.release()
```

Acquires the mutex on the shared resource, which guarantees that only one thread holding the mutex can run

Releases the mutex

Here we add a mutex to our two methods so that only one operation of the same type will be performed at a time. This ensures that there is no race condition: deposit() and withdraw(), which read or write the balance, do so while holding the lock. If a thread tries to get a lock that currently belongs to another thread, it is blocked until the other thread releases the lock. Hence, no more than one thread can own a mutex at a time. Therefore, there cannot be simultaneous reading/writing or writing/writing, which we see in the results of the execution:

```
Balance of synced account after concurrent transactions:
Actual: 0
Expected: 0
```

Synchronization is only effective when it is used consistently by all threads in the application. If we create a mutex to restrict access to a shared resource, all threads must receive the same mutex before attempting to manipulate the resource. Failing to do so would compromise the protection provided by the mutex, leading to potential errors.

Semaphores

A *semaphore* is another synchronization mechanism that can be used to control access to shared resources, similar to a mutex. But unlike a mutex, a semaphore can allow several tasks to access the resource at the same time; hence it can be locked and unlocked by multiple tasks, while a mutex can be locked and unlocked only by the same task.

Internally, a semaphore holds a counter that keeps track of how many times it has been acquired or released. As long as the value of the semaphore counter is positive, any task can acquire the semaphore, thus decreasing the value of the counter. If the counter reaches zero, tasks attempting to acquire the semaphore are blocked and wait until the semaphore becomes available (the counter becomes positive). When a task finishes using a shared resource, it releases the semaphore, increasing the counter's value. And if other threads are waiting to acquire the semaphore, they are told to wake up and do so.

In essence, a mutex can be viewed as a specialized type of semaphore called a *binary semaphore*. In the case of a mutex, the internal counter can have only two possible values: 0 or 1.

NOTE   The term *semaphore* was coined by computer scientist Edsger Dijkstra in the 1960s, who used the term to describe a synchronization primitive that can be used to signal between threads. The word comes from the use of flags and signal lamps to communicate between ships. Later, Dijkstra acknowledged that *semaphore* was not the best choice for the synchronization primitive he had described, as it was a more general concept that could be used for other purposes beyond signaling.

Let's use a semaphore to simulate a public parking garage with a certain number of parking spaces and two entrances. We have cars that want to enter and leave the garage. A car cannot enter if it is not guaranteed a parking space, but it can always leave the garage when desired.

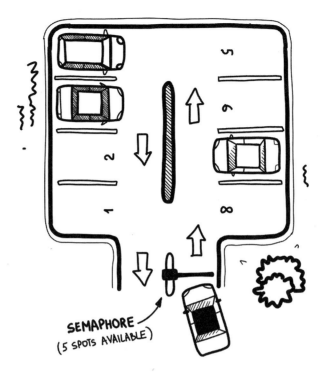

SEMAPHORE
(5 SPOTS AVAILABLE)

To enter the garage, a car must get a parking ticket, corresponding to acquiring a semaphore. If there are available parking spots, the car is assigned one, and the semaphore count is decreased. However, when the garage reaches full capacity, the semaphore count drops to zero, preventing additional cars from entering. Only when a car that currently holds the semaphore releases it, typically after leaving the garage, can another car acquire the semaphore and enter the garage. Here's the code:

```python
# Chapter 8/semaphore.py
import typing as T
import time
import random
from threading import Thread, Semaphore, Lock

TOTAL_SPOTS = 3
```

```
class Garage:

    def __init__(self) -> None:
        self.semaphore = Semaphore(TOTAL_SPOTS)
        self.cars_lock = Lock()
        self.parked_cars: T.List[str] = []

    def count_parked_cars(self) -> int:
        return len(self.parked_cars)

    def enter(self, car_name: str) -> None:
        self.semaphore.acquire()
        self.cars_lock.acquire()
        self.parked_cars.append(car_name)
        print(f"{car_name} parked")
        self.cars_lock.release()

    def exit(self, car_name: str) -> None:
        self.cars_lock.acquire()
        self.parked_cars.remove(car_name)
        print(f"{car_name} leaving")
        self.semaphore.release()
        self.cars_lock.release()
```

A semaphore controls the limited number of parking spots available in the garage.

Releases the semaphore to signal that a parking spot is available

Ensures that only one thread at a time can modify the list of parked cars

In this code, we use both a mutex and a semaphore! Although they are similar in their properties, we use them for different purposes. We use a mutex to coordinate access to an internal variable: a list of parked cars. The semaphore is used to coordinate the enter() and exit() methods of the parking garage to limit the number of cars based on the available parking spots—in our case, only three spots.

If the semaphore is unavailable (because its value is zero), a car waits until a parking space is available and the semaphore is released. When the car thread acquires the semaphore, it prints a message that it is parked and then goes to sleep for a random period. The car thread then prints a message that it is leaving and releases the semaphore, increasing its value so that another waiting thread can acquire it. Let's simulate a busy day in such a parking garage:

```
# Chapter 8/semaphore.py
def park_car(garage: Garage, car_name: str) -> None:
    garage.enter(car_name)
    time.sleep(random.uniform(1, 2))
    garage.exit(car_name)
```

A car parks in the garage, waits, and then exits.

```
def test_garage(garage: Garage, number_of_cars: int = 10) -> None:
    threads = []
    for car_num in range(number_of_cars):
        t = Thread(target=park_car,
                   args=(garage, f"Car #{car_num}"))
        threads.append(t)
        t.start()

    for thread in threads:
        thread.join()
```

Creates a number of threads to simulate multiple cars parking in the garage concurrently

```
if __name__ == "__main__":
    number_of_cars = 10
    garage = Garage()
    test_garage(garage, number_of_cars)
```

Simulates a busy day at the garage by spawning threads that represent cars entering and leaving the garage

```
    print("Number of parked cars after a busy day:")
    print(f"Actual: {garage.count_parked_cars()}\nExpected: 0")
```

Just as with a mutex, we get the expected result:

```
Car #0 parked
Car #1 parked
Car #2 parked
Car #0 leaving
Car #3 parked
Car #1 leaving
Car #4 parked
Car #2 leaving
Car #5 parked
Car #4 leaving
Car #6 parked
Car #5 leaving
Car #7 parked
Car #3 leaving
Car #8 parked
Car #7 leaving
Car #9 parked
```

```
Car #6 leaving
Car #8 leaving
Car #9 leaving
Number of parked cars after a busy day:
Actual: 0
Expected: 0
```

Another way to solve synchronization problems is to create more powerful operations that are executed in one step and thus eliminate the possibility of undesired interrupts. Such operations exist and are called *atomic*.

Atomic operations

Atomic operations are the simplest form of synchronization and work with primitive data types. *Atomic* means no other thread can see the operation in a partially completed state.

For certain simple operations, such as incrementing a counter variable, atomic operations can offer significant performance benefits compared to traditional locking mechanisms. Instead of acquiring a lock, modifying the variable, and releasing the lock, atomic operations provide a more streamlined approach. Consider an example using assembly code:

```
add 0x9082a1b, $0x1
```

Here the assembly instruction adds the value 1 to the memory location specified by the address 0x9082a1b. The hardware guarantees that this operation executes atomically without any interruption. When an interruption occurs, the operation either does not execute at all or executes to the end; there is no intermediate state.

The advantage of atomic operations is that they do not block competing tasks. This can potentially maximize concurrency and minimize synchronization costs. But these operations depend on special hardware instructions, and with good communication between hardware and software, guarantees of atomicity at the hardware level can be extended to the software level.

> **NOTE** Most programming languages provide atomic data structures, but you must be careful because not all data structures are atomic. For example, some Java collections are thread safe; in addition, Java has several nonblocking atomic data structures such as `AtomicBoolean`, `AtomicInteger`, `AtomicLong`, and `AtomicReference`. As another example, the C++ standard library provides atomic types such as `std::atomic_int` and `std::atomic_bool`.

But not all operations are atomic, so we should not assume that they are. When writing concurrent applications, there is a long tradition of pretending that we don't know anything but what the programming language standards tell us. When atomic operations are not available, use locks.

With this knowledge of synchronization in mind, in the next chapter, we look at some other common concurrency problems.

Recap

- When using shared resources, as is typical for concurrent programs, be careful to avoid concurrent access to shared resources since any task can be interrupted mid-execution. Those problems can lead to unexpected behavior and subtle bugs that don't appear until much later.

- A *critical section* of code can be executed concurrently by multiple tasks and has access to shared resources. To ensure the exclusive use of critical sections, a synchronization mechanism is required.

- The simplest method to prevent unexpected behavior in a critical section is using atomic operations. *Atomic* means no other thread can see the operation in a partially completed state. But these operations rely on the environment (hardware and runtime environment support).

- Another method of synchronization, and the most common, is using *locks*. A lock is an abstract concept. The basic premise is that a lock protects access to a shared resource. If you own a lock, you can access the protected shared resource. If you do not own the lock, you cannot access the shared resource.

- Tasks may require mutually exclusive operations, which can be protected by *mutually exclusive locks* or *mutexes* to prevent reading shared data in one task and updating it in another.

- A *semaphore* is a lock that can be used to control access to shared resources, similar to a mutex. But unlike a mutex, a semaphore can allow several tasks to access the resource at the same time; hence it can be locked and unlocked by multiple tasks, while a mutex is locked and unlocked by the same task.

- Synchronization is expensive. Therefore, if possible, try to design without synchronization of any kind.

- When two tasks access and manipulate a shared resource concurrently, and the resulting execution outcome depends on the order in which processes access the resource, this is called a *race condition*. (One thread is in a race with the other.) This condition can be avoided by properly synchronizing threads in critical sections using techniques such as locks, atomic operations, or switching to message-passing interprocess communication.

Solving concurrency problems: | 9
Deadlocks and starvation

In this chapter

- You learn how to identify and solve common concurrency problems: deadlocks, livelocks, and starvation

- You learn popular concurrency design patterns: the producer-consumer and readers-writer patterns

In the previous chapter, we explored the challenges that arise in concurrent programming, such as race conditions and the synchronization primitives used to address them. In this chapter, we focus on another set of common concurrency problems: deadlocks, livelocks, and starvation.

These problems can lead to extremely serious consequences, given that concurrency is used in all sorts of technology to which we quite literally entrust our lives. Two Boeing 737 Max airplanes crashed in 2018 and 2019 due to a software error caused by a concurrency problem. The airplanes' Maneuvering Characteristics Augmentation System (MCAS) was designed to prevent the airplane from stalling, but a race condition caused it to malfunction, leading to fatal crashes that killed 347 people. A decade earlier, in 2009 and 2010, Toyota vehicles experienced sudden, unintended acceleration linked to a software error that caused a concurrency problem in the electronic throttle control system. The error caused the throttle to open unexpectedly, leading to several accidents and fatalities.

In this chapter, we explore how to identify and solve common concurrency problems, providing you with the knowledge and tools to address them effectively. By the end of the chapter, you will have a comprehensive understanding of common concurrency problems and popular concurrency patterns, including the producer-consumer and readers-writer patterns, enabling you to implement appropriate solutions to avoid potential disasters.

Dining philosophers

Locks (mutexes and semaphores) are very tricky to use. Incorrect use of locks can break an application when the locks acquired are not released or the locks that need to be acquired never become available. A classic example used to illustrate synchronization problems, when several tasks compete for locks, is philosophers having lunch, formulated by computer scientist Edsger Dijkstra in 1965. This example is a standard test case for evaluating synchronization approaches.

Five silent philosophers sit at a round table with a plate of dumplings. Between each pair of neighboring philosophers lies a chopstick. The philosophers do what philosophers do best—think and eat.

Only one philosopher can hold each chopstick, so a philosopher can only use a chopstick if no other philosopher is using it. After a philosopher has finished eating, they must put down both chopsticks so the chopsticks are available to the others. A philosopher can only take the chopsticks to their right and left, can do so only when the chopsticks are available, and cannot start eating without taking both chopsticks.

The problem is designing a ritual (algorithm) so that every philosopher can keep alternating between eating and thinking, assuming that no philosopher can know when the others want to eat or think—making it a concurrent system.

The act of taking dumplings from the plate is a critical section, so we can develop a mutual exclusion process to protect it, using two chopsticks as mutexes. Thus, when a philosopher wants to bite into a dumpling, they will first take the chopstick on the left, if available, and put a lock on it. Then they will take the right chopstick, if it is available, and put a lock on it as well. Now they have two chopsticks—they are in the critical section, so they eat a dumpling. Then they put down the right chopstick to unlock it, followed by the left chopstick. Finally, being a philosopher, they will go back to philosophizing.

In the code, the process looks like this:

```python
# Chapter 9/deadlock/deadlock.py
import time
from threading import Thread

from lock_with_name import LockWithName

dumplings = 20


class Philosopher(Thread):
    def __init__(self, name: str, left_chopstick: LockWithName,
                 right_chopstick: LockWithName):
        super().__init__()
        self.name = name
        self.left_chopstick = left_chopstick
        self.right_chopstick = right_chopstick
```

Each philosopher is associated with two chopsticks, one on their left and one on their right.

```python
    def run(self) -> None:
        global dumplings

        while dumplings > 0:
            self.left_chopstick.acquire()
            print(f"{self.left_chopstick.name} grabbed by {self.name} "
                  f"now needs {self.right_chopstick.name}")
            self.right_chopstick.acquire()
            print(f"{self.right_chopstick.name} grabbed by {self.name}")
```

Eat until there are no dumplings left.

Acquires the left chopstick

Acquires the right chopstick

```
                      dumplings -= 1
                      print(f"{self.name} eats a dumpling. "
```
A dumpling
is gone.
```
                          f"Dumplings left: {dumplings}")
```
Releases the
right chopstick
```
                      self.right_chopstick.release()
                      print(f"{self.right_chopstick.name} released by {self.name}")
```
Releases the
left chopstick
```
                      self.left_chopstick.release()
                      print(f"{self.left_chopstick.name} released by {self.name}")
                      print(f"{self.name} is thinking...")
                      time.sleep(0.1)
```

In this code, the `Philosopher` thread represents a single philosopher. It contains the name of the philosopher and two mutexes named `left_chopstick` and `right_chopstick` to specify the order in which the philosopher acquires them.

We also have a shared variable, `dumplings`, to represent the remaining dumplings on the shared plate. The `while` loop makes the philosophers keep taking dumplings as long as some are left on the plate. As part of the loop, a philosopher takes and acquires a lock on their left chopstick and then on their right chopstick. Then, if there are still dumplings on the plate, the philosopher takes one, decreasing the `dumplings` variable, and displays a message saying how many dumplings are left.

Being philosophers, they keep alternating between eating and thinking. But because they operate as concurrent tasks, none of them know when the others want to eat or think, which can lead to problems. Let's look at some of the problems that may arise when running this code, as well as possible solutions.

Deadlocks

To simplify explanations in this section, let's decrease the number of philosophers to two, preserving the original algorithm:

```
# Chapter 9/deadlock/deadlock.py
if __name__ == "__main__":
    chopstick_a = LockWithName("chopstick_a")
    chopstick_b = LockWithName("chopstick_b")

    philosopher_1 = Philosopher("Philosopher #1", chopstick_a,
chopstick_b)
    philosopher_2 = Philosopher("Philosopher #2", chopstick_b,
chopstick_a)

    philosopher_1.start()
    philosopher_2.start()
```

When we run this program, we see output similar to the following:

```
Philosopher #1 eats a dumpling. Dumplings left: 19
Philosopher #1 eats a dumpling. Dumplings left: 18
Philosopher #2 eats a dumpling. Dumplings left: 17
...
Philosopher #2 eat a dumpling. Dumplings left: 9
```

The program doesn't finish—it's stuck, and there are still dumplings on the plate. What's going on?

Suppose the first philosopher gets hungry and takes chopstick A. The second philosopher, at the same time, also gets hungry and takes chopstick B. They each have one of the two locks they need, but they are both stuck waiting for the other thread to release the remaining lock.

This is an example of a situation called a *deadlock*. During a deadlock, multiple tasks are waiting for resources occupied by the others, and none of them can continue execution. The program is stuck in this state forever, so it is necessary to manually terminate its execution. Running the same program again will result in a deadlock after a different number of dumplings. The exact number at which the philosophers get stuck depends on how the system schedules the tasks.

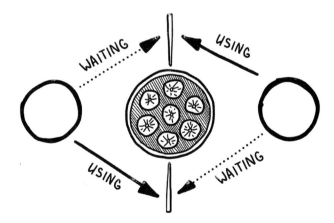

As with a race condition, you may be lucky enough never to run into this problem in your applications. However, if even the potential for deadlocks exists, they should be avoided. Every time a task tries to get more than one lock at a time, there is a possibility of a deadlock. Avoiding deadlocks is a common problem for concurrent programs using mutual exclusion mechanisms to protect critical code sections.

NOTE Never assume a specific order of execution. When there are multiple threads, as we have seen, the execution order is nondeterministic. If you care about the execution order of one thread relative to another, you must apply synchronization. But for the best performance, you should avoid synchronization as much as possible. In particular, you want highly detailed tasks that do not require synchronization; this will allow your cores to work as fast as possible on each task assigned to them.

To consider a more realistic example for a moment (it's not every day that we feed philosophers dumplings), let's imagine a real system: your home computer with two applications installed, such as video chat (like Zoom or Skype) and a movie-watching application (like Netflix or YouTube). The two programs serve different functions—one lets you chat with coworkers or friends, and the other lets you watch cool movies—but both access the same subsystems of your computer, such as the screen and audio. Imagine that they both want access to the screen and audio. They make their requests simultaneously, and the OS gives the screen to the movie app and the audio to the video chat. Both programs block the resource they have and then wait for the remaining resource to become available. They will wait forever, just like our poor philosophers! The deadlock is permanent unless the OS takes drastic action, such as killing one or more processes or forcing one or more processes to backtrack.

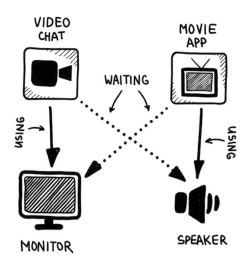

Arbitrator solution

Returning to our philosophers, to avoid a deadlock, we can make sure each philosopher can take either both chopsticks or none. The easiest way to achieve this is to introduce an *arbitrator*—someone in charge of the chopsticks, such as a waiter. To take a chopstick, the philosopher must ask the waiter for permission to grab it first. The waiter only gives permission to one philosopher at a time until they take both chopsticks. Putting down a chopstick is allowed at all times.

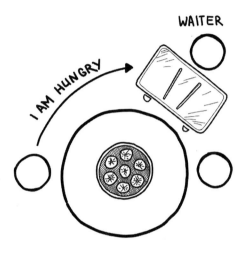

The waiter can be implemented with another lock:

```python
# Chapter 9/deadlock/deadlock_arbitrator.py
import time
from threading import Thread, Lock

from lock_with_name import LockWithName

dumplings = 20


class Waiter:
    def __init__(self) -> None:
        self.mutex = Lock()
```

```
def ask_for_chopsticks(self, left_chopstick: LockWithName,
                            right_chopstick: LockWithName) -> None:
    with self.mutex:
        left_chopstick.acquire()
        print(f"{left_chopstick.name} grabbed")
        right_chopstick.acquire()
        print(f"{right_chopstick.name} grabbed")
```

Internal mutex to safeguard a critical section, ensuring
that it can only be accessed by one thread at a time

```
def release_chopsticks(self, left_chopstick: LockWithName,
                           right_chopstick: LockWithName) -> None:
    right_chopstick.release()
    print(f"{right_chopstick.name} released")
    left_chopstick.release()
    print(f"{left_chopstick.name} released\n")
```

The waiter is now responsible for managing the allocation and release of chopsticks.

And we can use the waiter as a lock, as follows:

```
# Chapter 9/deadlock/deadlock_arbitrator.py
class Philosopher(Thread):
    def __init__(self, name: str, waiter: Waiter,
                 left_chopstick: LockWithName,
                 right_chopstick: LockWithName):
        super().__init__()
        self.name = name
        self.left_chopstick = left_chopstick
        self.right_chopstick = right_chopstick
        self.waiter = waiter

    def run(self) -> None:
        global dumplings

        while dumplings > 0:
            print(f"{self.name} asks waiter for chopsticks")
            self.waiter.ask_for_chopsticks(
                self.left_chopstick, self.right_chopstick)

            dumplings -= 1
            print(f"{self.name} eats a dumpling. "
                  f"Dumplings left: {dumplings}")
            print(f"{self.name} returns chopsticks to waiter")
            self.waiter.release_chopsticks(
                self.left_chopstick, self.right_chopstick)
            time.sleep(0.1)
```

A philosopher asks the waiter for chopsticks.

The philosopher returns the chopsticks to the waiter after eating.

```
if __name__ == "__main__":
    chopstick_a = LockWithName("chopstick_a")
    chopstick_b = LockWithName("chopstick_b")

    waiter = Waiter()
    philosopher_1 = Philosopher("Philosopher #1", waiter, chopstick_a,
                                chopstick_b)
    philosopher_2 = Philosopher("Philosopher #2", waiter, chopstick_b,
                                chopstick_a)

    philosopher_1.start()
    philosopher_2.start()
```

Because it introduces a new central entity—the waiter—this approach can lead to limited concurrency: if a philosopher eats and one of their neighbors requests chopsticks, all other philosophers must wait until this request is fulfilled, even if chopsticks are available to them. In a real computer system, the arbitrator does much the same thing, controlling access by the worker threads to ensure that access is orderly. This solution reduces concurrency—but we can do better than that.

Resource hierarchy solution

What if we set priorities on the locks so the philosophers try to take the same chopstick first? This way they won't have a deadlock problem, because they will be competing for the same first lock.

Both philosophers must agree that, out of the two chopsticks they plan to use, the chopstick with the highest priority should always be taken first. In our case, both philosophers compete simultaneously for the chopstick with the highest priority. When one philosopher wins the battle and takes the chopstick with the highest priority, only the chopstick with the lowest priority remains on the table. Because the philosophers have agreed to use the highest-priority chopstick first, the second philosopher cannot take the remaining chopstick. Furthermore, the philosopher who took the first chopstick now has access to the chopstick with the lowest priority, allowing them to start eating with both chopsticks. Genius!

Let's set priorities for our chopsticks. We'll say that chopstick A has the highest priority, and chopstick B, the second highest. Each philosopher should always get the chopstick with the highest priority first.

In our code, Philosopher #2 creates a problem by acquiring chopstick B before A. To fix that, we change the chopstick acquisition order without changing any other code. First we acquire chopstick A, and then we acquire chopstick B:

```
# Chapter 9/deadlock/deadlock_hierarchy.py
from lock_with_name import LockWithName

from deadlock import Philosopher

if __name__ == "__main__":
    chopstick_a = LockWithName("chopstick_a")
    chopstick_b = LockWithName("chopstick_b")

    philosopher_1 = Philosopher("Philosopher #1", chopstick_a,
chopstick_b)
    philosopher_2 = Philosopher("Philosopher #2", chopstick_a,
chopstick_b)

    philosopher_1.start()
    philosopher_2.start()
```

When we run the program after making this change, it runs to the end without any deadlocks.

NOTE Ordering locks is not always possible if a task does not know beforehand all the locks it needs to acquire. Deadlock avoidance mechanisms like resource allocation graphs (RAGs) and lock hierarchies can be used to prevent deadlocks. A RAG helps detect and prevent cycles in the relationships between processes and resources. Higher-level synchronization primitives in some programming languages and frameworks simplify lock management. However, careful design and testing are still necessary as these techniques do not guarantee the complete elimination of deadlocks.

Another method of preventing deadlocks is to set a timeout on blocking attempts. If the task cannot successfully get all the locks it needs within a certain time, we force the thread to release all the locks it currently holds. But that may cause another problem: a livelock.

Livelocks

A *livelock* is similar to a deadlock and occurs when two tasks are competing for the same set of resources—but in a livelock, a task gives up its first lock in an attempt to get a second lock. After getting the second lock, it comes back and tries to get the first lock again. The task is now in the same blocked state because it spends all its time releasing one lock and trying to get another instead of doing actual work.

Imagine that you are making a phone call, but the person on the other end is also trying to call you. You both hang up and try again at the same time, which creates the same situation. In the end, neither of you can get through to the other.

A livelock occurs when tasks are actively performing concurrent tasks, but these tasks do not affect moving the program's state forward. It is similar to a deadlock, but the difference is that the tasks are "polite" and let others do their work first.

Let's imagine that our philosophers have become a little more polite than they were—they can give up a chopstick if they can't get both:

```python
# Chapter 9/livelock.py
import time
from threading import Thread

from deadlock.lock_with_name import LockWithName

dumplings = 20


class Philosopher(Thread):
    def __init__(self, name: str, left_chopstick: LockWithName,
                 right_chopstick: LockWithName):
        super().__init__()
        self.name = name
        self.left_chopstick = left_chopstick
        self.right_chopstick = right_chopstick

    def run(self) -> None:
        global dumplings

        while dumplings > 0:
            self.left_chopstick.acquire()
            print(f"{self.left_chopstick.name} chopstick "
                f"grabbed by {self.name}")
            if self.right_chopstick.locked():
                print(f"{self.name} cannot get the "
                    f"{self.right_chopstick.name} chopstick, "
                    f"politely concedes...")
            else:
                self.right_chopstick.acquire()
                print(f"{self.right_chopstick.name} chopstick "
                    f"grabbed by {self.name}")
                dumplings -= 1
                print(f"{self.name} eats a dumpling. Dumplings "
                    f"left: {dumplings}")
                time.sleep(1)
                self.right_chopstick.release()
            self.left_chopstick.release()
```

The left chopstick is acquired by a philosopher. There are two philosophers, so they each grab one chopstick from the table.

A philosopher tries to acquire the right chopstick. If it is available, the philosopher grabs it and eats a dumpling; otherwise, they concede and release the left chopstick.

```
if __name__ == "__main__":
    chopstick_a = LockWithName("chopstick_a")
    chopstick_b = LockWithName("chopstick_b")

    philosopher_1 = Philosopher("Philosopher #1", chopstick_a, chopstick_b)
    philosopher_2 = Philosopher("Philosopher #2", chopstick_b, chopstick_a)

    philosopher_1.start()
    philosopher_2.start()
```

Unfortunately, these nice people are not destined to eat:

```
chopstick_a chopstick grabbed by Philosopher # 1
Philosopher # 1 cannot get the chopstick_b chopstick, politely concedes...
chopstick_b chopstick grabbed by Philosopher #  2
Philosopher # 2 cannot get the chopstick_a chopstick, politely concedes...
chopstick_b chopstick grabbed by Philosopher # 2
chopstick_a chopstick grabbed by Philosopher # 1
Philosopher # 2 cannot get the chopstick_a chopstick, politely concedes...
Philosopher # 1 cannot get the chopstick_b chopstick, politely concedes...
chopstick_b chopstick grabbed by Philosopher # 2
chopstick_a chopstick grabbed by Philosopher # 1
Philosopher # 2 cannot get the chopstick_a chopstick, politely concedes...
Philosopher # 1 cannot get the chopstick_b chopstick, politely concedes...
```

In addition to doing zero work, this approach can lead to system overloads with frequent context switching, reducing overall system performance. In addition, the OS scheduler cannot implement fairness because it does not know which task has been waiting longest for the shared resource.

To avoid this type of locking, we can order the locking sequence hierarchically as we did with resolving a deadlock. This way, only one process can block both locks successfully.

> **NOTE** Detecting and resolving livelocks is often more challenging than doing so for deadlocks because livelock scenarios involve complex and dynamic interactions among multiple entities, making them harder to identify and resolve.

Livelocks are a subset of a broader set of problems called *starvation*.

Starvation

Let's add a local variable to keep track of how many dumplings each `Philosopher` thread eats:

```python
# Chapter 9/starvation.py
from threading import Thread

from deadlock.lock_with_name import LockWithName

dumplings = 1000


class Philosopher(Thread):
    def __init__(self, name: str, left_chopstick: LockWithName,
                 right_chopstick: LockWithName):
        super().__init__()
        self.name = name
        self.left_chopstick = left_chopstick
        self.right_chopstick = right_chopstick

    def run(self) -> None:
        global dumplings

        dumplings_eaten = 0
        while dumplings > 0:
            self.left_chopstick.acquire()
            self.right_chopstick.acquire()
            if dumplings > 0:
                dumplings -= 1
                dumplings_eaten += 1
                time.sleep(1e-16)
            self.right_chopstick.release()
            self.left_chopstick.release()
        print(f"{self.name} took {dumplings_eaten} pieces")


if __name__ == "__main__":
    chopstick_a = LockWithName("chopstick_a")
    chopstick_b = LockWithName("chopstick_b")

    threads = []
    for i in range(10):
        threads.append(
            Philosopher(f"Philosopher #{i}", chopstick_a, chopstick_b))
```

The variable dumplings_eaten keeps track of the number of dumplings this philosopher has eaten.

```
for thread in threads:
    thread.start()

for thread in threads:
    thread.join()
```

We name the variable `dumplings_eaten` and initialize it to zero. We also added more philosophers this time. We increment `dumplings_eaten` each time a philosopher eats a dumpling. When the program finishes, we see that each of the philosophers has eaten a different number of dumplings, and that's not fair:

```
Philosopher #1 took 417 pieces
Philosopher #9 took 0 pieces
Philosopher #6 took 0 pieces
Philosopher #7 took 0 pieces
Philosopher #5 took 0 pieces
Philosopher #0 took 4 pieces
Philosopher #2 took 3 pieces
Philosopher #8 took 268 pieces
Philosopher #3 took 308 pieces
Philosopher #4 took 0 pieces
```

Philosopher #1 took a lot more dumplings than Philosopher #8—more than 400 pieces. It seems that Philosopher #8 is sometimes slow to take a chopstick, and Philosopher #1 thinks quickly and takes the chopstick back, while Philosopher #8 is again stuck waiting. Some philosophers never take both chopsticks. If this happens once in a while, it's probably okay, but if it happens regularly, the thread will starve.

Starvation is exactly what it sounds like: a thread is quite literally *starved*, never gaining access to required resources, and no progress is made. If another greedy task often holds a lock on a shared resource, the starving task will not get a chance to execute.

> **NOTE** Starvation is one of the basic ideas behind the most famous type of attacks against online services: denial of service (DOS) attacks. In these attacks, the attacker tries to deplete all of the server's resources. The service starts to run out of available resources (storage, memory, or computing resources), crashes, and cannot provide its services.

Starvation is usually caused by an oversimplified scheduling algorithm. The scheduling algorithm, as we learned in Chapter 6, is part of the runtime system. It should distribute resources equally among all the tasks; that is, the scheduler should distribute resources in such a way that no task is constantly blocked from accessing the resources it needs to complete its work. The treatment of different task priorities depends on the OS, but tasks with a higher priority are usually scheduled to run more often, and this can cause low-priority tasks to starve. Another thing that can lead to starvation is too many tasks in the system, when it takes a long time before a task starts execution.

A possible solution to starvation is to use a scheduling algorithm with priority queuing, which also uses the aging technique. *Aging* is a technique of gradually increasing the priority of threads waiting in the system for a long time. Eventually, a thread reaches a high enough priority to be scheduled to access resources/processors and terminate appropriately. We do not discuss this concept in detail, as it is very specific; if you're interested in learning more, see Andrew Tanenbaum's book *Modern Operating Systems*.[1] But don't feel limited to one book; by all means, see what is out there.

With all this knowledge of synchronization in mind, let's look at some concurrency design problems.

Designing synchronization

When designing systems, it is useful to relate the problem at hand to known problems. Several problems have gained importance in the literature and are often found in real-world scenarios. The first of these is the *producer-consumer problem*.

Producer-consumer problem

Suppose that one or more producers generate items and put them into a buffer. Some consumers take items from the same buffer, processing them one at a time. A single producer can generate and store items in the buffer at its own pace. The consumer acts similarly but must ensure that it does not read from an empty buffer. Thus, the system must be constrained to prevent conflicting operations for the buffer. Breaking this down, we need to make sure the producer does not try to add data to the buffer if it is full, and the consumer does not access data from an empty buffer. Concurrency programming is already at your fingertips, so try to solve this problem yourself before you go any further.

The basic implementation looks like this:

```
# Chapter 9/producer_consumer.py
import time
from threading import Thread, Semaphore, Lock

SIZE = 5
BUFFER = ["" for i in range(SIZE)]
producer_idx: int = 0
```

Shared buffer ←

---

[1]   Andrew S. Tanenbaum, *Modern Operating Systems*, 4th ed., Pearson Education, 2015.

```
mutex = Lock()
empty = Semaphore(SIZE)
full = Semaphore(0)


class Producer(Thread):
    def __init__(self, name: str, maximum_items: int = 5):
        super().__init__()
        self.counter = 0
        self.name = name
        self.maximum_items = maximum_items

    def next_index(self, index: int) -> int:
        return (index + 1) % SIZE

    def run(self) -> None:
        global producer_idx
        while self.counter < self.maximum_items:
            empty.acquire()
            mutex.acquire()
            self.counter += 1
            BUFFER[producer_idx] = f"{self.name}-{self.counter}"
            print(f"{self.name} produced: "
                  f"'{BUFFER[producer_idx]}' into slot {producer_idx}")
            producer_idx = self.next_index(producer_idx)
            mutex.release()
            full.release()
            time.sleep(1)


class Consumer(Thread):
    def __init__(self, name: str, maximum_items: int = 10):
        super().__init__()
        self.name = name
        self.idx = 0
        self.counter = 0
        self.maximum_items = maximum_items

    def next_index(self) -> int:
        return (self.idx + 1) % SIZE

    def run(self) -> None:
        while self.counter < self.maximum_items:
            full.acquire()
            mutex.acquire()
```

There is at least one empty slot in the buffer.

Enters a critical section that modifies the shared buffer

A new item has been added to the buffer, and there is one less empty slot.

Gets the next buffer index to consume

There is at least one item in the buffer that can be consumed.

Enters a critical section that modifies the shared buffer

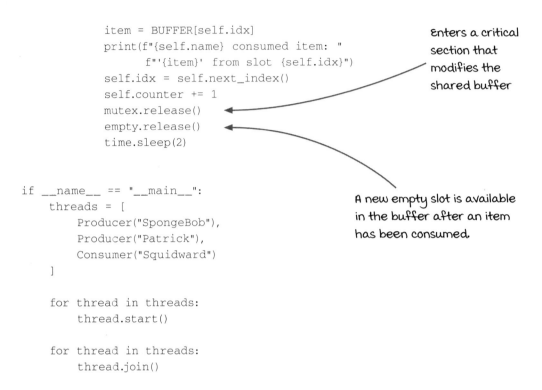

```
        item = BUFFER[self.idx]
        print(f"{self.name} consumed item: "
            f"'{item}' from slot {self.idx}")
        self.idx = self.next_index()
        self.counter += 1
        mutex.release()
        empty.release()
        time.sleep(2)
```

Enters a critical section that modifies the shared buffer

A new empty slot is available in the buffer after an item has been consumed.

```
if __name__ == "__main__":
    threads = [
        Producer("SpongeBob"),
        Producer("Patrick"),
        Consumer("Squidward")
    ]

    for thread in threads:
        thread.start()

    for thread in threads:
        thread.join()
```

Let's analyze this code. We use three synchronizations:

- full—The semaphore keeps track of the space the Producer fills. At the beginning of the program, it is initialized as locked (the counter equals zero) because the buffer is completely empty: producers haven't had time to fill it yet.

- empty—The semaphore tracks empty slots in the buffer. Initially it is set to its maximum value (SIZE in the code) because at the beginning, the buffer is empty.

- mutex—The mutex is used for mutual exclusion so that only one thread can access the shared resource—the buffer—at a time.

The producer can insert a buffer at any time. In a critical section, the producer adds an element to the buffer and increases the buffer index used for all producers; the mutex controls access to the critical section. But before putting data into the buffer, the producer tries to get an empty semaphore and decrease its value by 1. If the value of this semaphore is 0, it means the buffer is full, and the semaphore will block all producers until the buffer has available space (the empty semaphore is greater than 0). The producer releases the full semaphore after adding one element to it.

On the other hand, the consumer tries to get a full semaphore before consuming data from the buffer. If the value of this semaphore is 0, the buffer is empty, and our full semaphore blocks any consumer until the value of the full semaphore is greater than 0. Then the consumer takes the element from the buffer and works with it in its critical section. After the consumer has processed all the data from the buffer, it releases the `empty` semaphore, increasing its value by 1 to let producers know that there is free space for a new element.

If the producer is ahead of the consumer, which is the usual situation, the consumer will rarely block on the `empty` semaphore because the buffer usually will not be empty. Consequently, both the producer and the consumer work without problems with a shared buffer.

> **NOTE** The same problem arises in the implementation of pipe interprocess communication (IPC) in Linux. Each pipe has its own pipe buffer, which is guarded by semaphores.

In the next section, we look at another classic problem: the *readers-writer problem*.

Readers-writer problem

Not all operations are born equal. Simultaneous reading of the same data by any number of tasks will not cause concurrency problems if the data being accessed does not change. The data can be a file, a block of memory, or even a CPU register. It is possible to allow multiple simultaneous reads of data as long as anyone writing the data does so exclusively—that is, as long as there are no simultaneous writers.

For example, suppose the shared data is the library catalog. Regular library users read the catalog to find a book they are interested in. One or more librarians may update the catalog. Generally, each access to the catalog is treated as a critical section, and users are forced to take turns reading the catalog. This clearly leads to unacceptable delays. At the same time, it is important to prevent librarians from interfering with each other, and it is necessary to prevent reading while writing to prevent access to conflicting information.

If we generalize, we can say that some tasks only read data (readers = library users) and some tasks only write data (writers = librarians):

- Any number of readers can read shared data at the same time.
- Only one writer can write to the shared data at a time.
- While a writer is writing to shared data, no reader can read it.

This way, we prevent any race conditions or bad interleaving due to read/write or write/write errors.

Thus, readers are tasks that must not exclude each other, and writers are tasks that must exclude all other tasks, both readers and writers. In this way, we achieve an efficient solution to the problem instead of simply mutually excluding a shared resource for any operation.

Libraries and programming languages often include a readers-writer lock (RWLock) that solves such problems. This type of lock is usually used in large operations and can greatly improve performance if the protected data structure is read often and changed only occasionally. Since there is no such thing in Python, let's implement it ourselves:

```
# Chapter 9/reader_writer/rwlock.py
from threading import Lock

class RWLock:
    def __init__(self) -> None:
        self.readers = 0
        self.read_lock = Lock()
        self.write_lock = Lock()

    def acquire_read(self) -> None:
        self.read_lock.acquire()
        self.readers += 1
        if self.readers == 1:
            self.write_lock.acquire()
        self.read_lock.release()

    def release_read(self) -> None:
        assert self.readers >= 1
        self.read_lock.acquire()
        self.readers -= 1
        if self.readers == 0:
            self.write_lock.release()
        self.read_lock.release()

    def acquire_write(self) -> None:
        self.write_lock.acquire()

    def release_write(self) -> None:
        self.write_lock.release()
```

Acquires the read lock for the current thread. If a writer is waiting for the lock, the method blocks until the writer releases the lock.

Releases the read lock held by the current thread. If no more readers are holding the lock, the method releases the write lock.

Acquires the write lock for the current thread. If a reader or a writer is holding the lock, the method blocks until the lock is released.

Releases the write lock held by the current thread

During normal operation, a lock can be accessed by several readers at the same time. However, when a thread wants to update the shared data, it blocks until all readers release the lock, after which the writer gets the lock and updates the shared data. While a thread is updating the shared data, new reader threads are blocked until the writer thread is finished.

Here is an example of the reader and writer threads implementation:

```
# Chapter 9/reader_writer/reader_writer.py
import time
import random
from threading import Thread

from rwlock import RWLock                    Shared
                                             data
counter = 0
lock = RWLock()

class User(Thread):
    def __init__(self, idx: int):
        super().__init__()
        self.idx = idx

    def run(self) -> None:
        while True:
            lock.acquire_read()
            print(f"User {self.idx} reading: {counter}")
            time.sleep(random.randrange(1, 3))
            lock.release_read()
            time.sleep(0.5)

class Librarian(Thread):
    def run(self) -> None:
        global counter
        while True:
            lock.acquire_write()
            print("Librarian writing...")
            counter += 1
            print(f"New value: {counter}")
            time.sleep(random.randrange(1, 3))
            lock.release_write()

if __name__ == "__main__":
    threads = [
        User(0),
        User(1),
        Librarian()
    ]

    for thread in threads:
        thread.start()

    for thread in threads:
        thread.join()
```

Here we have two user threads that read shared memory and one librarian thread that changes it. The output is as follows:

```
User 0 reading: 0
User 1 reading: 0
Librarian writing...
New value: 1
User 0 reading: 1
User 1 reading: 1
Librarian writing...
New value: 2
User 0 reading: 2
User 1 reading: 2
User 0 reading: 2
User 1 reading: 2
User 0 reading: 2
User 1 reading: 2
User 0 reading: 2
Librarian writing...
New value: 3
```

The output shows that no user reads while the librarian is writing, and no librarian writes while any of the users are still reading the shared memory.

A last few words

This was a long chapter! Let's review the main points.

When it comes to thread safety, good design is the best protection a developer can have. Avoiding shared resources and minimizing communication between tasks makes it less likely that these tasks will mess with each other. However, it is not always possible to create an application that does not use shared resources. In that case, proper synchronization is required.

Synchronization helps ensure that the code is correct, but it comes at the expense of performance. The use of locks introduces delays even in nonconflicting cases. For a task to access shared data, it must first obtain a lock associated with that data. To get the lock, synchronize it between tasks, and monitor the shared objects, the processor has to do a lot of work hidden from the developer. Locks and atomic operations usually involve memory barriers and kernel-level synchronization to ensure proper code protection. If multiple tasks are trying to get the same lock, the overhead increases even more. Global locks can also become scalability inhibitors.

Therefore, if possible, try to design without synchronization of any type. In the case of communication, instead of shared memory, consider using message-passing IPC—in that case, you can avoid sharing memory between different tasks so each task has its own copy of the data to work with safely. You can do this with algorithmic improvements, good design models, proper data structures, or synchronization-independent classes.

Recap

- Concurrency is not an easy concept, and when developers implement concurrency in their applications, they may encounter various problems. A few of the most common are as follows:

    - Careless use of synchronization primitives can lead to deadlocks. During a deadlock, several tasks are waiting for resources occupied by the others, and none of them can continue execution.

    - A situation similar to deadlock occurs in livelock, another frequent concurrency implementation problem. Livelock is a situation where a request for an exclusive lock is repeatedly rejected because there are multiple overlapping locks that keep interfering with each other. Tasks keep running but don't complete their work.

    - An application thread can also experience starvation, where it never gets CPU time or access to shared resources because other "greedy" threads hog the resources. Tasks are starved, never receiving resources, and, in turn, their work does not get done. Starvation can be caused by errors in the scheduling algorithm or use of synchronization.

- Concurrency is not a new field, so many common design problems have already been solved and have become best practices or design patterns that need to be learned. Some of the best known are the *producer-consumer problem* and the *readers-writer problem*. They can be solved most efficiently with the use of semaphores and mutexes.

Part 3
Asynchronous octopuses: A pizza-making tale of concurrency

Picture this: You're at a pizza restaurant, and you see the chef (of course, the octopus) working in the kitchen, preparing several pizzas at once. The chef is moving swiftly, with tentacles flowing in perfect harmony, and you can't help but marvel at their multitasking abilities: from dough tossing to sauce spreading and toppings sprinkling. But how does the restaurant handle dozens, or even hundreds, of orders at the same time? The answer lies in its use of asynchronous communication!

As we enter the final part of this book on concurrency, we turn our attention to a different breed of octopus: the asynchronous ones. Just like their synchronous counterparts, these creatures are experts at multitasking and juggling multiple tasks simultaneously. But what sets them apart is their ability to do so without blocking and waiting for one task to finish before starting the next.

In Chapters 10 through 13, we explore the world of nonblocking I/O, event-based concurrency, and asynchronous communication through the lens of a pizza joint. We show you how different approaches to concurrency can affect the speed and efficiency of your application and how to write concurrent applications that can handle high volumes of requests.

But don't worry as you navigate the various techniques and approaches to handling concurrency. You'll start to see the bigger picture—much like an orchestra conductor bringing together all the different instruments to create a harmonious symphony.

So grab your tentacles—er, I mean, grab a slice of pizza, and let's dive in!

Nonblocking I/O | **10**

In this chapter

- You learn about message-passing interprocess communication in a distributed network of computers

- You learn about client-server applications

- You learn the limits on using multiple threads or processes in I/O operations

- You learn about nonblocking operations and how they can help hide I/O-bound operations

As processor speeds have historically increased, allowing for the execution of more operations in a given time, I/O speeds have struggled to keep up. Applications today heavily rely on I/O rather than CPU operations, resulting in longer durations for tasks such as writing to the hard disk or reading from the network, compared to CPU operations. Consequently, the processor remains idle while waiting to complete I/O, preventing the application from performing other tasks. This limitation creates a significant bottleneck for high-performance applications.

In this chapter, we explore a potential solution to this problem by delving into message-passing interprocess communication (IPC). We use our current understanding of the thread-based model and examine its application in high-load I/O scenarios, focusing on its popular use in web server development. Web servers are an excellent example for demonstrating asynchronous programming functions and the underlying concepts that empower developers to fully utilize concurrency for such tasks. We further enhance this approach in subsequent chapters.

The distributed world

Concurrency has long gone beyond a single computer. The internet and the World Wide Web have become the backbone of modern life, and modern technology makes it possible to connect hundreds or thousands of distributed computers. This has led to the emergence of distributed systems and distributed computing. Tasks in such systems can run on the same computer or different computers in the same local network or geographically distant from each other. All of this is based on different interrelated technologies, the most important of which is message-passing IPC (introduced in Chapter 5).

In this context, the component is a task on a single machine; the resources are all the hardware components of the computer and the individual functions delegated to a given computational node. Data is stored in the memory of the application process, and communication between nodes occurs through specialized protocols over the network. The most common design for communication between such nodes is the *client-server model*.

Client-server model

This model has two kinds of processes: *clients* and *servers*. Server applications provide services to client applications. A client initiates communication by connecting to the server. Then a client can request a service by sending a message to the server. The server repeatedly receives service requests from clients, performs the service, and (if necessary) returns a completion message to the client. Finally, the client disconnects.

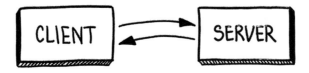

Many network applications work this way: web browsers are clients for web servers, an e-mail program is a client for an e-mail server, and so on. The client and server can communicate via network sockets.

Network sockets

We talked about the concept of sockets when we discussed message-passing IPC in Chapter 5, but in this case, we are talking about a different type of sockets: *network sockets*. Network sockets are the same as UNIX domain sockets, but they are used to send messages over a network. A network can be a logical network, the local network of a computer, or a network physically connected to an outside network with its own connections to other networks. The obvious example is the internet.

There are different types of network sockets, but in this chapter, we focus on TCP/IP sockets. This kind of socket guarantees data delivery and is therefore the most popular. With TCP/IP sockets, a connection is established. This means two processes must agree before information can be sent between them. Both processes maintain this connection throughout the communication session.

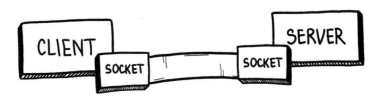

The network socket is an abstraction used by the OS to communicate with the network. For developers, it represents the end point of this connection. The socket takes care of reading and writing data to/from the network and then sends data to the network. Every socket contains two important things: an IP address and a port.

IP addresses

Each device (host) connected to the network has a unique identifier. This unique identifier is represented as an IP address. IP addresses (version 4) have a common format: a set of four numbers separated by dots, such as 8.8.8.8. Using the IP address, we can connect a socket to a specific host anywhere on the network, including printers, cash registers, refrigerators, servers, mainframes, PCs, and so on.

In many ways, IP addresses are similar to the mailing address of a house on a street. A street may have a name, such as 5th Avenue, and there may be several houses on it. Each house has a unique number; thus, 175 5th Avenue is uniquely different from 350 5th Avenue by house number.

Ports

To accommodate multiple server applications on a single machine that clients wish to connect to, a mechanism is required to route traffic from the same network interface to different applications. This is achieved through the use of multiple *ports* on each machine.

Each port serves as an entry point for a specific application, actively listening for incoming requests. The server process is bound to a particular port and remains in a listening state, ready to handle client connections. Clients, in turn, need to be aware of the port number on which the server is listening to establish a connection.

Certain well-known ports are reserved for system-level processes and serve as standard ports for specific services. These reserved ports provide a consistent and recognizable means for clients to connect to the corresponding services. Think of offices in a business center: each business has its own facility where it provides services.

Both client and server have their own socket connected to the other socket. The server socket listens on a specific port, and the client socket connects to the server socket on that port. Once a connection is established, the data exchange begins. This is similar to a business center where business A has its own office, and clients connect to that office to receive services.

The sender process puts the information it needs into a message and sends the message explicitly over the network to the receiver socket; the receiver process then reads it as we described regarding UDS sockets (Chapter 5). The processes in this exchange can be executed on the same machine or different machines connected by a network.

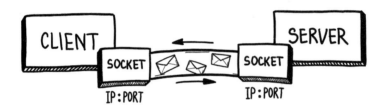

We use the server implementation as a good exercise and a concrete example to help us understand how concurrency has evolved and the new challenges it presents. We do not go much deeper into the network model and protocol stack for this communication. Networking and sockets are big topics, and volumes have been written about them. If you are new to sockets or networking, it is normal to feel overwhelmed by all the terms and details. If you want to dive deep into the topic, you can find more in the book *Modern Operating Systems* by Andrew Tanenbaum.[1]

Now that you have a basic understanding of network sockets and client-server communication, you are ready to build your first server. We start with the simplest, sequential version and later modify this implementation to see how and why the transition from concurrency to asynchrony has happened.

---

[1]   Andrew S. Tanenbaum, *Modern Operating Systems*, 4th ed., Pearson Education, 2015.

Pizza-ordering service

In the 1980s, the Santa Cruz Operation (which did more to create the internet than Al Gore) ordered a lot of pizza for developers from a particular pizza parlor in downtown Santa Cruz, California. The process of ordering on the phone took too long, so the developers created the world's first commerce app in which they could order and pay for pizza by communicating between their terminals and another terminal they set up at the pizza parlor. That was back in the era of dumb terminals connected via a wide area network rather than personal computers. Today, the process is a bit more complicated. Let's take a moment to replicate that effort with more modern technology. We will implement a pizza-ordering service for our local pizza joint: a server that accepts pizza orders from clients and responds with a "Thank you for ordering" message.

A server application must provide a server socket for clients to connect to. We do this by binding the server socket to an IP address and port on the server machine. The server application must then listen for incoming connections:

```
# Chapter 10/pizza_server.py
from socket import socket, create_server

BUFFER_SIZE = 1024
ADDRESS = ("127.0.0.1", 12345)


class Server:
    def __init__(self) -> None:
        try:
            print(f"Starting up at: {ADDRESS}")
```

Sets the maximum amount of data to be received at once

Defines the address and port of the host machine

```
        self.server_socket: socket = create_server(ADDRESS)
    except OSError:
        self.server_socket.close()
        print("\nServer stopped.")

def accept(self) -> socket:
    conn, client_address = self.server_socket.accept()
    print(f"Connected to {client_address}")
    return conn

def serve(self, conn: socket) -> None:
    try:
        while True:
            data = conn.recv(BUFFER_SIZE)
            if not data:
                break
            try:
                order = int(data.decode())
                response = f"Thank you for ordering {order} pizzas!\n"
            except ValueError:
                response = "Wrong number of pizzas, please try again\n"
            print(f"Sending message to {conn.getpeername()}")
            conn.send(response.encode())
    finally:
        print(f"Connection with {conn.getpeername()} has been closed")
        conn.close()

def start(self) -> None:
    print("Server listening for incoming connections")
    try:
        while True:
            conn = self.accept()
            self.serve(conn)
    finally:
        self.server_socket.close()
        print("\nServer stopped.")


if __name__ == "__main__":
    server = Server()
    server.start()
```

Creates a server socket object bound to the specified address

Blocks until a client connects to the server socket and returns a new connection and the socket for that client.

Continuously receives data from the client socket until there is incoming data

Sends a response to the client socket

Closes the client socket after the serve method has finished executing for that client

Accepts incoming connections and serves each client until the server is stopped

Here we use the local computer address 127.0.0.1 (our local machine) and port 12345. We bind our socket to this host and port with a `create_server()` call. It allows the server to accept incoming client connections. The `accept()` method waits for a client connection, and the server waits at this point until it receives an incoming client connection.

When the client connects, it returns a new `socket` object representing the connection and client address. When this happens, the server socket creates a new socket that will be used to communicate with the client. That's it. Now we have established a connection with the client and can communicate with it. The server is ready.

Now we can start the server:

```
$ python pizza_server.py
```

When we run this command, our terminal hangs because the server is blocked on the `accept()` call—it is waiting for a new client to connect.

We are using Netcat (http://netcat.sourceforge.net) as a client (alternatively, you can use Chapter 10/pizza_client.py). To run the client, open another terminal window and start the client as follows on UNIX/macOS:

```
$ nc 127.0.0.1 12345
```

> **NOTE** In Windows, use `ncat`: `$ ncat 127.0.0.1 12345`.

Once it's running, we can start typing messages—pizza orders. If the server works, we'll see a response from the server

```
$ nc 127.0.0.1 12345
10
Thank you for ordering 10 pizzas!
```

and the server output:

```
Starting up on: 127.0.0.1:12345
Server listening for incoming connections
Connected to ('127.0.0.1', 52856)
Sending message to ('127.0.0.1', 52856)
Connection with ('127.0.0.1', 52856) has been closed
```

The server listens for incoming connections; when a client connects, the server communicates with it until the connection is closed (close the client to close the connection). It then continues to listen for new connections. Take a moment to study this code.

Our server is working—the client can now order pizzas with it! But there is a problem in the implementation that we've missed.

A need for concurrency

Similar to the Santa Cruz Operation, this version of the server is not concurrent. When several clients try to connect to the server at about the same time, one client connects and occupies the server while other clients wait for the current client to disconnect. In the previous code, the server is essentially blocked by a single client connection!

Try it yourself: try running a new client in a separate terminal. You will notice that the second client's connection remains pending until the first client terminates its connection. This lack of concurrency hampers the server's ability to handle multiple client connections concurrently.

In a real web application, however, concurrency is unavoidable: multiple clients and multiple servers are networked together, simultaneously sending and receiving messages and waiting for timely responses. Thus, a web application is also inherently a concurrent system requiring concurrent approaches. Consequently, concurrency is not only a feature of the web architecture but also a necessary and decisive principle for implementing large-scale web applications to maximize the use of hardware.

Threaded pizza server

One standard solution is to use threads or processes. As we discussed earlier, threads are
generally more lightweight, so we use them for the implementation:

```python
# Chapter 10/threaded_pizza_server.py
from socket import socket, create_server
from threading import Thread


BUFFER_SIZE = 1024
ADDRESS = ("127.0.0.1", 12345)


class Handler(Thread):
    def __init__(self, conn: socket):
        super().__init__()
        self.conn = conn

    def run(self) -> None:
        print(f"Connected to {self.conn.getpeername()}")
        try:
            while True:
                data = self.conn.recv(BUFFER_SIZE)
                if not data:
                    break
                try:
                    order = int(data.decode())
                    response = f"Thank you for ordering {order} pizzas!\n"
                except ValueError:
                    response = "Wrong number of pizzas, please try again\n"
                print(f"Sending message to {self.conn.getpeername()}")
                self.conn.send(response.encode())
        finally:
            print(f"Connection with {self.conn.getpeername()} "
                  f"has been closed")
            self.conn.close()


class Server:
    def __init__(self) -> None:
        try:
            print(f"Starting up at: {ADDRESS}")
            self.server_socket = create_server(ADDRESS)
```

```
        except OSError:
            self.server_socket.close()
            print("\nServer stopped.")

    def start(self) -> None:
        print("Server listening for incoming connections")
        try:
            while True:
                conn, address = self.server_socket.accept()
                print(f"Client connection request from {address}")
                thread = Handler(conn)
                thread.start()
        finally:
            self.server_socket.close()
            print("\nServer stopped.")

if __name__ == "__main__":
    server = Server()
    server.start()
```

For each client, when a client connection request is received, a new thread is created to handle the connection.

In this implementation, the main thread contains a listening server socket that accepts incoming connections from clients. Each client connecting to the server is handled in a separate thread. The server creates another thread that communicates with the client. The rest of the code remains unchanged.

Concurrency is achieved by using multiple threads. The OS overlaps multiple threads with preemptive scheduling. We already know this approach; it leads to a simple programming model because all the threads needed to process the requests can be written consistently. Moreover, it provides a simple abstraction, freeing the developer from low-level scheduling details. Instead, the developer can rely on the OS and the execution environment.

> **NOTE**   This approach is used in many technologies, such as the popular Apache web server MPM Prefork module, servlets in Jakarta EE (< version 3), the Spring Framework (< version 5), Ruby on Rails' Phusion Passenger, Python Flask, and many others.

The threaded server we've described seems to solve the problem of serving multiple clients perfectly, but at a price.

C10k problem

A modern server application processes hundreds, thousands, or tens of thousands of client requests (threads) concurrently, waiting for timely responses. Although threads are relatively cheap to create and manage, the OS spends significant time, precious RAM space, and other resources managing them. For small tasks such as processing single requests, the overhead associated with thread management may outweigh the benefits of concurrent execution.

> **NOTE** Many OSs have trouble handling more than a few thousand threads, usually much less. You can try your machine with the code from Chapter 10/ thread_cost.py.

The OS constantly shares CPU time with all threads, regardless of whether a thread is ready to continue execution. For example, a thread may be waiting for data on a socket, but the OS scheduler may switch to that thread and back a thousand times before any useful work is done. Responding to thousands of connection requests simultaneously using multiple threads or processes takes up a significant amount of system resources, reducing responsiveness.

Recall the preemptive scheduler from Chapter 6, which pulls up the CPU core for a thread. This may require a short wait time if the machine is heavily loaded. After that, the thread usually uses the time allocated to it and returns to the Ready state to wait for new portions of CPU time.

Now imagine that you define the scheduler period as 10 milliseconds, and you have two threads; each thread gets 5 milliseconds separately. If you have five threads, each thread will get 2 milliseconds. But what happens if you have 1,000 threads? You give each thread a time slice of 10 microseconds. In that case, the threads will spend a lot of time switching contexts and won't be able to do any real work.

You need to limit the length of the time slice. In the latter scenario, if the minimum time slice is 2 milliseconds and there are 1,000 threads, the scheduler cycle needs to be increased to 2 seconds. If there are 10,000 threads, the scheduler cycle is 20 seconds.

In this simple example, if each thread uses its full time slice, it will take 20 seconds for all threads to run concurrently. That's too long.

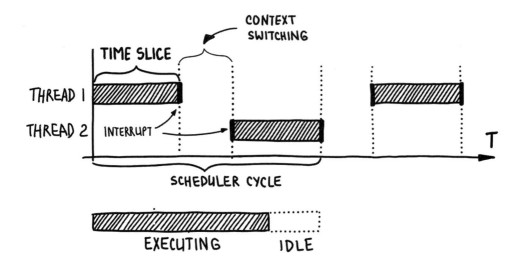

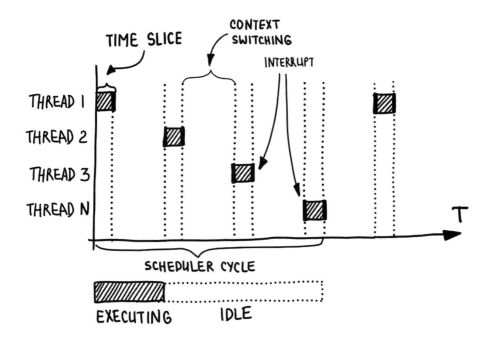

Context-switching threads takes precious CPU time. The more threads we have, the more time we spend switching instead of doing actual work. Thus, the overhead of starting and stopping threads can become quite high.

With a high level of concurrency (say, 10,000 threads, if you can configure the OS to create that many threads), having many threrads can affect throughput due to the frequent context-switching overhead. This is a scalability problem, specifically named *the*

C10k problem,[2] which prevents servers from handling more than 10,000 simultaneous connections.

> **NOTE** As technology has evolved from that time, this problem has been extended to C10m: that is, how to support 10 million simultaneous connections or handle 1 million connections per second.

With threads, unfortunately, we can't solve the C10k problem. To solve it, we need to change our approach. But first, let's understand why we need threads in the first place: we need them to handle blocking operations.

Blocking I/O

When we wait for data from I/O, we get a delayed response. This delay can be small when requesting a file on a hard disk and longer when requesting data from the network because the data has to travel a greater distance to the calling party. For example, a file stored on a hard disk must reach the CPU through SATA cables and motherboard buses; data from a network resource located on a remote server must travel through miles of network cables, routers, and eventually the network interface card (NIC) in our computer to the CPU. This means the application is *blocked* until the I/O system call is complete. The calling application is in a state where it is not using the CPU and is just waiting for a response, so it is inefficient from a processing standpoint. And the more I/O operations, the more we run into the same problem discussed—the processor becomes idle and doesn't do any real work.

> **NOTE** Any input/output operation is inherently sequential—sending a signal and waiting for a response. Nothing is concurrent in this process, so Amdahl's law (discussed in Chapter 2) is in full force here.

An example

Let's say that instead of ordering, you decide to make pizza at home. To cook it, you place sauce, cheese, pepperoni, and olives on the dough (pineapple on pizza is forbidden in our house). You put the pizza in the oven and wait for the cheese to melt and the dough to brown. Nothing else is required of you; from this point on, the oven takes care of the cooking. All you have to do is wait for the right moment to take the pizza out of the oven.

---

[2]   Daniel Kegel, "The C10K problem," http://www.kegel.com/c10k.html.

So, you place a chair in front of the oven, take a seat, and keep a vigilant eye on the pizza, ensuring you don't miss the critical moment just before it starts to burn.

In this approach, you can't do anything else since most of your time is spent waiting in front of the oven. It is a *synchronized* task; you are "in sync" with the oven. You have to wait and be there until the moment the oven finishes with the pizza.

Similarly, traditional send() and recv() socket calls are blocking in nature. If there is no message to receive, recv() system calls block the program until it receives the data. It just gets a chair, sits down, and waits for the client to send the data.

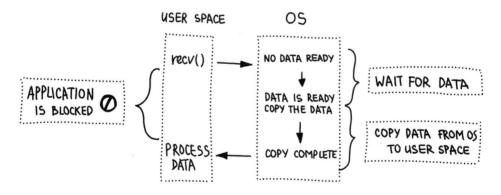

Unless otherwise specified, almost all I/O interfaces (including network socket interfaces) are blocking. For conventional desktop applications, I/O-bound operations are usually an occasional task. For web servers, I/O is the primary task, and it turns out the server doesn't use the CPU while it's waiting for a response from the client. This communication is very inefficient because it is blocking.

OS optimization

Why would we use the CPU to just sit and wait for a request? When a task is blocked, the OS puts it in a Blocked state until the I/O operation completes. To make efficient use of physical resources, the OS immediately "parks" the blocked task, removing it from the CPU core and storing it in the system, while another Ready task is allocated CPU time. As soon as the I/O is complete, the task exits the Blocked state and goes to the Ready state and possibly to the Running state if the OS scheduler decides so.

If a program is CPU-bound, context switching will become a performance nightmare, as we've seen. Since a computational task always has something to do, it doesn't need to wait for anything; context switching stops that useful work from getting done.

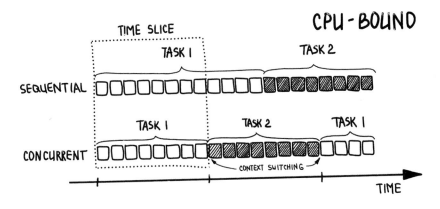

If a program has a lot of I/O-bound operations, context switching is an advantage. As soon as a task goes into a Blocked state, another task in a Ready state takes its place. This allows the processor to stay busy if work (tasks in the Ready state) needs to be done. This situation is fundamentally different from what happens with CPU-bound tasks.

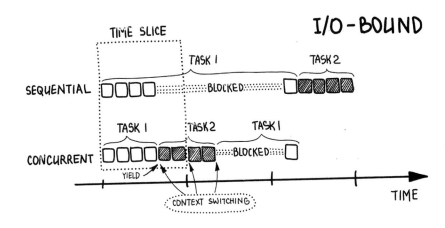

So, if a function is blocked (for whatever reason), it can delay other tasks, and the overall progress of the entire system may suffer. If a function is blocked because it's performing a CPU task, there's not much we can do. But if it is blocked because of I/O, we know that the CPU is idle and can be used to perform another task that needs the CPU.

Blocking occurs in all concurrent programs, not only in I/O (interaction in and out of a process, possibly over a network, writing/reading to/from a file, with a user at the command line or GUI, etc.). Concurrent modules do not work synchronously like sequential programs. They usually have to wait for each other when coordinated actions are required.

Now imagine that we can create an operation that will not be blocked.

Nonblocking I/O

Recalling Chapter 6, it is possible to achieve concurrency without any parallelism. This can be handy when dealing with a large number of I/O-bound tasks. We can abandon thread-based concurrency to achieve more scalability, avoiding the C10k problem with *nonblocking I/O.*

The idea of nonblocking I/O is to request an I/O operation and not wait for a response so we can move on to other tasks. For example, with a nonblocking read, we can request data over a network socket while the execution thread is doing other things (such as working with another connection) until the data is placed in buffers, ready to be consumed. The disadvantage is that we need to periodically ask whether the data is ready to be read.

Since one of the problems with previous implementations was that each thread had to block and wait for the I/O to return with data, let's use another socket access mechanism: *nonblocking sockets.* All the blocking socket calls can be put into nonblocking mode.

Going back to the pizza cooking analogy, this time you don't constantly monitor the pizza. Instead, you periodically go over to the oven and "ask" it whether the pizza is ready—turn on the light in the oven, and check whether the pizza is done.

The same with sockets—by putting a socket in nonblocking mode, we can effectively poll it. The consequence of nonblocking is that the I/O command cannot be executed immediately—if we try to read data from a nonblocking socket and there is no data, it will return an error (depending on the implementation, it may return a special values such as EWOULDBLOCK or EAGAIN). The simplest nonblocking approach is to create an infinite loop by repeatedly calling I/O operations on the same socket. If any I/O operations are marked as complete, we process them. This approach is called *busy-waiting*.

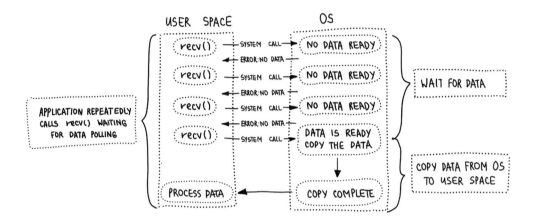

In Python's nonblocking implementation, when calling send(), recv(), or accept(), if the device has no data to read, it raises a BlockingIOError exception instead of blocking the execution. This indicates that it should have been blocked here, and the caller should try to repeat the operation in the future.

We can also remove the creation of new threads; they don't give us any particular advantage in the nonblocking I/O approach. On the contrary, they only consume more RAM and waste time by context switching. Here's an example implementation:

```
# Chapter 10/pizza_busy_wait.py
import typing as T
from socket import socket, create_server

BUFFER_SIZE = 1024
ADDRESS = ("127.0.0.1", 12345)


class Server:
    clients: T.Set[socket] = set()
```

```python
    def __init__(self) -> None:
        try:
            print(f"Starting up at: {ADDRESS}")
            self.server_socket = create_server(ADDRESS)
            self.server_socket.setblocking(False)
        except OSError:
            self.server_socket.close()
            print("\nServer stopped.")
```

Sets the server socket to nonblocking mode so it doesn't block while waiting for incoming connections

```python
    def accept(self) -> None:
        try:
            conn, address = self.server_socket.accept()
            print(f"Connected to {address}")
            conn.setblocking(False)
            self.clients.add(conn)
        except BlockingIOError:
            pass
```

This exception is caught to handle nonblocking sockets when no data is available to read from the socket. This allows the program to avoid blocking and instead continue execution for other clients with data available to be read.

```python
    def serve(self, conn: socket) -> None:
        try:
            while True:
                data = conn.recv(BUFFER_SIZE)
                if not data:
                    break
                try:
                    order = int(data.decode())
                    response = f"Thank you for ordering {order} pizzas!\n"
                except ValueError:
                    response = "Wrong number of pizzas, please try again\n"
                print(f"Sending message to {conn.getpeername()}")
                conn.send(response.encode())
        except BlockingIOError:
            pass

    def start(self) -> None:
        print("Server listening for incoming connections")
        try:
            while True:
                self.accept()
                for conn in self.clients.copy():
                    self.serve(conn)
```

```
        finally:
            self.server_socket.close()
            print("\nServer stopped.")


if __name__ == "__main__":
    server = Server()
    server.start()
```

In this server implementation, we make the socket nonblocking by calling `setblock-ing(False)`, so the server application will never wait for the operation to complete. Then, for each nonblocking socket, we try to perform `accept()`, `read()`, and `send()` operations in an endless `while` loop—a *polling loop*. The polling loop should keep trying to perform the operations again and again because they are no longer blocking—during `send()`, we don't know if the socket is ready—we have to keep trying until the attempt is successful. The same is true for the other calls. Thus `send()`, `recv()`, and `accept()` calls can pass control back to the main thread without doing anything.

> **NOTE** It is a common misconception that nonblocking I/O results in faster I/O operations. Although nonblocking I/O does not block the task, it does not necessarily execute faster. Instead, it enables the application to perform other tasks while waiting for I/O operations to complete. This allows for better utilization of processing time and efficient handling of multiple connections, ultimately enhancing overall performance. Nonetheless, the speed of the I/O operation is primarily determined by hardware and network performance characteristics, and nonblocking I/O does not affect these factors.

Since there is no blocking I/O, multiple I/O operations overlap, even if a single thread is used. This creates the illusion of parallelism because multiple tasks run concurrently (similar to how it was done in Chapter 6).

Using nonblocking I/O in the right situation hides latency and improves our application's throughput and/or responsiveness. It also allows us to work with a single thread, potentially saving us from synchronization problems between threads and the costs of thread management and associated system resources.

Recap

- In client-server applications interacting via message-passing IPC, concurrency is unavoidable: multiple clients and servers are networked together, simultaneously sending and receiving messages and waiting for timely responses.

- When I/O-bound code runs in a program, the processor often spends a lot of time doing nothing because the only thing currently running is waiting for I/O to complete.

- *Blocking* interfaces do all their work before returning to the calling party; *nonblocking* interfaces start some work but return immediately, thus allowing other work to be done. In workloads with more I/O work than CPU work, the efficiency gains from nonblocking I/O are much higher, as expected.

- OS threads (especially processes) are suitable for a small number of long-running tasks, since the use of a large number of threads is limited by increasing performance degradation due to constant context switching and memory consumption related to the thread stack size. One simple approach to overcome the costly creation of threads or processes is to use the busy-waiting approach, where, with a single thread, we can concurrently process multiple client requests, using nonblocking operations.

Event-based concurrency | 11

In this chapter

- You learn how to overcome the difficulties of the inefficient busy-waiting approach from Chapter 10

- You learn more about synchronization in message-passing IPC

- You learn about event-based concurrency

- You learn the reactor design pattern

Concurrency is a critical aspect of modern software development, allowing applications to perform multiple tasks simultaneously and maximize hardware utilization. While traditional thread/process-based concurrency is a well-known technique, it is not always the best approach for every application. In fact, for high-load I/O-bound applications, event-based concurrency is often a more effective solution.

Event-based concurrency involves organizing an application around events or messages rather than threads or processes. When an event occurs, the application responds by invoking a handler function, which performs the necessary processing. This approach has several advantages over traditional concurrency models, including lower resource usage, better scalability, and improved responsiveness.

Real-world examples of event-based concurrency can often be found in many high-performance applications, such as web servers, messaging systems, and gaming platforms. For instance, a web server can use event-based concurrency to handle a large number of simultaneous connections with minimal resource consumption, while a messaging system can use it to efficiently process a high volume of messages.

In this chapter, we explore event-based concurrency in more detail, comparing it with traditional thread/process-based concurrency and discussing its most popular use in client-server applications. We examine the benefits and drawbacks of event-based concurrency and discuss how to design and implement event-driven applications effectively. By the end of this chapter, you will have a solid understanding of event-based concurrency and its applications, allowing you to choose the right approach for your projects.

Events

Looking back at our pizza cooking analogy from Chapter 10, we can see that using the busy-waiting approach to cook pizza is inefficient and tedious. This approach requires constantly polling all sockets, regardless of their state. If we have 10,000 sockets, and only the last socket is ready to send/receive data, we may go through them all only to find a message waiting impatiently on the last one. The CPU constantly runs as we poll each socket to check its status. This means 99% of our CPU time is spent polling rather than executing other CPU-bound tasks, which is inefficient.

We need an efficient mechanism. We need *event-based concurrency.*

What we want to know is when the pizza will be ready, right? Why don't we just set a timer to notify us when the pizza is cooked? That way, we can do something else while waiting for the event. When the timer notifies us that the pizza is ready, we can process the event and eat that hot, fresh pizza.

Event-based concurrency focuses on *events*. We simply wait for something to happen—that is, an event. It may be an I/O event, such as data ready to consume or a socket ready for writing, or any other event, such as the timer trigger. When it happens, we check what type of event it is and do a small amount of work processing that event (which can include executing I/O requests, scheduling other events, etc.).

NOTE User interfaces are almost always designed as event-driven programs because their purpose is to respond to user actions. For example, JavaScript has historically been used to interact with the document object model (DOM) and with the user in the browser, so an event-driven programming model is natural for this language. But this style has also become popular in some modern systems, including server-side frameworks such as Node.js. Another example of event-based concurrency is the React.js library, commonly used for building user interfaces. React.js uses a virtual DOM and event handlers to update the user interface in response to user input or other events rather than updating the DOM directly. This approach allows React.js to minimize the number of DOM updates and improve performance by batching updates together.

Callbacks

In an event-driven program, we need to specify the code that will be run when each event occurs. This code is called a *callback*.

Callback translates as "Call me back," and the principle of callbacks is similar to the order of a phone callback. Imagine that you call an operator to order a pizza, but an answering machine responds with a pleasant voice that asks you to either stay on the line until the operator is free or request a callback. If you request a callback, when the operator is free, they call you back and take your order. Instead of waiting for an operator to answer, you can request a callback and do other things. Once the callback happens, you can do what you set out to do and order a pizza.

NOTE   Callback-based code often makes the control flow less obvious and more difficult to debug. We no longer have clean and readable code. We used to be able to read the code sequentially, but now we need to spread the logic across multiple callbacks. This chain of operations in the code can cause a series of nested callbacks, also known as *callback hell*.

Now we have events, and we have callbacks. How do we make them work together? Event-based concurrency depends on an event loop.

Event loop

Combining different events and callbacks to these events means introducing a controlling entity that tracks different events and runs their appropriate callbacks. Such an entity is usually called an *event loop*.

Instead of polling for events as we did in the busy-waiting implementation, events are queued as they arrive in an *event queue*. The event loop waits for events, continuously retrieves them from the queue, and invokes the appropriate callback.

The following diagram shows an example of a typical flow that an event-oriented program executes. The event loop continuously fetches events from the event queue and makes appropriate callbacks. Although this diagram shows only one specific event mapped to one callback, it should be noted that in some event-driven applications, the number of events and callbacks could theoretically be infinite.

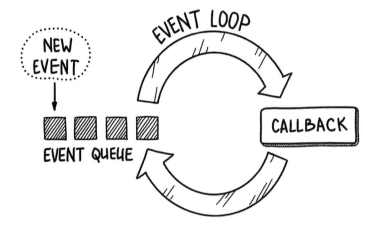

Essentially, all the event loop does is wait for events to occur, map each event to a callback we have registered in advance, and run this callback.

NOTE The event loop is the heart and soul of JavaScript. In JavaScript, we are not allowed to create new threads. Instead, concurrency in JavaScript is achieved through the mechanism of event loops. This is how JavaScript can bridge the gap between multithreading and concurrency, making JavaScript a serious contender in an arena filled with concurrent languages such as Java, Go, Python, Rust, and so on. Many GUI toolkits, such as Java Swing, also have an event loop.

Let's try to implement the same idea in code:

```python
# Chapter 11/event_loop.py
from collections import deque
from time import sleep
import typing as T
```

The Event class represents an action to be executed by the event loop.

```python
class Event:
    def __init__(self, name: str, action: T.Callable[..., None],
                 next_event: T.Optional[Event] = None) -> None:
        self.name = name
        self._action = action
        self._next_event = next_event

    def execute_action(self) -> None:
        self._action(self)
        if self._next_event:
            event_loop.register_event(self._next_event)
```

Creates a queue to store events to be executed by the event loop

```python
class EventLoop:
    def __init__(self) -> None:
        self._events: deque[Event] = deque()
```

Adds an event to the event queue

```python
    def register_event(self, event: Event) -> None:
        self._events.append(event)

    def run_forever(self) -> None:
        print(f"Queue running with {len(self._events)} events")
        while True:
            try:
                event = self._events.popleft()
            except IndexError:
                continue
            event.execute_action()
```

Runs the event loop forever, executing each event in the queue as it becomes available

```
def knock(event: Event) -> None:
    print(event.name)
    sleep(1)


def who(event: Event) -> None:
    print(event.name)
    sleep(1)
```

Registers with event loop callbacks that represent actions to be executed when events with the corresponding names are triggered

```
if __name__ == "__main__":
    event_loop = EventLoop()
    replying = Event("Who's there?", who)
    knocking = Event("Knock-knock", knock, replying)
    for _ in range(2):
        event_loop.register_event(knocking)
    event_loop.run_forever()
```

Starts the event loop and runs it indefinitely until interrupted, continuously checking the event queue for new events to execute

Here, we create an event loop and register two events: `knock` and `who` (note that the `knock` event can produce a `who` event). Then we manually generate two `knock` events as though they just happened and started the infinite execution of the event loop. We see that the event loop executes them one after the other:

```
Queue running with 2 events
Knock-knock
Knock-knock
Who's there?
Who's there?
```

Ultimately, the flow of the application depends on events. But how can the server know which event it should process next?

I/O multiplexing

Modern OSs typically include event notification subsystems, commonly called *I/O multiplexing*. These subsystems collect and queue I/O events from monitored resources and block them until the user application is available to process them. This allows the user application to perform a simple check for incoming I/O events that require attention.

Using I/O multiplexing, we don't need to keep track of all the socket events as we did in the previous chapter using the busy-waiting approach. We can rely on the OS to tell us what events happen on which sockets. The application can ask the OS to monitor the socket and queue the events until the data is ready. The application can check for events at any time, perhaps doing something else in the meantime. This mechanism is provided by the granddad of system calls: `select`.

When we use a `select` system call, we don't make any socket calls on a given socket until the `select` tells us that something has happened on that socket: for example, data has arrived and is ready to be read. However, the biggest advantage of I/O multiplexing is that we can process multiple socket I/O requests concurrently using the same thread. We can register multiple sockets and wait for incoming events from all of them.

If sockets are ready when `select` is called, it returns control to the event loop immediately. Otherwise, it is blocked until some of the registered sockets are ready. When a new `read` event arrives or a socket is available for writing, `select` returns new events, places these new events in the event queue, and returns control to the event loop. This way, the application can receive new requests while processing a previous request. This ensures that the processing of the previous request is not blocked, but control can be quickly returned to the event loop to process the new request.

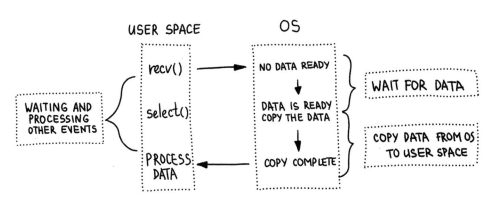

NOTE Many OSs provide a more efficient interface for event notification: POSIX provides `poll`, Linux has `epoll`, FreeBSD and macOS use `kqueue`, Windows has IOCP, Solaris has `/dev/poll`, and so on. These basic primitives allow us to build a nonblocking event loop that simply checks incoming packets, reads socket messages, and responds as needed.

By using I/O multiplexing, we concurrently perform several I/O operations with different sockets using the same execution thread without constantly polling for incoming events. Instead, the OS manages incoming events, notifying the application only when necessary. It is still blocking with the `select` system call, but it does not waste time waiting for data to arrive or waste CPU time in the constant event-polling loop, as we see in the busy-waiting approach.

Event-driven pizza server

We are now ready to implement a single-threaded concurrent version of the pizza server using I/O multiplexing! The core of the program is again the event loop—an infinite loop that, at each iteration, gets ready to read/write sockets from the `select` system call and invokes the corresponding registered callbacks:

```python
# Chapter 11/pizza_reactor.py
class EventLoop:
    def __init__(self) -> None:
        self.writers = {}
        self.readers = {}

    def register_event(self, source: socket, event: Mask,
                       action: Action) -> None:
        key = source.fileno()
        if event & select.POLLIN:
            self.readers[key] = (source, event, action)
        elif event & select.POLLOUT:
            self.writers[key] = (source, event, action)

    def unregister_event(self, source: socket) -> None:
        key = source.fileno()
        if self.readers.get(key):
            del self.readers[key]
        if self.writers.get(key):
            del self.writers[key]

    def run_forever(self) -> None:
        while True:
            readers, writers, _ = select.select(
                self.readers, self.writers, [])
            for reader in readers:
                source, event, action = self.readers.pop(reader)
                action(source)
```

Keeps track of sockets that are ready for either write or read I/O operations

Gets a unique identifier associated with the socket

Indicates that data is available to be read from the socket

Indicates that the socket is ready to write data

Removes the socket from the readers and/or writers when the client closes the connection

Runs an infinite loop, waiting for sockets in readers or writers to become ready for I/O using select

For each read-ready socket, the corresponding action is executed, and then the socket is removed from the readers.

```
for writer in writers:
    source, event, action = self.writers.pop(writer)
    action, msg = action
    action(source, msg)
```

For each write-ready socket, the corresponding action is executed, and then the socket is removed from the writers.

Inside the `run_forever` method of the event loop, we call the `select` system call, waiting for it to tell us when clients have new events to process. This is a blocking operation, which means the event loop does not run inefficiently. It waits for at least one event to happen. `select` tells us when the socket is ready to read/write, and we call the corresponding callback.

We need to encapsulate sending and receiving data into independent functions (callbacks, for each of the expected event types) _on_accept(), _on_read(), and _on_write(). Then we let the OS monitor the state of the client sockets instead of our application. All we need to do is register all client sockets with all expected events with corresponding callbacks. That's exactly what we do inside the `Server` class:

```
# Chapter 11/pizza_reactor.py
class Server:
    def __init__(self, event_loop: EventLoop) -> None:
        self.event_loop = event_loop
        try:
            print(f"Starting up at: {ADDRESS}")
            self.server_socket = create_server(ADDRESS)
            self.server_socket.setblocking(False)
        except OSError:
            self.server_socket.close()
            print("\nServer stopped.")

    def _on_accept(self, _: socket) -> None:
        try:
            conn, client_address = self.server_socket.accept()
        except BlockingIOError:
            return
        conn.setblocking(False)
        print(f"Connected to {client_address}")
        self.event_loop.register_event(conn, select.POLLIN, self._on_read)
        self.event_loop.register_event(self.server_socket, select.POLLIN,
                                       self._on_accept)
```

Callback that is called when a new client connects to the server; it registers the connection with the event loop to monitor for incoming data.

```
def _on_read(self, conn: socket) -> None:
    try:
        data = conn.recv(BUFFER_SIZE)
    except BlockingIOError:
        return
    if not data:
        self.event_loop.unregister_event(conn)
        print(f"Connection with {conn.getpeername()} has been closed")
        conn.close()
        return
    message = data.decode().strip()
    self.event_loop.register_event(conn, select.POLLOUT,
                                   (self._on_write, message))
```

Callback that is called when data is
received from a client connection

Callback that is called when a response
is ready to be sent to the client

```
def _on_write(self, conn: socket, message: bytes) -> None:
    try:
        order = int(message)
        response = f"Thank you for ordering {order} pizzas!\n"
    except ValueError:
        response = "Wrong number of pizzas, please try again\n"
    print(f"Sending message to {conn.getpeername()}")
    try:
        conn.send(response.encode())
    except BlockingIOError:
        return
    self.event_loop.register_event(conn, select.POLLIN, self._on_read)

def start(self) -> None:
    print("Server listening for incoming connections")
    self.event_loop.register_event(self.server_socket, select.POLLIN,
                                   self._on_accept)
```

```
if __name__ == "__main__":
    event_loop = EventLoop()
    Server(event_loop= event_loop).start()
    event_loop.run_forever()
```

Starts the server by registering
the server socket with the
event loop and setting the
callback function for accepting
new client connections

In this implementation, we start by creating a server socket, similar to the previous approach. However, instead of monolithic code, we represent the application as a set of callbacks, each of which handles a specific type of event request. Once these components are set up, we initiate the server to listen for incoming connections.

The core of the implementation lies in the event loop, which handles events from the event queue and invokes the corresponding event handlers. The event loop transfers control to the appropriate callback function and resumes control once the callback has finished executing. This process continues as long as there are pending events in the event queue. When all events have been processed, the event loop returns control to the `select` function, which becomes blocked again, waiting for new operations to complete.

By implementing this event-driven architecture and utilizing the event loop, we successfully address the challenge of handling multiple clients concurrently by running the event loop within a single thread. Hooray!

Reactor pattern

This use of the event loop, which waits for events to happen and then processes them, is so common that it has achieved the status of a design pattern: the *reactor pattern*. By executing a single-threaded event loop using I/O multiplexing to handle nonblocking I/O and employing appropriate callbacks, we effectively employ the reactor pattern.

The reactor pattern handles incoming requests that arrive in the application from one or more clients. Here, an application is represented by callbacks, each responsible for processing event-specific requests. For the reactor pattern, we need several components: event sources, event handlers, a synchronous event demultiplexer, and a reactor structure.

Event sources are entities that generate events, such as files, sockets, timers, or synchronization objects. Our pizza server code has two event sources: the server socket and the client sockets.

Event handlers, which are essentially callback functions, are responsible for processing requests from specific event sources. In our code, we have three types of event handlers:

- `_on_accept`—Handles the server socket and accepts a new connection

- `_on_read`—Handles a new message from the client connection

- `_on_write`—Handles writing messages to the client connection

Synchronous event demultiplexer is a fancy name for getting events from an event notification mechanism provided by the OS, such as `select` or any of its flavors. It waits for specific events to occur on a set of handles.

The *reactor,* aka the *event loop,* is the one who runs the show. It registers callbacks for specific events and responds to events by passing the work to the appropriate registered event handler or callback. In our code, the `EventLoop` class serves as the reactor, as it waits for events and "reacts" to them. When the `select` call returns a list of resources ready for I/O operations, the reactor calls the corresponding registered callbacks.

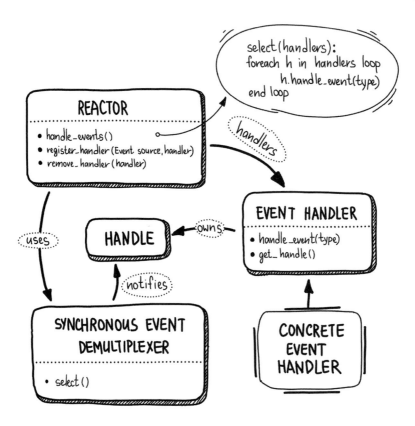

In summary, an application following the reactor pattern registers event sources and event types it is interested in. For each event, it provides a corresponding event handler, which is a callback. The synchronous event demultiplexer waits for events and notifies the reactor, which then invokes the appropriate event handler to handle the event.

> **NOTE** A lot of popular core libraries and frameworks have been built on the ideas we outline here. Libevent is a widely used, long-standing cross-platform event library; `libuv` (an abstraction layer on top of `libeio`, `libev`, `c-ares`, and `iocp`) implements low-level I/O in Node.js, Java NIO, NGINX, and Vert.x using nonblocking models with an event loop implementation to achieve a high level of concurrency.

The reactor pattern allows for an event-driven concurrency model, avoiding the overhead of creating and managing system threads, context switching, and complexities associated with shared memory and locks in traditional thread-based models. By utilizing events for concurrency, resource consumption is significantly reduced, as only one execution thread is employed. However, it requires a different programming style that involves callbacks and handling events that occur later.

To sum up, the reactor pattern targets synchronous processing of events but asynchronous I/O processing and relies on the OS event notification system. As we've touched on the concept of synchronization, let's talk more about it.

Synchronization in message passing

Synchronization in message passing refers to the coordination and sequencing of tasks that rely on a specific order of execution. When tasks are synchronized, they run in order, and subsequent tasks must wait for the completion of preceding tasks before proceeding. It's important to note that synchronization refers to the start and end points of tasks rather than their actual execution.

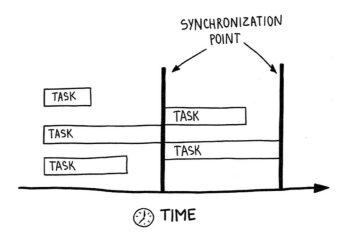

Synchronous communication requires both parties to be ready to exchange data at the same time, creating an explicit synchronization point for both tasks. This approach blocks program execution until the communication is completed, leaving system resources idle. In contrast, asynchronous communication occurs when the caller initiates a task and does not wait for it to complete but moves on. Asynchronous communication does not require synchronization when sending and receiving, and the sender is not blocked until the receiver is ready. The calling application accesses the results asynchronously and can check for events at any convenient time. This approach allows the processor to spend time processing other tasks instead of waiting.

To illustrate the difference between synchronous and asynchronous communication, think of how different people use mobile phones. During a call, while one person is talking, the other person is listening. When the first person finishes talking, the second person usually answers right away. Until the second person answers, the first person waits for an answer. This means the first person cannot continue until the second person has finished.

In this example, the first person's end point is synchronized with the second person's start point. However, while this provides immediate satisfaction to both participants, it takes longer to conclude a conversation because the average person can consume 10 times more information while reading as opposed to listening. That's one reason texting has become so popular among younger people.

Text messaging represents an asynchronous method of communication. One person can send a message, and the recipient can reply at their convenience. In the meantime, the sender can perform other tasks while waiting for a response.

In programming, asynchronous communication occurs when the caller initiates a task and does not wait for it to complete but moves on (like an inattentive partner). It does not require synchronization when sending and receiving: the sender is not blocked until the receiver is ready. If it cares about the results (or partner) provided by such a task, it must have a way to get them (by providing a callback or in any other way). Regardless of which method is used, we say that the calling application accesses the results *asynchronously*. The application can check for events at any convenient time, perhaps by running other tasks in the meantime (or coming up with the answer to a loaded question like "How much do you love me?"). This is an asynchronous process since the application expresses interest at one point and uses data at another point.

Asynchronous tasks don't have synchronized start and end points. Instead of waiting, the CPU time spent in synchronous communication is utilized for processing other tasks. Thus, the processor is never left idle when there is work to be done.

All asynchronous I/O operations boil down to the same pattern. It's not about how the code is executed but where the waiting occurs. Multiple I/O operations can combine their waiting efforts so that the waiting occurs at the same place in the code. When an event occurs, the asynchronous system must resume the part of the code that was waiting for that event.

Asynchronous messaging decouples the communication between entities and allows senders to send messages without waiting for recipients. In particular, no synchronization is required for messaging between senders and receivers, and both entities can work independently. With multiple recipients, the advantage of asynchronous messaging becomes even more apparent. It would be very inefficient to wait until all message recipients are ready to communicate simultaneously or even to send a message synchronously to one recipient at a time.

I/O models

The terms *blocking/synchronous* and *nonblocking/asynchronous* are often used interchangeably. But even though they describe similar concepts, they are different—they are used at different levels with different meanings. We distinguish them, at least to describe I/O operations:

- *Blocking vs. nonblocking*—Using these properties, an application can tell the OS how to access the device. When using blocking mode, the I/O operation does not return to the caller until the operation completes. In nonblocking mode, all calls are returned immediately but only show the state of the operation. Thus, it may take several calls to ensure that the operation has been completed successfully.

- *Synchronous vs. asynchronous*—These properties describe the high-level flow of control during an I/O operation. A synchronous call retains control because it does not return until the operation completes, thus making a synchronization point. An asynchronous call returns immediately, allowing further operations to be performed.

Combining these properties gives four different models of I/O operations. Each of them has different uses that are advantageous for certain applications.

Synchronous blocking model

This is the most common model of operation for many typical applications. In this model, an application in the user space makes a system call that causes the application to block. The application is blocked until the system call (data transfer or error) completes.

Synchronous nonblocking model

In this model, the application accesses the I/O device in nonblocking mode. This causes the OS to immediately return the I/O call. Normally, the device is not yet ready, and the response to the call indicates that the call should be repeated later. By doing so, application code often implements busy-waiting behavior, which is highly inefficient. Once the I/O operations are complete and the data is available in the user space, the application can continue to work and use the data.

Asynchronous blocking model

An example of this model is a reactor pattern. Surprisingly, the asynchronous blocking model still uses nonblocking mode for I/O operations. However, instead of busy-wait, a special blocking system call, `select`, is used to send a notification about the I/O status. However, it blocks just the notification, not the I/O call. If this notification mechanism is reliable and performant, it is a good model for highly performant I/O.

Asynchronous nonblocking model

Finally, in the asynchronous nonblocking I/O model, an I/O request is returned immediately, indicating that the operation was successfully initiated. The application performs other operations while the background operation completes. When the response arrives, a signal or callback can be generated to complete the I/O operation.

An interesting feature of this model is that there is no blocking or waiting at the user level. The whole operation is moved elsewhere (to the OS or a device). This allows the application to take advantage of the extra processor time while I/O operations occur in the background. Not surprisingly, this model also performs well with high performance I/O.

These models describe I/O operations in OSs at a low level only. From a more abstract, developer point of view, the application framework can provide I/O access using synchronous blocking through background threads but provide an asynchronous interface for developers using callbacks and vice versa.

NOTE   Asynchronous I/O (AIO) in Linux is a relatively recent addition to the Linux kernel. The basic idea behind AIO is to allow a process to initiate a series of I/O operations without having to block or wait for any operation to complete. Later, or after receiving an I/O completion notification, the process can retrieve the I/O results. We get a notification that the socket can be read or written without a lock. We then perform an I/O operation that is not blocked. Windows uses the completion notification model (I/O completion ports [IOCPs]).

Recap

- *Event-based concurrency* is more suitable for high-load I/O applications because it provides better scalability with higher concurrency. Such applications require less memory, even if they handle thousands of simultaneous connections.

- *Synchronous* communication refers to tasks that run in order and depend on that order. It blocks program execution for the duration of data exchange, leaving system resources idle. In synchronous communication, both parties must be ready to exchange data at the same time, and the application is blocked until the communication is completed.

- *Asynchronous* communication occurs when the caller initiates a task and does not wait for it to complete but moves on. It does not require synchronization when sending and receiving, and the sender is not blocked until the receiver is ready. Asynchronous communication allows the CPU time spent waiting in synchronous communication to be spent processing other tasks instead. The application can check for events at any convenient time, and asynchronous tasks do not have synchronized start and end points.

- The *reactor pattern* is the most popular pattern for implementing event-based concurrency for handling I/O-bound applications. Simply put, it uses a single-threaded event loop and nonblocking events, and it sends those events to the appropriate callbacks.

Asynchronous communication | 12

In this chapter

- You learn about asynchronous communication and when to use an asynchronous model

- You learn the difference between preemptive and cooperative multitasking

- You learn how to implement an asynchronous system using cooperative multitasking via coroutines and futures

- You learn to combine event-based concurrency and concurrency primitives to implement an asynchronous system that efficiently runs I/O and CPU tasks

People are impatient by nature and want systems to respond immediately. But this is not always necessary. In many programming scenarios, we can postpone processing or move it elsewhere so that it happens *asynchronously*. When we do this, we reduce the latency constraints on systems that have to run in real time. Part of the goal of moving to asynchronous operations is to reduce the workload, but it's not always a simple step.

For example, there is a popular steakhouse in San Jose, California, called Henry's Hi-Life, which has been an institution in the city since 1950. It is popular but has limited space, so it has developed an innovative, asynchronous method for moving patrons through quickly without making them feel rushed.

Diners enter through a small dive bar and are greeted by a host at a podium at the back of the bar. The diner tells the host how many are in their party, and the host hands them the number of menus needed. Patrons can then grab a drink at the bar while they make their choices, which are written on a checklist with any special requests and then handed to the host. The order is taken directly to the kitchen, and as soon as it is ready, the host guides the diners to their table; before they can put napkins in their laps, the food is delivered piping hot (no microwaves allowed).

This process reduces the latency constraints on the kitchen, improves the overall dining experience for customers, and maximizes revenue for the restaurant. Implementing asynchronous systems can improve the performance and scalability of a system, even in scenarios where people are accustomed to immediate service.

In this chapter, we learn how to implement asynchronous systems by borrowing the "event loop plus callback" model described in Chapter 11 and turning it into its own implementation. We take an in-depth look at coroutines and futures, popular abstractions for implementing asynchronous calls. And we look at when to use the asynchronous model and present examples to help you better understand this computer science term and the scenarios for which it is useful.

A need for asynchrony

At first glance, the event-based approach to programming seems like a great solution. With a simple event loop, events are handled as they occur. However, a significant problem arises when an event requires a system call that could be blocked, such as a CPU-bound operation. This problem is compounded by the fact that instead of a single, cohesive codebase, the application is represented as a collection of callbacks, each responsible for a specific type of event request. This approach sacrifices readability and maintainability.

When it comes to servers that use threads or processes, this problem is easily solved. While one thread is busy with a blocking operation, other threads can run in parallel, enabling the server to continue functioning. The OS handles the scheduling of threads on available CPU cores.

However, in the event-based approach, there is only a main thread with an event loop that listens for events. This means no operation should block execution, as doing so would result in the entire system being blocked. As a result, asynchronous programming techniques must be used to ensure that operations do not block the event loop and that the system remains responsive.

Asynchronous procedure calls

By default, in most programming languages, when a method is invoked, it is executed synchronously. This means the code runs sequentially, and control is not returned to the environment until the entire method completes. However, this can become problematic when the method takes a long time to execute, such as a network call or long-running computation. In such cases, the calling thread becomes blocked until the method finishes. When this is undesirable, you can start a worker thread and call the method from it; but in most cases, it is not worth an additional thread with its complexities and overhead.

Let's imagine a very inefficient example. You arrive at the front desk of a hospital to check in for a procedure. If this were done with synchronous communication, the receptionist would require you to stand at the counter for as long as you needed to fill out multiple forms while the receptionist just sat and waited for you. You'd be in the way of them serving other patients. The only way to scale this approach would be to hire more receptionists and make room for them. Doing so would be costly and inefficient, as the receptionists would be doing nothing most of the time. Fortunately, that is not the way it is done.

Generally, medical facilities are asynchronous systems. When you walk up to a counter and find out you need to fill out additional forms, the receptionist hands you the forms, a clipboard, and a pen and tells you to come back when you've finished. You sit down to fill out the forms while the receptionist helps the next person in line. You do not block a receptionist from serving others. When you finish, you go back to the line and wait to talk to the receptionist again. If you've done something wrong or need to fill out another form, they give you a new form or tell you what needs fixing, and you repeat the process: sit, do your work, and then get back in line. This system already scales well. If the queue gets too long, the facility can add another receptionist, making it even more scalable.

A sequential programming model can be extended to support concurrency by overloading synchronous calls with asynchronous semantics. The call does not create a synchronization point; instead, the runtime scheduler passes the results to the handler later or asynchronously. A synchronous call with asynchronous semantics added is called an *asynchronous call* or *asynchronous procedure call* (APC). APC augments a potentially long-running (synchronous) method with an asynchronous version that returns immediately and with additional methods that make it easy to get a completion notification or wait for completion at a later time.

Several software constructs and operations that make up the asynchronous structure have emerged in the programming world. Perhaps one of the most widely used is cooperative multitasking.

Cooperative multitasking

According to the Oxford English Dictionary, *a-syn-chro-nous* means "of or requiring a form of computer control timing protocol in which a particular operation begins upon receiving an indication (signal) that the preceding operation has been completed." It is clear from the definition that the main problem is not how and where operations take place but how to restart this or that part of the code after the event completion.

Up to this point, when we've talked about threads, threads that relate one-to-one to system-level threads are managed by the OS itself. But we can also have logical threads at the user or application level; these are threads managed by developers. The OS knows nothing about user-level threads. It treats applications utilizing user-level threads as if they were single-threaded processes. User-level threads usually form the simplest kind of multitasking: *cooperative multitasking,* also known as *non-preemptive multitasking.*

In cooperative multitasking, the OS never initiates context switching. Instead, each task decides when to hand over control to the scheduler, allowing other tasks to run by explicitly saying to the scheduler, "I'm pausing my work for a while; please keep running other tasks." The scheduler's job is only to assign tasks to available processing resources.

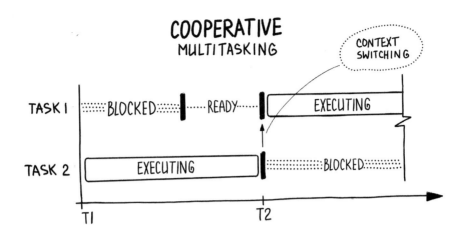

Thus, we have only one worker thread, and no other thread can replace the currently running thread. The system is called cooperative multitasking because, to be successful, the developer and the runtime environment work together in harmony to make the most of the available processing resources.

> **NOTE** This simple approach has found its way into all versions of macOS up to macOS X, and Windows up to Windows 95 and Windows NT.

Since there is only one execution thread, but multiple tasks need to be completed, there is the problem of resource sharing. In this case, thread management is the resource that needs to be shared. But the cooperative scheduler cannot take control away from the executing task unless the task itself gives it.

Coroutines (user-level threads)

In our threaded server implementation (Chapter 10), the OS threads do not impose control-transfer responsibility on us: they provide concurrency even if we have only one processor core. The key here is the OS's ability to pause and resume thread execution using preemptive multitasking (Chapter 6). If we could have functions capable of pausing and resuming execution like OS threads, we could write concurrent single-threaded code. Guess what? We can do it with *coroutines*!

   Coroutines are a programming construct that allows for cooperative multitasking, where a single thread of execution can be paused and resumed at specific points in the code. This approach offers several advantages, including more efficient and flexible code capable of handling asynchronous tasks without explicit threading.

The key difference between coroutines and OS threads is that coroutine switching is cooperative rather than preemptive. This means the developer, along with the programming language and its execution environment, has control over when the switch between coroutines occurs. At the right moment, a coroutine can be paused, allowing another task to start executing instead.

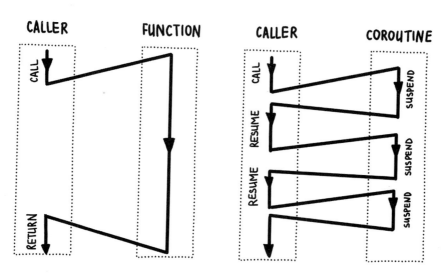

Coroutines are particularly useful in scenarios where certain operations are expected to block for a significant duration, such as network requests. Instead of involving the system scheduler, coroutines allow immediate switching to another task. This cooperative nature of coroutines enables developers to write code that is more elegant, readable, and reusable.

> **NOTE** The core idea of coroutines came out of work called *continuations*. Continuations can be thought of as a snapshot of the program's execution context at a specific point in time, including the current call stack, local variables, and other relevant information. By capturing this information, continuations enable a program to save its execution state and resume it later, potentially on a different thread or even a different machine.

To illustrate the usefulness of coroutines, let's consider an example of generating the Fibonacci sequence. The following Python code showcases an elegant and readable implementation using coroutines, highlighting the concept's benefits in terms of elegance, readability, and code reuse:

```
# Chapter 12/coroutine.py
from collections import deque
import typing as T

Coroutine = T.Generator[None, None, int]


class EventLoop:
    def __init__(self) -> None:
        self.tasks: T.Deque[Coroutine] = deque()

    def add_coroutine(self, task: Coroutine) -> None:
        self.tasks.append(task)

    def run_coroutine(self, task: Coroutine) -> None:
        try:
            task.send(None)
            self.add_coroutine(task)
        except StopIteration:
            print("Task completed")

    def run_forever(self) -> None:
        while self.tasks:
            print("Event loop cycle.")
            self.run_coroutine(self.tasks.popleft())


def fibonacci(n: int) -> Coroutine:
    a, b = 0, 1
    for i in range(n):
        a, b = b, a + b
        print(f"Fibonacci({i}): {a}")
        yield
    return a

if __name__ == "__main__":
    event_loop = EventLoop()
    event_loop.add_coroutine(fibonacci(5))
    event_loop.run_forever()
```

Contains the list of all the coroutines to be executed

Adds a new coroutine task to the event loop for the execution

Executes the coroutine until it reaches the next yield statement

An exception is raised when a coroutine has completed its execution and returned a value.

Enters a loop that executes coroutines from the event loop's deque object until none remain

Temporarily pauses the execution of the function and allows other coroutines to be executed

Returns the final value computed by the function after it has completed execution

The output of the program is as follows:

```
Event loop cycle.
Fibonacci(0): 1
Event loop cycle.
Fibonacci(1): 1
Event loop cycle.
Fibonacci(2): 2
Event loop cycle.
Fibonacci(3): 3
Event loop cycle.
Fibonacci(4): 5
Event loop cycle.
Task completed
```

In this code, we introduce a simple event loop and a coroutine. We call the coroutine just like a regular function, but it executes instructions until it reaches a pause point marked by the `yield` instruction. This special instruction temporarily halts the current function execution, returns control to the caller, and preserves the current instruction stack and pointer in memory, effectively saving the execution context. Consequently, the event loop remains unblocked by a single task and executes the next task while waiting for the awaited event to occur. Once the event is complete, the event loop resumes execution from the exact line it paused on.

Over time, the main thread can invoke the same coroutine again, and it will start execution not from the beginning but from the last pause point. Therefore, a coroutine is a partially executed function that, under appropriate conditions, can be resumed at some point in the future until it completes.

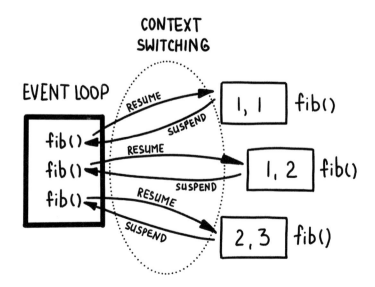

In our code example, the `Fibonacci()` coroutine pauses and returns control to the event loop, which then waits and pauses with a resume marker. Upon resumption, the `fibonacci` coroutine yields the result, and the event loop then resumes execution, passing the yielded value to the appropriate destination.

By employing coroutines and an event loop, we achieve cooperative multitasking, where tasks can be efficiently scheduled and executed without relying on multiple threads or processes. Coroutines allow us to write concurrent code with improved control flow, making it easier to handle asynchronous tasks and optimize resource utilization.

> **NOTE** *Fibers*, *light threads*, and *green threads* are other names for coroutines or coroutine-like concepts. Sometimes they may look (usually on purpose) like OS threads, but they don't run like real threads; instead, they run coroutines. Depending on the language or implementation, there may be more specific technical features or differences between these concepts: Python (generator-based and native coroutines), Scala (coroutines), Go (goroutines), Erlang (Erlang processes), Elixir (Elixir processes), Haskell GHC (Haskell threads), and many others.

Cooperative multitasking benefits

Cooperative multitasking offers several advantages over preemptive multitasking, making it a desirable approach in certain scenarios.

Uses fewer resources

User-level threads are less resource intensive. Context switching occurs when the OS needs to switch between threads or processes. System threads are relatively heavyweight, and context switching between system threads results in significant overhead. In contrast, user-level threads are lighter in both aspects. With cooperative scheduling, because tasks maintain their own lifecycles, the scheduler does not need to monitor the state of each task, so task switching is cheaper: switching tasks is not much more expensive than calling a function. This makes it possible to create millions of coroutines without significant management overhead. Applications with this approach usually boast scalability even while being single-threaded (in the OS sense).

Avoids blocking shared resources

With cooperative multitasking, tasks can switch between themselves at specific points in the code, mitigating the problems of blocking shared resources. By carefully choosing these switch points, we ensure that tasks never interrupt each other in the middle of critical sections.

Greater efficiency

Context switching in cooperative multitasking is more efficient because the task knows when to pause and pass control to another task. But this requires the task to be tremendously aware that it is not working alone—other tasks are waiting, and it decides when to hand over control. We need only one centralized sequence of operations to lose everything (see the mall example in Chapter 2).

The scheduler can't make global decisions about how long tasks should run. That's why in cooperative multitasking, it's important not to run long operations—or, if we do, to periodically return control. When multiple programs do small chunks of work and voluntarily switch between each other, we can achieve a level of concurrency that no scheduler can achieve. Now we can have thousands of coroutines working together instead of dozens of threads.

But preemptive multitasking and cooperative multitasking are not mutually exclusive; they are often used in the same systems at different levels of abstraction. For example, a cooperative computation may be periodically preempted to provide a fairer distribution of CPU time.

Future objects

Imagine that you go to a burger joint. There you place an order for a fancy burger for lunch. The cashier says something to the cook in the kitchen to let them know to make your burger. The cashier gives you your order number and a promise that your burger will be cooked and you'll get it sometime in the future. You will receive your order once your order number is displayed at the counter, indicating that the cook has finished preparing it. While you wait, you pick a table, and you sit and mind your own business. But if there is no callback method, how do you know when the burger is ready? In other words, how do you get the result of an asynchronous call?

As the return value of an asynchronous call, we can make an object that guarantees a future result (expected result or error). This object is returned as a "promise" of a future result: a placeholder object for the result that is initially unknown because the computation of its value is not yet complete. Once the result is obtained, we can put it inside the placeholder object. Such objects are called *future objects*.

Future objects can be thought of as results that will eventually become available. They also act as a synchronization mechanism because they allow us to send independent computations but be synchronized with the source control and eventually return the result.

> **NOTE**　*Future, promise, delay,* and *deferred* generally refer to roughly the same synchronization mechanism in different programming languages, where the object acts as a proxy for an as-yet-unknown result. When a result becomes available, the waiting code is executed. Over the years, these terms have come to have slightly different meanings in different languages and ecosystems.

Back to your burger order. From time to time, you check the number on the counter to see if your order is ready. At some point, it's finally ready for pickup. You walk over to the counter, grab your burger, return to the table, and enjoy your meal.

In code, it looks like this:

```
# Chapter 12/future_burger.py
from __future__ import annotations

import typing as T
from collections import deque
from random import randint

Result = T.Any
Burger = Result
Coroutine = T.Callable[[], 'Future']
```

```
class Future:
    def __init__(self) -> None:
        self.done = False
        self.coroutine = None
        self.result = None

    def set_coroutine(self, coroutine: Coroutine) -> None:
        self.coroutine = coroutine

    def set_result(self, result: Result) -> None:
        self.done = True
        self.result = result

    def __iter__(self) -> Future:
        return self

    def __next__(self) -> Result:
        if not self.done:
            raise StopIteration
        return self.result


class EventLoop:
    def __init__(self) -> None:
        self.tasks: T.Deque[Coroutine] = deque()

    def add_coroutine(self, coroutine: Coroutine) -> None:
        self.tasks.append(coroutine)

    def run_coroutine(self, task: T.Callable) -> None:
        future = task()
        future.set_coroutine(task)
        try:
            next(future)
            if not future.done:
                future.set_coroutine(task)
                self.add_coroutine(task)
        except StopIteration:
            return

    def run_forever(self) -> None:
        while self.tasks:
            self.run_coroutine(self.tasks.popleft())
```

Sets the coroutine associated with the Future object

Sets the Future as done, and assigns the computation result to the object

Checks whether the Future is done, and returns the result if it is

Runs a coroutine by calling it, creating a Future object, and executing its coroutine. If the future is not done, adds the coroutine to the task queue to be executed again later.

```python
def cook(on_done: T.Callable[[Burger], None]) -> None:
    burger: str = f"Burger #{randint(1, 10)}"
    print(f"{burger} is cooked!")
    on_done(burger)
```

Cooks a burger, and calls the function that handles the next step, which is the cashier

```python
def cashier(burger: Burger, on_done: T.Callable[[Burger], None]) -> None:
    print("Burger is ready for pick up!")
    on_done(burger)
```

Notifies the customer that their burger is ready for pickup, and calls the function that handles the next step

```python
def order_burger() -> Future:
    order = Future()

    def on_cook_done(burger: Burger) -> None:
        cashier(burger, on_cashier_done)

    def on_cashier_done(burger: Burger) -> None:
        print(f"{burger}? That's me! Mmmmmm!")
        order.set_result(burger)

    cook(on_cook_done)
    return order
```

Creates a Future object to represent the customer's order

Calls the function to cook the burger, and returns the Future object. The callbacks passed as arguments to the cook and cashier functions are called when the corresponding operation is done.

```python
if __name__ == "__main__":
    event_loop = EventLoop()
    event_loop.add_coroutine(order_burger)
    event_loop.run_forever()
```

The program consists of calling the cook coroutine, in which the chef cooks the burger and then passes the result to the second coroutine—cashier, which informs you that the burger is ready. Each coroutine returns a Future object and returns control to the main function. The function pauses until the value is ready and then resumes and completes its operation. This is what makes coroutines asynchronous.

The Future object describes the idea of separating the computation and its final result by providing a proxy entity that returns the result as soon as it becomes available. The Future object has a result property that stores future execution results. There is also a set_result method, which sets the result after the value is bound to the result.

While waiting until the `Future` object is filled with the result, we can perform other computations. This provides a simple way to call an operation that takes a long time to execute or can be delayed because of costly operations such as I/O, which can slow down other program elements.

> **NOTE**   There is also a related scatter-gather method of I/O. It involves using a single procedure call to efficiently read data from multiple buffers and write it to a single data stream or vice versa. This technique offers benefits such as improved efficiency and convenience. For example, this pattern is particularly useful for running multiple independent web requests concurrently. Scattering the requests as background tasks and gathering the results through proxy entities enables the concurrent processing of operations, similar to how `promise.all()` works in JavaScript. With `promise.all()`, we can pass an array of promises, and it waits for them to resolve before returning the results as an array.

If we combine `Future` objects with the concept of coroutines—functions whose execution can be paused and then resumed—we can write asynchronous code, which is close to sequential code in its form.

Cooperative pizza server

In Chapter 10, we talked about the first e-commerce app developed by the Santa Cruz Operation in the 1980s to order pizza for developers. That was a simple synchronous approach, but it was limited in scope because of a lack of computing resources. Since then, programmers have learned how to run coroutines and have created future implementations, giving us all the building blocks we need to create an asynchronous server via cooperative multitasking.

Event loop

Let's take a look at our main component—the event loop:

```
# Chapter 12/asynchronous_pizza/event_loop.py
from collections import deque
import typing as T
import socket
import select
```

```
from future import Future

Action = T.Callable[[socket.socket, T.Any], Future]
Coroutine = T.Generator[T.Any, T.Any, T.Any]
Mask = int


class EventLoop:
    def __init__(self):
        self._numtasks = 0
        self._ready = deque()
        self._read_waiting = {}
        self._write_waiting = {}

    def register_event(self, source: socket.socket, event: Mask, future,
                       task: Action) -> None:
        key = source.fileno()
        if event & select.POLLIN:
            self._read_waiting[key] = (future, task)
        elif event & select.POLLOUT:
            self._write_waiting[key] = (future, task)

    def add_coroutine(self, task: Coroutine) -> None:
        self._ready.append((task, None))
        self._numtasks += 1

    def add_ready(self, task: Coroutine, msg=None):
        self._ready.append((task, msg))

    def run_coroutine(self, task: Coroutine, msg) -> None:
        try:
            future = task.send(msg)
            future.coroutine(self, task)
        except StopIteration:
            self._numtasks -= 1

    def run_forever(self) -> None:
        while self._numtasks:
```

```
if not self._ready:
    readers, writers, _ = select.select(
        self._read_waiting, self._write_waiting, [])
    for reader in readers:
        future, task = self._read_waiting.pop(reader)
        future.coroutine(self, task)

    for writer in writers:
        future, task = self._write_waiting.pop(writer)
        future.coroutine(self, task)

task, msg = self._ready.popleft()
self.run_coroutine(task, msg)
```

Checks if there are any ready coroutines to be executed. If there are ready coroutines, executes the next one. If there are none, waits until one or more of the registered sockets are ready for I/O operations, and then executes the corresponding coroutine(s).

In addition to the same event notification loop in our main entry point method `run_forever`, we run the `run_coroutine` method for all coroutines ready to run. As soon as all the tasks are done (a future is returned and control is given back or the result returned), we remove all completed tasks from the task queue. If there are no ready tasks, we call `select` as before, blocking the event loop until some event happens on the client sockets we have registered. As soon as that happens, we run the appropriate callbacks and start a new iteration of the loop.

As stated earlier, a cooperative scheduler cannot take control away from the executing task, as the event loop cannot interrupt a running coroutine. A running task runs until it passes control. The event loop selects the next task and keeps track of the blocked tasks that cannot run until I/O is complete, but only when no tasks are currently running.

To implement a cooperative server, we need to implement coroutines for each server socket method (`accept`, `send`, and `recv`). There we create a `Future` object and return it to the event loop. We put the result into the future when the desired event has been completed. To make it easier to operate, let's put the asynchronous socket implementation into a separate class:

```
# Chapter 12/asynchronous_pizza/async_socket.py
from __future__ import annotations

import select
import typing as T
import socket
```

```
from future import Future

Data = bytes


class AsyncSocket:
    def __init__(self, sock: socket.socket):
        self._sock = sock
        self._sock.setblocking(False)

    def recv(self, bufsize: int) -> Future:
        future = Future()

        def handle_yield(loop, task) -> None:
            try:
                data = self._sock.recv(bufsize)
                loop.add_ready(task, data)
            except BlockingIOError:
                loop.register_event(self._sock, select.POLLIN, future, task)

        future.set_coroutine(handle_yield)
        return future

    def send(self, data: Data) -> Future:
        future = Future()

        def handle_yield(loop, task):
            try:
                nsent = self._sock.send(data)
                loop.add_ready(task, nsent)
            except BlockingIOError:
                loop.register_event(self._sock, select.POLLOUT, future, task)

        future.set_coroutine(handle_yield)
        return future

    def accept(self) -> Future:
        future = Future()

        def handle_yield(loop, task):
            try:
                r = self._sock.accept()
                loop.add_ready(task, r)
            except BlockingIOError:
                loop.register_event(self._sock, select.POLLIN, future, task)
```

```
            future.set_coroutine(handle_yield)
            return future

    def close(self) -> Future:
        future = Future()

        def handle_yield(*args):
            self._sock.close()

        future.set_coroutine(handle_yield)
        return future

    def __getattr__(self, name: str) -> T.Any:
        return getattr(self._sock, name)
```

We make our server socket nonblocking, and in each method, we execute the corresponding operation without waiting for it to complete. We simply release control by returning a Future object in which we write the result of the operation later. We have prepared the generic boilerplate and are ready to create our cooperative server application.

Cooperative pizza server implementation

Let's implement our asynchronous server with cooperative multitasking:

```
# Chapter 12/asynchronous_pizza/cooperative_pizza_server.py
import socket

from async_socket import AsyncSocket
from event_loop import EventLoop

BUFFER_SIZE = 1024
ADDRESS = ("127.0.0.1", 12345)


class Server:
    def __init__(self, event_loop: EventLoop):
        self.event_loop = event_loop
        print(f"Starting up on: {ADDRESS}")
        self.server_socket = AsyncSocket(socket.create_server(ADDRESS))

    def start(self):
        print("Server listening for incoming connections")
        try:
            while True:
                conn, address = yield self.server_socket.accept()
                print(f"Connected to {address}")
```

Suspends execution until a connection request arrives at the server socket. When a connection request arrives, the accept method returns a new socket object for the connection, and the method resumes execution.

```
                    self.event_loop.add_coroutine(
                        self.serve(AsyncSocket(conn)))
            except Exception:
                self.server_socket.close()
                print("\nServer stopped.")

    def serve(self, conn: AsyncSocket):
        while True:
            data = yield conn.recv(BUFFER_SIZE)
            if not data:
                break

            try:
                order = int(data.decode())
                response = f"Thank you for ordering {order} pizzas!\n"
            except ValueError:
                response = "Wrong number of pizzas, please try again\n"

            print(f"Sending message to {conn.getpeername()}")
            yield conn.send(response.encode())
            print(f"Connection with {conn.getpeername()} has been closed")
        conn.close()


if __name__ == "__main__":
    event_loop = EventLoop()
    server = Server(event_loop=event_loop)
    event_loop.add_coroutine(server.start())
    event_loop.run_forever()
```

Suspends execution until data is received from the client. When data is received, the method resumes execution, and the received data is returned.

Suspends execution of the serve method until the response can be sent back to the client. When the response has been sent, the method resumes execution.

We follow an approach similar to the previous versions by creating an event loop and assigning our `server` function to it for execution. Once the event loop starts running, we run clients and submit orders to the server.

However, in our cooperative multitasking approach, we don't rely on threads or processes that require control transfer, as all execution occurs within a single thread. Instead, we manage multiple tasks by transferring control to a central function that coordinates these tasks—the event loop.

To sum up, cooperative multitasking significantly reduces CPU and memory overhead, especially for workloads with a large number of I/O-related tasks such as servers and databases. All other things being equal, we can have orders of magnitude more tasks than OS threads because the cooperative-multitasking approach uses one expensive thread to handle a large number of cheap tasks.

Asynchronous pizza joint

For the last two chapters, you've probably been thinking, "What kind of pizza joint is this if we're not actually making pizza, but just saying 'Thanks for ordering'?" Time to put on an apron and start the oven!

As you can imagine, making pizza is a lengthy process. Let's use this `Kitchen` class to simulate the cooking process:

```
# Chapter 12/asynchronous_pizza/asynchronous_pizza_joint.py

class Kitchen:
    @staticmethod
    def cook_pizza(n):
        print(f"Started cooking {n} pizzas")
        time.sleep(n)
        print(f"Fresh {n} pizzas are ready!")
```

Simulates the time required to cook n pizzas

If we run this in our cooperative server implementation, our server will be busy making pizza for one customer for a long time and only then serve other customers! There's a blocking call lurking in a dark corner of our beautiful asynchronous system. Bummer!

We want to continue getting customer orders while making pizza in the background. The oven and the order server should not be blocked by each other. Yes, we are going back to basics—to threads—but this time, we are using concurrency with asynchronous communication. How exciting!

The idea is to create an asynchronous method that returns a future that encapsulates a long operation that will complete at some point in the future. Once the job is sent, the `Future` object is returned, and the caller's execution thread can continue working, separated from the new computation.

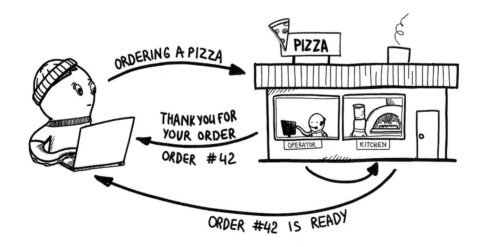

For the implementation, we use the same approach to event notification; we can return a Future object that promises the result will arrive sometime in the future:

```python
# Chapter 12/asynchronous_pizza/event_loop_with_pool.py
import socket
from collections import deque
from multiprocessing.pool import ThreadPool
import typing as T
import select

from future import Future

Data = bytes
Action = T.Callable[[socket, T.Any], None]
Mask = int

BUFFER_SIZE = 1024


class Executor:
    def __init__(self):
        self.pool = ThreadPool()

    def execute(self, func, *args):
        future_notify, future_event = socket.socketpair()
        future_event.setblocking(False)

        def _execute():
            result = func(*args)
            future_notify.send(result.encode())

        self.pool.apply_async(_execute)
        return future_event


class EventLoop:
    def __init__(self):
        self._numtasks = 0
        self._ready = deque()
        self._read_waiting = {}
        self._write_waiting = {}
        self.executor = Executor()
```

Uses a thread pool to run blocking tasks in separate threads

Creates a pair of connected sockets for interprocess communication. One socket is used to send notifications about task completion, and the other socket is used to wait for those notifications.

Submits a function to be executed in a worker thread of a thread pool, and returns a future event socket to wait for notification

```python
def register_event(self, source: socket.socket, event: Mask, future,
                   task: Action) -> None:
    key = source.fileno()
    if event & select.POLLIN:
        self._read_waiting[key] = (future, task)
    elif event & select.POLLOUT:
        self._write_waiting[key] = (future, task)

def add_coroutine(self, task: T.Generator) -> None:
    self._ready.append((task, None))
    self._numtasks += 1

def add_ready(self, task: T.Generator, msg=None):
    self._ready.append((task, msg))

def run_coroutine(self, task: T.Generator, msg) -> None:
    try:
        future = task.send(msg)
        future.coroutine(self, task)
    except StopIteration:
        self._numtasks -= 1

def run_in_executor(self, func, *args) -> Future:
    future_event = self.executor.execute(func, *args)
    future = Future()

    def handle_yield(loop, task):
        try:
            data = future_event.recv(BUFFER_SIZE)
            loop.add_ready(task, data)
        except BlockingIOError:
            loop.register_event(
                future_event, select.POLLIN, future, task)

    future.set_coroutine(handle_yield)
    return future

def run_forever(self) -> None:
    while self._numtasks:
        if not self._ready:
            readers, writers, _ = select.select(
                self._read_waiting, self._write_waiting, [])
            for reader in readers:
                future, task = self._read_waiting.pop(reader)
                future.coroutine(self, task)
```

Runs an operation in the Executor, and adds a corresponding callback for when data becomes available

```
            for writer in writers:
                future, task = self._write_waiting.pop(writer)
                future.coroutine(self, task)

        task, msg = self._ready.popleft()
        self.run_coroutine(task, msg)
```

Here we combine the thread pool with the event loop. When we get a CPU-heavy task, we can run it inside the thread pool and return a Future object. Once the task is done, an execution thread sends a notification that it's ready, and we can set the result of the Future object.

Finally, our pizza joint server looks like this:

```
# Chapter 11/asynchronous_pizza_joint.py
import socket
import time

from async_socket import AsyncSocket
from event_loop_with_pool import EventLoop

BUFFER_SIZE = 1024
ADDRESS = ("127.0.0.1", 12345)


class Server:
    def __init__(self, event_loop: EventLoop):
        self.event_loop = event_loop
        print(f"Starting up on: {ADDRESS}")
        self.server_socket = AsyncSocket(socket.create_server(ADDRESS))

    def start(self):
        print("Server listening for incoming connections")
        try:
            while True:
                conn, address = yield self.server_socket.accept()
                print(f"Connected to {address}")
                self.event_loop.add_coroutine(
                    self.serve(AsyncSocket(conn)))
        except Exception:
            self.server_socket.close()
            print("\nServer stopped.")

    def serve(self, conn: AsyncSocket):
        while True:
            data = yield conn.recv(BUFFER_SIZE)
            if not data:
                break
```

Runs a blocking operation in a separate thread to cook pizza
while continuing to serve other clients

```python
    try:
        order = int(data.decode())
        response = f"Thank you for ordering {order} pizzas!\n"
        print(f"Sending message to {conn.getpeername()}")
        yield conn.send(response.encode())
        yield self.event_loop.run_in_executor(
            Kitchen.cook_pizza, order)
        response = f"Your order of {order} pizzas is ready!\n"
    except ValueError:
        response = "Wrong number of pizzas, please try again\n"

    print(f"Sending message to {conn.getpeername()}")
    yield conn.send(response.encode())
    print(f"Connection with {conn.getpeername()} has been closed")
    conn.close()


if __name__ == "__main__":
    event_loop = EventLoop()
    server = Server(event_loop=event_loop)
    event_loop.add_coroutine(server.start())
    event_loop.run_forever()
```

Although this implementation is not yet suitable for production use due to various limitations, such as insufficient exception handling and the restriction that only socket events can trigger event loop iteration, it provides a glimpse into the mechanics of concurrency using asynchronous calls. Using our current knowledge, we can utilize hardware resources more efficiently, leading to increased performance. This example serves as a foundation for building next-generation asynchronous frameworks in any programming language you choose. By employing similar principles and techniques, you can develop more robust and scalable systems capable of handling a multitude of tasks concurrently.

> **NOTE** JavaScript is single-threaded, so the only way to achieve multithreading is to run multiple instances of the JavaScript engine. But then how do we communicate between these instances? This is where *web workers* come in. They allow tasks to run in a separate thread in the background, isolated from the main thread of the web application. This multithreading capability is provided by the browser container, so not all browsers support web workers yet. Node.js is another container for the JavaScript engine, which provides multithreading with the OS.

Asynchronous programming is complex, but many complexities can be covered by asynchronous libraries and frameworks. As an example, we can take a look at the same logic, but using the built-in Python `asyncio` library:

```
# Chapter 12/asynchronous_pizza/aio.py
import asyncio
import socket

from asynchronous_pizza_joint import Kitchen

BUFFER_SIZE = 1024
ADDRESS = ("127.0.0.1", 12345)


class Server:
    def __init__(self, event_loop: asyncio.AbstractEventLoop) -> None:
        self.event_loop = event_loop
        print(f"Starting up at: {ADDRESS}")
        self.server_socket = socket.create_server(ADDRESS)
        self.server_socket.setblocking(False)

    async def start(self) -> None:
        print("Server listening for incoming connections")
        try:
            while True:
                conn, client_address = \
                    await self.event_loop.sock_accept(
                        self.server_socket)
                    self.server_socket)
                self.event_loop.create_task(self.serve(conn))
        except Exception:
            self.server_socket.close()
            print("\nServer stopped.")

    async def serve(self, conn) -> None:
        while True:
            data = await self.event_loop.sock_recv(conn, BUFFER_SIZE)
            if not data:
                break
            try:
                order = int(data.decode())
                response = f"Thank you for ordering {order} pizzas!\n"
                print(f"Sending message to {conn.getpeername()}")
                await self.event_loop.sock_sendall(
                    conn, f"{response}".encode())
                await self.event_loop.run_in_executor(
                    None, Kitchen.cook_pizza, order)
                response = f"Your order of {order} pizzas is ready!\n"
            except ValueError:
                response = "Wrong number of pizzas, please try again\n"
```

The keyword async means the function is asynchronous.

The keyword await is used to wait for a coroutine to complete while allowing other tasks to run in the meantime.

```
        print(f"Sending message to {conn.getpeername()}")
        await self.event_loop.sock_sendall(conn, response.encode())
    print(f"Connection with {conn.getpeername()} has been closed")
    conn.close()
```

The keyword await is used to wait for a coroutine to complete while allowing other tasks to run in the meantime.

```
if __name__ == "__main__":
    event_loop = asyncio.get_event_loop()
    server = Server(event_loop=event_loop)
    event_loop.create_task(server.start())
    event_loop.run_forever()
```

The application code is greatly simplified—all the boilerplate code is gone. Everything from sockets to the event loop and concurrency is now hidden under the library calls and managed by the library developers.

> **NOTE** This does not mean `async/await` is the only correct approach to communication in concurrent systems. Take as an example the communicating sequential processes (CSP) model implemented in Go and Clojure or the actor model implemented in Erlang and Akka. However, `async/await` seems to be the best model in Python today.

This was definitely not easy code, so let's step back and talk about the asynchronous model in general.

Conclusions on the asynchronous model

Asynchronous operations generally do not wait for results to be completed. Instead, they delegate tasks to other locations, such as devices, threads, processes, or external systems, that can handle them independently. This allows the program to continue executing other tasks without waiting, and it receives a notification when a delegated task finishes or encounters an error.

It's important to note that asynchrony is a characteristic of an operation call or communication and is not tied to a specific implementation. Various asynchronous mechanisms exist, but they all adhere to the same underlying model. They differ in how they structure code to enable pausing when a blocking operation is requested and resuming once the operation is complete. This flexibility allows developers to choose the most suitable approach for their specific requirements and programming environment.

When should you use an asynchronous model? Asynchronous communication is a powerful tool for optimizing a heavily loaded system with frequent blocking system calls. But like any complex technology, it should not be used just because it exists.

Asynchrony adds complexity and makes the code less maintainable. Compared to the synchronous model, the asynchronous model works best in the following situations:

- You have a large number of tasks. In that case, there's probably always at least one task that can move forward. Using an asynchronous model often results in faster response times and improved overall performance, which can be good for the system's end users.

- The application spends most of its time doing I/O rather than processing. For example, you have a lot of slow requests—web sockets, long pooling, or slow external synchronous backends for which you don't know when the requests will run out.

- Tasks are largely independent, so there's no need for intertask communication (and therefore no need to wait for one task to run before running another).

These conditions almost perfectly characterize a typical busy server (such as a web server) in a client-server system (so the pizza examples make perfect sense). In server-side programs, asynchronous communication allows us to efficiently handle massive concurrent I/O operations, intelligently utilizing resources during their downtime and avoiding the creation of new resources. Server-side implementation is a prime candidate for the asynchronous model, which is why Python's `asyncio` and JavaScript's Node.js, along with other asynchronous libraries, have become so popular in recent years. Front-end and UI applications can also benefit from asynchrony because it enhances the flow of an application, particularly in high-volume independent I/O tasks.

Recap

- Asynchronous communication is a software development method that enables a single process to continue running without being blocked by time-consuming tasks such as I/O operations or network requests. Instead of waiting for a task to finish before moving on to the next one, an asynchronous program can execute other code while the task is being performed in the background. This approach optimizes system resources, resulting in improved program performance and responsiveness.

- Asynchrony is a property of an operation call or communication, not a specific implementation. The asynchronous model allows efficient handling of massive concurrent I/O operations, optimizing resource utilization, reducing system delay, and increasing scalability and system throughput. But without good libraries and frameworks, asynchronous programs may be difficult to write and debug.

- *Cooperative multitasking* is one method used to implement asynchronous systems. It allows multiple tasks to share processing time and CPU resources. In cooperative multitasking, tasks must cooperate by yielding control to the system once they complete a portion of their work.

- Compared to preemptive multitasking, cooperative multitasking offers several advantages. User-level threads, used in cooperative multitasking, are less resource intensive than system threads. This allows for the creation of a large number of coroutines without significant management overhead. However, it is crucial for tasks to be aware that they are not working alone and must decide when to hand over control to other tasks.

- Cooperative multitasking significantly reduces CPU and memory overhead, particularly for workloads involving numerous I/O-related tasks like servers and databases. By using a small number of threads to handle a large number of tasks, cooperative multitasking allows for more efficient utilization of hardware resources. This, combined with asynchronous communication, leads to better resource utilization.

- Popular abstractions for implementing asynchronous calls are coroutines and futures. A *coroutine* is a function that is partially executed and paused and, under appropriate conditions, resumed at some point in the future until its execution is complete. A *future* is a promise of a future result—a proxy object for the result, which is initially unknown, usually because the computation of its value is not yet complete.

In this chapter

- You learn about a framework for designing concurrent systems illustrated by two sample problems

- We connect all the knowledge we have learned together

Throughout this book, we have examined various approaches for implementing concurrent applications and associated problems. Now it's time to apply that knowledge to real-world scenarios.

In this chapter, we focus on the practical application of concurrent programming by introducing a methodical approach to designing concurrent systems. We also illustrate this approach through the examination of sample problems. By the end of this chapter, we will have the knowledge and skills needed to methodically design a simple concurrent system and recognize and address any potential flaws that reduce efficiency or scalability. But before we begin, let's take a moment to review the key concepts and principles we've previously covered on the topic of concurrency.

So, what is concurrency?

Concurrency is a big, sometimes dizzying puzzle. Early in the history of computers, programs were written for *sequential* computations. To solve a problem in this tradition, an algorithm is constructed and implemented as a sequential stream of instructions. These instructions are executed on the CPU of a single computer. This is the simplest style of programming and a straightforward execution model. Each task is executed in turn, with one task completed before the next begins. If the tasks are always executed in a certain order, then when the subsequent task starts executing, it can be assumed that all previous tasks have completed without errors and all their results are available for use—a certain simplification of logic.

Concurrent programming means splitting a program into tasks and running them in any order with the same result. That makes concurrency a challenging area of software development. Decades of research and practice have led to a wide variety of concurrency models with different goals. These models are primarily designed to optimize performance, efficiency, correctness, and usability. Depending on the context, concurrency units have different terms, such as *tasks, coroutines, processes,* or *threads.*

The processing elements can vary and include resources such as a single computer with multiple processors, multiple computers connected via a network, specialized hardware, or any combination. The execution process is controlled by the runtime system (OS); in a system with multiple processors or multiple cores, it can run in *parallel* or *multitask* on a single processor core. The point is that the execution details are handled by the runtime system, and the developer simply thinks in terms of independent tasks that can execute concurrently.

Now that we have a way to safely run tasks concurrently, we also need a way to coordinate them with shared resources. This is where concurrency causes problems. Tasks using old data may make inconsistent updates, systems can *deadlock,* data in different systems may never converge to consistent values, and so on. The order in which tasks access shared resources is fully controlled not by the developer but by how tasks are allocated to processors. That is, when each task executes and for how long is decided automatically by the implementation of the programming language in the OS. As a result, concurrency errors are very difficult to reproduce but can be avoided by implementing proper design practices in our application, minimizing task communication, and employing effective synchronization techniques.

We have a way to safely coordinate tasks, but they often need to communicate with one another. Communication between tasks can be *synchronous* or *asynchronous.* A synchronous call retains control because it does not return until the operation completes, thus making a *synchronization point.* An asynchronous call asks for something to happen and then is notified when it does, releasing resources to do other stuff in the meantime. In the asynchronous model, a task runs until it explicitly passes control to other tasks. Note that we can mix asynchronous and concurrent models and use both in the same system.

Now let's learn a methodology that will help us create concurrent programs: Foster's methodology.

Foster's methodology

In 1995, Ian Foster proposed a set of steps for designing concurrent systems, known as *Foster's design methodology.*[1] It is a four-step design process. Let's walk through the steps with an abstract approach, followed by some examples.

Suppose you are planning a road trip with your friends. Your task is to ensure that the trip is enjoyable and all necessary arrangements are made. Consider these four steps:

1. *Partitioning.* It is possible to partition the road trip into smaller tasks, such as planning the route, booking accommodation, and researching places to visit. This allows for better organization and ensures that all necessary tasks are completed.

   Applying that to concurrency, we identify portions of work that can be performed concurrently. We decompose the problem into many tasks. This decomposition is achieved using data or task decomposition approaches (Chapter 7). Practical problems, such as the number of processors in the target computer, are ignored, and attention is focused on recognizing opportunities for independent execution.

---

[1] Ian Foster, "Designing and Building Parallel Programs," https://www.mcs.anl.gov/~itf/dbpp.

2. *Communication.* When preparing for the road trip, you need to communicate with everyone involved to obtain the necessary data to execute tasks. You can create a group chat or email thread to discuss everyone's preferences for the route, accommodations, and places to visit.

   Likewise, we organize the communications necessary to obtain the data needed to execute a task. The communication required to coordinate task execution is determined, and appropriate communication structures and algorithms are defined.

3. *Agglomeration.* Agglomeration refers to establishing responsibility areas by dividing tasks and responsibilities into specific domains. Tasks are grouped based on similarity or relatedness, such as booking accommodations and researching places to visit. This allows for easier communication and coordination between team members and simplifies the planning process, as each person is responsible for a specific area.

   The tasks and communication structures defined in the first two stages of our design are evaluated with respect to performance requirements and implementation costs. It may involve grouping tasks into larger tasks to reduce communication or simplify implementation while maintaining flexibility if possible.

4. *Mapping.* Finally, you need to assign tasks to the members of your road trip. For example, one person can be assigned to navigate and drive the car, while someone else can be responsible for booking accommodations and admission tickets. The goal is to minimize overall execution time and ensure that everyone has a role in making the road trip successful.

   When we assign tasks to physical processors, usually our goal is to minimize overall execution time. Load-balancing or task-scheduling techniques can be used to improve the quality of the mapping. Each task is assigned to a processor in a manner that attempts to satisfy the competing goals of maximizing processor utilization and minimizing communication costs. Mapping can be specified statically or determined at runtime by load-balancing algorithms.

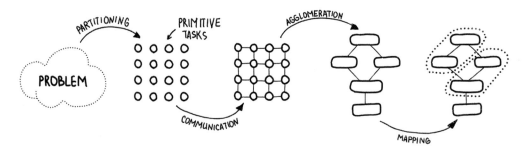

Foster's methodology

NOTE A common mistake in designing concurrent systems is choosing the specific mechanisms for concurrency too early in the design process. Each mechanism has advantages and disadvantages, and the best mechanism for a particular use case is often determined by subtle compromises and concessions. The earlier a mechanism is chosen, the less information we have on which to base a choice.

Thus, machine-independent aspects of design methodology, such as task independence, are considered early on, and machine-specific aspects of the design are deferred until the end of the design process. In the first two stages, we focus on concurrency and scalability and seek to find algorithms with these qualities. In the third and fourth stages, the focus shifts to efficiency and performance. Implementing a concurrent program is the final step to ensure effective implementation of the intended algorithm, perhaps with machine- or algorithm-specific features in mind. In the rest of this chapter, we dive deep into these steps with examples to illustrate their application.

Matrix multiplication

Consider using Foster's methodology on the example of matrix multiplication. Each matrix is represented as a two-dimensional array of arrays. Two matrixes can be multiplied if the number of columns in the first matrix, A, equals the number of rows in the second matrix, B.

The product of A by B, which we call matrix C, will have dimensions based on the number of rows in A and the number of columns in B. Each element in matrix C is the product of the corresponding row in A and the column in B.

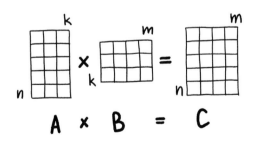

So, for example, the element $c_{2,3}$ is the product of the second row from matrix A and the first column from B. Written as a formula, $c_{2,3} = a_{2,1} \times b_{1,3} + a_{2,2} \times b_{2,3}$.

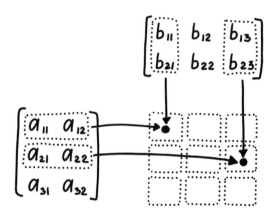

To give you something to compare this to, let's first use as an example the sequential algorithm:

```python
# Chapter 13/matmul/matmul_sequential.py
import random
from typing import List


Row = List[int]
Matrix = List[Row]


def matrix_multiply(matrix_a: Matrix, matrix_b: Matrix) -> Matrix:
    num_rows_a = len(matrix_a)
    num_cols_a = len(matrix_a[0])
    num_rows_b = len(matrix_b)
    num_cols_b = len(matrix_b[0])
    if num_cols_a != num_rows_b:
        raise ArithmeticError(
            f"Invalid dimensions; Cannot multiply "
            f"{num_rows_a}x{num_cols_a}*{num_rows_b}x{num_cols_b}"
        )
    solution_matrix = [[0] * num_cols_b for _ in range(num_rows_a)]
    for i in range(num_rows_a):
        for j in range(num_cols_b):
            for k in range(num_cols_a):
                solution_matrix[i][j] += matrix_a[i][k] * matrix_b[k][j]
    return solution_matrix

    if __name__ == "__main__":
        cols = 3
        rows = 2
```

Creates a new matrix filled with zeros, with the number of rows from matrix A and the number of columns from matrix B

For each row in matrix A ...

For each column in matrix B ...

For each column in matrix A ...

```
A = [[random.randint(0, 10) for i in range(cols)]
        for j in range(rows)]
print(f"matrix A: {A}")
B = [[random.randint(0, 10) for i in range(rows)]
        for j in range(cols)]
print(f"matrix B: {B}")
C = matrix_multiply(A, B)
print(f"matrix C: {C}")
```

... *generates a random matrix*

Here, we implement a sequential version of matrix multiplication that takes two matrixes A and B and produces the result of the multiplication, matrix C. The function uses a set of nested `for` loops that iterates over rows in A and columns in B. The third `for` loop sums the products of the elements from row A and column B. In this way, the program fills the result matrix C with values. The goal is to design and build a concurrent program that calculates the product of two matrixes, a common mathematical problem that can greatly benefit from concurrency.

Partitioning

The first step of Foster's methodology, partitioning, is designed to identify opportunities for concurrency. Consequently, the focus is on identifying a large number of small tasks to obtain a fine-grained decomposition of the problem (Chapter 7). Just as fine sand is easier to pile than bricks, so fine-grained decomposition provides the greatest flexibility in terms of potential concurrent algorithms.

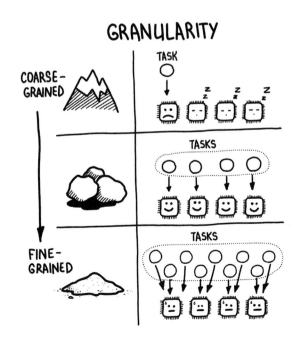

The goal

The goal of partitioning is to discover tasks that are as granular as possible. Partitioning is the only way to do this; the other steps usually reduce the amount of concurrency, so the goal of this step is to find all of it. At this initial stage, we are not concerned with practical problems such as the number of processor cores and the type of target machine, and our attention is focused on recognizing opportunities for parallel execution.

> **NOTE** The partitioning step must produce at least an order of magnitude more tasks than the processors in the target machine. Otherwise, we will have fewer options in the later stages of the design.

Data vs. task decomposition

When we implement a concurrent algorithm, we assume that it will be executed by multiple processing units. To do this, we need to isolate sets of operations in the algorithm that can be executed independently; that is, we *decompose* it. Two types of decomposition exist: data decomposition and task decomposition (Chapter 7).

  If the algorithm is used to process large amounts of data, we can try to divide the data into parts, each of which allows independent processing by a separate processing unit. This is *data decomposition*. Another approach involves dividing calculations based on their functionality. This is *task decomposition*.

> **NOTE**   Decomposition is not always possible. Some algorithms do not allow the participation of several executors in their implementation. To speed up those algorithms, there is vertical scaling, but it has physical limitations (Chapter 1).

Remember that data and task decomposition are complementary ways of approaching a problem, and it's natural to combine the two. Developers usually start with data decomposition because it is the basis for many concurrent algorithms. But sometimes, task decomposition can provide a different perspective on problems. Task decomposition may reveal problems or opportunities for better optimization that an inexperienced programmer may miss by looking at just the data.

Example

Let's return to our matrix multiplication example. We have a program in front of us, and we can start thinking about how to decompose it and where the dependencies are. What parts of the program can we run independently?

  As is clear from the definition of matrix multiplication, all elements of matrix C may be computed independently. As a result, a possible approach for partitioning matrix multiplication is to define the basic computational subtask as the problem of computing a single element of result matrix C. In that case, the total number of subtasks appears equal to $n \times m$ (based on the number of elements of matrix C).

The concurrency level achieved using this approach may seem excessive—the number of subtasks may greatly exceed the number of available processor cores. But that is fine at this stage; we have a follow-up stage (agglomeration) where we aggregate the computations for our specific needs.

Communication

The next step in our design process is to establish communication, which involves figuring out how to coordinate execution and set up a communication channel between tasks.

The goal

When all computations are a single sequential program, all data is available to all parts of the program. When a computation is divided into independent tasks that may run in separate processors or even in separate processor cores, some of the data a task needs may reside in its local memory and some in the memory of other tasks. In either case, these tasks need to exchange data with each other. Organizing this communication efficiently can be a challenge. Even simple decomposition can have complex communication structures. We want to minimize this overhead in our program, so it is important to define it.

> **NOTE** As we said before, the best way to implement concurrency is to reduce communication and interdependencies between concurrent tasks. If each task works with its own dataset, it does not need to protect that data with locks. Even when two tasks share a dataset, we might consider splitting that dataset or giving each task its own copy. Of course, there are also costs associated with copying datasets, so we need to weigh those costs against the costs of synchronization before making a decision.

Example

Our concurrent algorithm at this stage is formulated as a set of tasks where each task calculates the value of an element of matrix C and expects a single row of matrix A and a single column of matrix B to be the input.

In the agglomeration stage, we may consider combining the tasks to calculate not just one element of matrix C but the whole matrix row. In that case, a row of matrix A and all the columns of matrix B must be available for carrying out the necessary computations of the tasks. The simple solution is duplicating matrix B in all the tasks, but doing so may be unacceptable because of the sizeable memory expense of data storage. Another option is to use shared memory all the time, as the algorithm only uses matrixes A and B for read access, and elements of matrix C will be executed independently. In the later stages, we consider those options and think about the best solution for the use case at hand.

Agglomeration

In the first two stages of the design process, computation is broken down to maximize concurrency, and communication between tasks is introduced so that tasks have the data they need. The resulting algorithm is still an abstraction since it is not designed to run on any particular computer. The design obtained at this point probably doesn't map well onto a real machine. If the number of tasks greatly exceeds the number of processors, the overhead will be strongly affected by how the tasks are assigned to the processors. This third step, agglomeration, revisits the decisions made in the partitioning and communication steps.

The goal

The goal of this step is to improve performance and simplify development efforts, often by combining groups of tasks into larger tasks. The goals are often contradictory, and compromises have to be made.

In some cases, combining tasks with very different execution times can lead to performance problems. For example, if a long-running task is combined with many short-running tasks, the short-running tasks may have to wait a long time for the long-running task to complete. On the other hand, separating tasks may simplify the design but result in lower performance. In such cases, a compromise may be necessary between the benefits of simplicity and performance.

Let's consider the snow-shoveling example from Chapter 7. Shoveling snow is harder and slower than scattering salt, so in coming up with a plan of attack, the worker with the salt bag may want to give the shoveler a head start and then start scattering salt. When they catch up to the shoveler, they can switch jobs, giving the shoveler a breather as they take the bag of salt and wait for the other worker to get a head start. They continue this pattern until all the jobs are done. This reduces communication between the workers and improves overall performance.

Reducing communication overhead is one way to improve performance. When two tasks exchanging data with each other are combined into one task, the data communication becomes part of one task, and that communication and overhead are removed. This is called *increasing locality.*

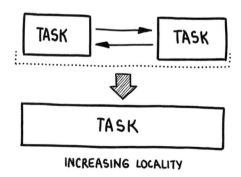

INCREASING LOCALITY

Another way to reduce communication overhead is to group tasks that send data, and group tasks that receive data, where possible. In other words, suppose task T1 sends data to task T3, and T2 sends to T4. If we merge T1 and T2 into one task T1, and we merge T3 and T4 into one task T3, the communication overhead decreases. The transmission time is not reduced, but we halve the total waiting time. Remember that when a task is waiting for data, it cannot compute, so the time spent waiting is lost.

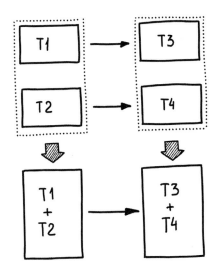

Example

When we partitioned our matrixes earlier, we used a fine-grained approach. Each element of the resulting matrix needs to be calculated. We divided the multiplication task into separate tasks according to the number of elements in the resulting matrix, one for each matrix element. In evaluating the communication, we determined that each subtask should have a row of matrix A and a column of matrix B. For a single instruction, multiple data (SIMD) computer (Chapter 3), it may be great if we can share A and B matrixes between threads; and on this type of machine, the solution will work better if we use a large number of threads. A natural choice is for each thread to compute one element of the result.

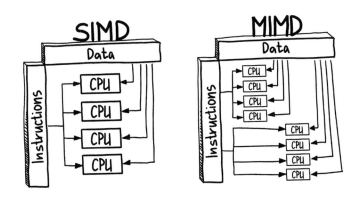

But if we have ordinary hardware—a multiple instruction, multiple data (MIMD) computer (Chapter 3)—the number of tasks is greater than the number of processors (p). If the number of elements in the matrix $n \times m$ is greater than p, the tasks can be aggregated by combining several neighboring rows and columns of multiplied matrixes into one subtask. In this case, the original matrix A is split into a number of horizontal strips, and matrix B is represented as a set of vertical strips. The band size (d) ideally should be equal to $d = n \times m/p$ (provided n is a multiple of p) because this ensures an equal distribution of computational load among processors. This reduces the communication between these tasks since everything else is handled locally within the task.

> **NOTE** Too much agglomeration is not good either. It's easy to make a short-sighted decision that could limit the program's scalability. A well-designed parallel program must adapt to changes in the number of processors. Try not to put unnecessarily strict limits on the number of tasks in the program. You should design your system to take advantage of more cores as they appear. Make the number of cores an input variable, and design based on it.

Mapping

The last step in Foster's methodology is assigning each task to a processing unit. Of course, this problem does not arise on single-processor computers or shared-memory computers whose OSs provide automatic task scheduling. If we are just writing programs to run on a desktop computer, as in the examples we've used throughout the book, scheduling isn't something we need to consider. Scheduling becomes a factor if we're using a distributed system or specialized hardware with many processors for large-scale tasks. We touch on that aspect in the next example.

The goal

The goal of mapping the algorithm is twofold: to minimize the overall program execution time and optimize resource utilization. There are two basic strategies for achieving that: place tasks that can run in parallel on different processors to increase overall concurrency, or focus on placing tasks that often interact with each other on the same processor to increase locality by keeping them close to each other. In some situations, we can use both approaches; but they often conflict, which means we have to make design tradeoffs. Designing a good mapping algorithm depends heavily on the program's structure and the hardware on which it runs, which is, unfortunately, beyond the scope of this book.

Example

In our example of matrix multiplication, we delegate the mapping and scheduling of tasks to the OS, so it's not our concern.

Implementation

There are a few steps left in the design process. First, we need to do some simple performance analyses to choose between alternative algorithms and check that our design meets our requirements and performance goals. We also need to think hard about the cost of implementing our algorithm, the reusability of existing code when we implement it, and how it all fits into the larger systems of which the algorithm may become a part. These questions are specific to the use case at hand, and real-world systems will likely bring more complications that need to be considered on a case-by-case basis. Such considerations are also beyond the scope of this book.

The example implementation of the concurrent matrix multiplication is as follows:

```
# Chapter 13/matmul/matmul_concurrent.py
from typing import List
import random
from multiprocessing import Pool


Row = List[int]
Column = List[int]
Matrix = List[Row]


def matrix_multiply(matrix_a: Matrix, matrix_b: Matrix) -> Matrix:
    num_rows_a = len(matrix_a)
    num_cols_a = len(matrix_a[0])
    num_rows_b = len(matrix_b)
    num_cols_b = len(matrix_b[0])
    if num_cols_a != num_rows_b:
        raise ArithmeticError(
            f"Invalid dimensions; Cannot multiply "
            f"{num_rows_a}x{num_cols_a}*{num_rows_b}x{num_cols_b}"
        )

    pool = Pool()
    results = pool.map(
        process_row,
        [(matrix_a, matrix_b, i) for i in range(num_rows_a)])
    pool.close()
    pool.join()
    return results
```

Creates a new process pool to calculate the matrix concurrently

Applies a function to each row in the matrix, passing in matrixes A and B and the current row index i, and returns a list of results

```
def process_row(args: tuple) -> Column:
    matrix_a, matrix_b, row_idx = args
    num_cols_a = len(matrix_a[0])
    num_cols_b = len(matrix_b[0])

    result_col = [0] * num_cols_b
    for j in range(num_cols_b):
        for k in range(num_cols_a):
            result_col[j] += matrix_a[row_idx][k] * matrix_b[k][j]
    return result_col


if __name__ == "__main__":
    cols = 4
    rows = 2
    A = [[random.randint(0, 10) for i in range(cols)] for j in range(rows)]
    print(f"matrix A: {A}")
    B = [[random.randint(0, 10) for i in range(rows)] for j in range(cols)]
    print(f"matrix B: {B}")
    C = matrix_multiply(A, B)
    print(f"matrix C: {C}")
```

multiplies a row of matrix A by each column of matrix B and returns the resulting column

This program defines a function `matrix_multiply` that takes in two matrixes and calculates their product concurrently. It uses a process pool to break down the calculation into smaller tasks of calculating individual columns of the solution matrix concurrently. The program collects the results of these tasks and stores them in the result matrix.

This is cool, but many frameworks and libraries already solve those math problems. Let's tackle another problem that's a bit more realistic; some big data engineering courses consider it a "Hello world" application, but we do it purely in Python.

Distributed word count

The distributed word count problem is a classic example of a big data problem that can be solved using distributed computing. The objective is to count the occurrences of each word in a large dataset, typically a text file or a collection of text files. While seemingly simple, this task can become time consuming and resource intensive when dealing with massive datasets.

To illustrate the significance of this challenge, consider the infamous incident that occurred during the reprint of the King James Bible in 1631. The printing process involved placing each letter (a total of 3,116,480) carefully in the lower platen of the printing press to create all 783,137 words in the Bible. However, a mistake was made, and the word *not* was omitted from a well-known verse. The resulting work became known as "The Wicked Bible" because, in the Ten Commandments, it said, "Thou shall commit adultery." If the printers had a way to automate the counting of all the words and letters that were supposed to be in the final product, the crucial mistake might have been avoided. This incident underscores the importance of accurate and efficient word count processes, especially when dealing with large datasets.

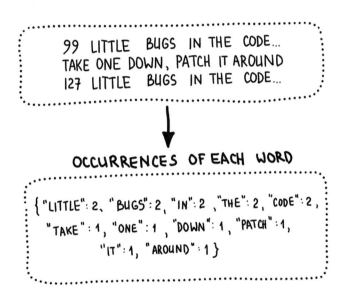

As a starting point, let's create a simple sequential program:

```python
# Chapter 13/wordcount/wordcount_seq.py
import re
import os
import glob
import typing as T

Occurrences = T.Dict[str, int]

ENCODING = "ISO-8859-1"


def wordcount(filenames: T.List[str]) -> Occurrences:
    word_counts = {}
```

```
for filename in filenames:
    print(f"Calculating {filename}")
    with open(filename, "r", encoding=ENCODING) as file:
        for line in file:
            words = re.split("\W+", line)

            for word in words:
                word = word.lower()
                if word != "":
                    word_counts[word] = 1 + word_counts.get(word, 0)
    return word_counts


if __name__ == "__main__":
    data = list(
        glob.glob(f"{os.path.abspath(os.getcwd())}/input_files/*.txt"))
    result = wordcount(data)
    print(result)
```

For each filename ...

For each line in
the current file ...

... splits the line into
individual words using a
regular expression pattern
that matches only word
characters (not punctuation)

... counts the word
if it is not empty

For each file, our application reads the text, divides it into words (ignoring punctuation and capitalization), and adds it to the total count of each word in the dictionary. From each word, it creates a key-value pair (word, 1). That is, the word is treated as a key, and the associated value of 1 means we have seen that word once.

The goal is to design and build a concurrent program that calculates the number of occurrences of each word in each document, with gigabytes of files and a distributed computer cluster. Let's run through the four stages again, this time applied to our new problem.

> **NOTE** The word count problem has been used to demonstrate several generations of distributed data engines. It was introduced in MapReduce and then used in many others, including Pig, Hive, and Spark.

Partitioning

To create a solution that associates each word with its frequency in a dataset, we must tackle two main challenges: breaking down the text files into individual words and counting the number of occurrences of each word. The second task depends on completing the first, as we cannot begin counting word occurrences until the text has been divided into individual words. This situation is a prime example of task decomposition, where we can break down the problem into smaller tasks based on their functionality. In this approach, the focus is primarily on the type of task to be performed rather than on the data needed for the computation.

This also looks like a great example for applying the map/reduce pattern we learned about in Chapter 7. We can express the computation in two steps or phases: *map* and *reduce*.

Here, the map phase plays a role in reading the text files and splitting them into word pairs. We can achieve maximum concurrency (what we are looking for in this step) in the map phase by splitting the input data into multiple chunks. For *M* workers, we want to have *M* chunks so that each worker has something to work on. The number of workers depends mainly on the number of machines at our disposal.

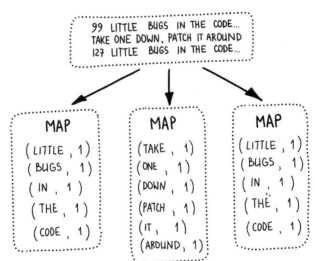

No matter how complex the data you are trying to process, the map phase produces events consisting of a key and a value. The key is important in the reduce phase.

The reduce task takes the output from the map task, a list of key-value pairs, and combines all the values for each unique key. For example, if the map task's output is [("the", 1), ("take", 1), ("the", 1)], the reduce task combines the values for the key "the" to produce the output [("the", 2)]. This is known as *reducing* or *aggregating* the data. The reduce output is a list of unique keys and their associated total count.

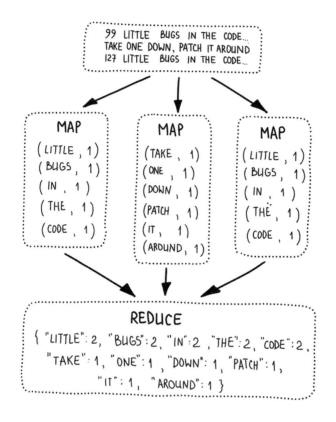

We can build the algorithm differently here by creating multiple reduce tasks and assigning each of them a list of words to handle. It's up to the next steps to decide on the best implementation.

There is no predicting which worker will get which file to read. It can be any file in any order. This gives our program ample horizontal scaling capability. Just add more worker nodes, and we can read more files simultaneously. If we had infinite hardware, we could read each file in parallel, reducing data read time to the length of the longest text.

Communication

All worker nodes in our cluster are assigned chunks of data to read. In our word count example, imagine that we are reading an enormous number of text files, such as a complete collection of books, where each book is a separate file.

To store and distribute this text data, we can use *network attached storage* (NAS). NAS can be described as a combination of a large storage drive and a special hardware platform that allows us to connect this storage drive to the local computer network. This way, we do not need to worry about complex communication protocols, and each node in the cluster can access files as if they were on a local disk.

The map and reduce tasks are expected to run on arbitrary machines of our cluster without any common context. They can run on the same machine or completely different machines. This means all the data that the map phase outputs must be transferred to the reduce phase and possibly written to disk if it's too big to fit in memory (which is often the case), and we can have several options for that situation. The first is interprocess communication (IPC) with message passing (Chapter 5). We can also use shared data to store intermediate data map tasks, and reduce tasks can use this shared NAS volume. That is what we do.

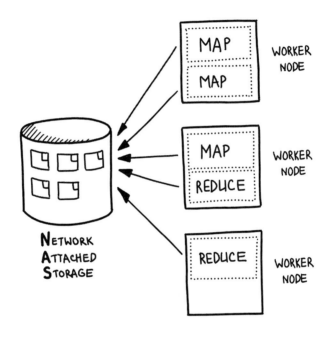

Another factor to consider is whether communications are synchronous or asynchronous. In synchronous communications, all tasks must wait until the entire communication process is complete before they can continue to do other work. This can potentially cause tasks to spend a lot of time waiting for data exchange instead of doing useful work.

In asynchronous communications, on the other hand, once a task sends an asynchronous message, it can immediately do other work regardless of when the receiving task receives the message. Also consider the amount of processing overhead that a particular communication strategy entails. After all, CPU cycles spent sending and receiving data are cycles not spent processing data.

For our problem, it is beneficial to use asynchronous communication. We have long-running tasks that do not require blocking execution, and we have a lot of communication between them.

Agglomeration

Currently, each of our map tasks yields word pairs (word, 1). A very easy way to speed things up is to pre-aggregate those pairs locally on each map task before the map phase ends and the reduce phase begins. This step, known as *combine,* is similar to reduce. It takes an arbitrary list of intermediate key-value pairs grouped by key, performs a value aggregation operation (if possible), and outputs fewer key-value pairs. In other words, it can opportunistically pre-aggregate some of the intermediate values to reduce the communication overhead between map tasks and reduce tasks.

Also, going back to our previous thoughts about the number of reduce tasks to simplify the algorithm, we use only one reduce task: we agglomerate all the reduce tasks into one big reduce task. This won't be as much data to compute since we just added the combine task, so that should be fine.

Mapping

After the agglomeration phase, we are in the state of a composer who has prepared everything to perform a symphony. But the beautiful sound of the orchestra is only possible with a conductor who coordinates the individual musicians and brings the conductor's own style to the performance. Yes, we are talking about scheduling our tasks on the actual processing resources that we have.

The most important (and complex) aspect of the task-scheduling algorithm is the strategy used to distribute tasks among workers. Typically, the strategy chosen is a compromise between the conflicting demands of independent work (to reduce communication costs) and global knowledge of the state of computation (to improve the load balance).

We implement the simplest idea: a central scheduler. The central scheduler sends tasks to workers, tracks progress, and returns results. It selects idle workers and assigns them either a map task or a reduce task. When all workers have finished their map task, the scheduler notifies them to start the reduce task (in our case, it is only one worker).

Each worker repeatedly requests and completes a task from the scheduler and returns the results of the work to the scheduler. The efficiency of this strategy depends on the number of workers and the relative costs of receiving and completing the tasks. We use a somewhat complex strategy of dynamic task allocation because we do not know the number of files and their sizes in advance. Therefore, we cannot guarantee optimal task allocation before the job starts.

Implementation

The following diagram provides an overview of the entire program in action. The server initiates the execution and creates a central scheduler. Each map worker is assigned a file for processing. If there are more files than workers, a worker is assigned another file once it has finished processing. Before completing the map task, combine tasks are triggered to aggregate the output of the map tasks, thereby reducing communication overhead. Once the map phase is finished, the scheduler commences the reduce phase, in which all the map outputs are combined into a single output.

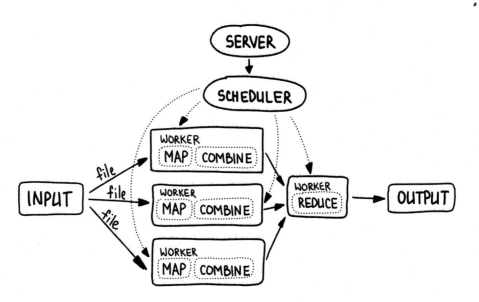

Our main server functionality is as follows:

```
# Chapter 13/wordcount/server.py
import os
import glob
import asyncio
```

```
from scheduler import Scheduler
from protocol import Protocol, HOST, PORT, FileWithId


class Server(Protocol):
    def __init__(self, scheduler: Scheduler) -> None:
        super().__init__()
        self.scheduler = scheduler

    def connection_made(self, transport: asyncio.Transport) -> None:
        peername = transport.get_extra_info("peername")
        print(f"New worker connection from {peername}")
        self.transport = transport
        self.start_new_task()

    def start_new_task(self) -> None:
        command, data = self.scheduler.get_next_task()
        self.send_command(command=command, data=data)

    def process_command(self, command: bytes,
                        data: FileWithId = None) -> None:
        if command == b"mapdone":
            self.scheduler.map_done(data)
            self.start_new_task()
        elif command == b"reducedone":
            self.scheduler.reduce_done()
            self.start_new_task()
        else:
            print(f"Unknown command received: {command}")


def main():
    event_loop = asyncio.get_event_loop()

    current_path = os.path.abspath(os.getcwd())
    file_locations = list(
        glob.glob(f"{current_path}/input_files/*.txt"))
    scheduler = Scheduler(file_locations)

    server = event_loop.create_server(
        lambda: Server(scheduler), HOST, PORT)
```

Defines the method to be called when a new worker connects to the server

Gets the next task from the scheduler and sends a command and data to the worker

Gets the event loop

Gets a list of the files in the input directory

Creates a Scheduler instance with the list of filenames in the data

Creates a server

```
        server = event_loop.run_until_complete(server)

        print(f"Serving on {server.sockets[0].getsockname()}")
        try:
            event_loop.run_forever()
        finally:
            server.close()
            event_loop.run_until_complete(server.wait_closed())
            event_loop.close()


if __name__ == "__main__":
    main()
```

Runs the
server

Tries to run the event loop forever. In the finally
clause, closes the server, waits for it to close,
and then closes the event loop.

This is `Server`—our main execution process that is responsible for communication with every worker process. It also calls `Scheduler` to get the next task for each worker and coordinate the map and reduce phases.

Our worker functionality is as follows:

```
# Chapter 13/wordcount/worker.py
import re
import os
import json
import asyncio
import typing as T
from uuid import uuid4

from protocol import Protocol, HOST, PORT, FileWithId, \
    Occurrences

ENCODING = "ISO-8859-1"
RESULT_FILENAME = "result.json"


class Worker(Protocol):
    def connection_lost(self, exc):
        print("The server closed the connection")
        asyncio.get_running_loop().stop()

    def process_command(self, command: bytes, data: T.Any) -> None:
        if command == b"map":
```

Runs when the
connection to
the server is lost

```
            self.handle_map_request(data)
        elif command == b"reduce":
            self.handle_reduce_request(data)
        elif command == b"disconnect":
            self.connection_lost(None)
        else:
            print(f"Unknown command received: {command}")


    def mapfn(self, filename: str) -> T.Dict[str, T.List[int]]:
        print(f"Running map for {filename}")
        word_counts: T.Dict[str, T.List[int]] = {}
        with open(filename, "r", encoding=ENCODING) as f:
            for line in f:
                words = re.split("\W+", line)
                for word in words:
                    word = word.lower()
                    if word != "":
                        if word not in word_counts:
                            word_counts[word] = []
                        word_counts[word].append(1)
        return word_counts


    def combinefn(self, results: T.Dict[str, T.List[int]]) -> Occurrences:
        combined_results: Occurrences = {}
        for key in results.keys():
            combined_results[key] = sum(results[key])
        return combined_results


    def reducefn(self, map_files: T.Dict[str, str]) -> Occurrences:
        reduced_result: Occurrences = {}
        for filename in map_files.values():
            with open(filename, "r") as f:
                print(f"Running reduce for {filename}")
                d = json.load(f)
                for k, v in d.items():
                    reduced_result[k] = v + reduced_result.get(k, 0)
        return reduced_result
```

map function. Takes a filename as input, opens the file, reads each line, splits it into words, and returns each word with a count of 1.

Combiner function. Takes a dictionary of results, sums the counts for each word, and returns a dictionary of combined results.

Reduce function. Takes a dictionary of filenames (where each key is an ID and each value is a filename), reads each file, and combines the results into a single dictionary.

Runs a map function

Combines the intermediate results of the map function

```python
def handle_map_request(self, map_file: FileWithId) -> None:
    print(f"Mapping {map_file}")
    temp_results = self.mapfn(map_file[1])
    results = self.combinefn(temp_results)
    temp_file = self.save_map_results(results)
    self.send_command(
        command=b"mapdone", data=(map_file[0], temp_file))
```

Sends a message to the server indicating that the map stage is complete

Saves the combined results to a temporary file and returns the file path

```python
def save_map_results(self, results: Occurrences) -> str:
    temp_dir = self.get_temp_dir()
    temp_file = os.path.join(temp_dir, f"{uuid4()}.json")
    print(f"Saving to {temp_file}")
    with open(temp_file, "w") as f:
        d = json.dumps(results)
        f.write(d)
    print(f"Saved to {temp_file}")
    return temp_file


def handle_reduce_request(self, data: T.Dict[str, str]) -> None:
    results = self.reducefn(data)
    with open(RESULT_FILENAME, "w") as f:
        d = json.dumps(results)
        f.write(d)
    self.send_command(command=b"reducedone",
                      data=("0", RESULT_FILENAME))
```

Calls the reducefn function with the intermediate map files results

Sends a message to the server indicating that the reduce stage is complete

Saves the reduced results to a JSON file

```python
def main():
    event_loop = asyncio.get_event_loop()
    coro = event_loop.create_connection(Worker, HOST, PORT)
    event_loop.run_until_complete(coro)
    event_loop.run_forever()
    event_loop.close()


if __name__ == "__main__":
    main()
```

Workers during the map phase invoke the `mapfn` function to parse the data and then invoke the `combinefn` function to merge the results and write intermediate (key, value) results. During the reduce phase, a worker gets the intermediate data, calls the `reducefn` function once for each unique key, and gives it a list of all values generated for that key. It then writes its final output to a single file that the user's program can access once the program has completed.

Here is our scheduler implementation:

```python
# Chapter 13/wordcount/scheduler.py
import asyncio
from enum import Enum
import typing as T

from protocol import FileWithId


class State(Enum):
    START = 0
    MAPPING = 1
    REDUCING = 2
    FINISHED = 3


class Scheduler:
    def __init__(self, file_locations: T.List[str]) -> None:
        self.state = State.START
        self.data_len = len(file_locations)
        self.file_locations: T.Iterator = iter(enumerate(file_locations))
        self.working_maps: T.Dict[str, str] = {}
        self.map_results: T.Dict[str, str] = {}

    def get_next_task(self) -> T.Tuple[bytes, T.Any]:
        if self.state == State.START:
            print("STARTED")
            self.state = State.MAPPING

        if self.state == State.MAPPING:
            try:
                map_item = next(self.file_locations)
                self.working_maps[map_item[0]] = map_item[1]
                return b"map", map_item
            except StopIteration:
                if len(self.working_maps) > 0:
                    return b"disconnect", None
                self.state = State.REDUCING
```

Gets the next task

```
        if self.state == State.REDUCING:
            return b"reduce", self.map_results

        if self.state == State.FINISHED:
            print("FINISHED.")
            asyncio.get_running_loop().stop()
            return b"disconnect", None

    def map_done(self, data: FileWithId) -> None:
        if not data[0] in self.working_maps:
            return
        self.map_results[data[0]] = data[1]
        del self.working_maps[data[0]]
        print(f"MAPPING {len(self.map_results)}/{self.data_len}")

    def reduce_done(self) -> None:
        print("REDUCING 1/1")
        self.state = State.FINISHED
```

Callback for when a file has finished being mapped

Callback for when all the files have been mapped and reduced

This is the central scheduler. In our implementation, it is divided into several states:

- *Start state*—Where the scheduler initializes the necessary data structures.

- *Mapping state*—Where the scheduler distributes all map tasks. Each task is a separate file, so when the server requests the next task, the scheduler simply returns the next unprocessed file.

- *Reducing state*—Where the scheduler stops all but one workflow for a single reduce task.

- *Finished state*—Where the scheduler stops the server and, therefore, the program.

NOTE For testing, I used books from Project Gutenberg (https://www.gutenberg.org/help/mirroring.html), and the overall system was able to work quite fast with a couple of gigabytes of data.

Recap

- The first 12 chapters of this book laid out a puzzle called *concurrency*. This chapter connected all the pieces of knowledge we learned previously.

- Before starting to write a concurrent program, we first examine the problem to be solved and make sure the effort to create a concurrent program is justified by the task at hand.

- The next steps are to be sure the problem can be divided into tasks and make communication and coordination of the tasks possible.

- In the third and fourth steps, the abstract algorithm becomes tangible and efficient when we consider the class of parallel computers on which it is to run. Is it a centralized multiprocessor or a multicomputer? What communication paths are supported? How should we combine tasks to efficiently distribute them across processors?

Epilogue

Throughout this book, we've utilized a variety of abstract concepts to illustrate the intricacies of designing concurrent systems. From symphony orchestras to hospital waiting rooms, and from fast food processes to home maintenance, we've drawn comparisons to help you understand complex topics. While we acknowledge that this book has only scratched the surface of this vast field, even this nominal level of detail emphasizes multiple strategies for developing concurrent applications.

After reading these 13 chapters, you should have a solid foundation to go deeper into the field of concurrency. There is still a lot to discover there! Now, hit it! (♫♫ Start the music! ♫♫).

index

T

U

V

W